# THE BUCKET LIST
# BEER

First published in the United States of America in 2019 by
Universe Publishing, A Division of
Rizzoli International Publications, Inc.
300 Park Avenue South
New York, NY 10010
www.rizzoliusa.com

2019 2020 2021 2022 / 10 9 8 7 6 5 4 3 2 1

ISBN: 978-0-7893-3685-9
Library of Congress Control Number: 2019940137

Visit us online:
Facebook.com/RizzoliNewYork
Twitter: @Rizzoli_Books
Instagram.com/RizzoliBooks
Pinterest.com/RizzoliBooks
Youtube.com/user/RizzoliNY
Issuu.com/Rizzoli

Conceived, designed, and produced by
The Bright Press, an imprint of the Quarto Group
The Old Brewery
6 Blundell Street
London N7 9BH
United Kingdom
T 00 44 20 7700 6700
www.QuartoKnows.com

Publisher: Mark Searle
Creative Director: James Evans
Art Director: Eoghan O'Brien
Design Assistance: Ginny Zeal
Managing Editor: Jacqui Sayers
Project Editor: Rica Dearman
Senior Editor: Caroline Elliker
Publishing Assistant: Chloe Porter
Picture Researchers: Katie Greenwood, Jane Roe

Printed and bound in Singapore

# THE BUCKET LIST

# BEER

## 1000 Adventures · Pubs · Breweries · Festivals

JUSTIN KENNEDY

GOA
BREWING
CO.
CRAFT BEER

UNIVERSE

# Contents

## How to use this book

This book is organized by areas of the world. Within each chapter you will then find entries organized under individual countries—or in the case of the US and Canada, states, provinces, and territories. If you have a specific brewery in mind, simply turn to page 406 to search for it in the index.

### A note about opening hours

Due to the changing nature of establishments, we haven't included details of opening times, but would advise you to visit a company's website or contact them directly for this and any other information. This is also the case for events such as beer festivals—dates will vary from year to year, so be sure to check in advance. You may also wish to check the price with the organizers and how far in advance you will need to purchase tickets.

### Color code

Each entry number in the book has been given a color that relates to one of five categories, as shown below, allowing you to select activities based on the type of element you are interested in, i.e. a brewery, specific beer, or event.

### Color key

■ Specific beer/drink type

■ Brewery/museum/bottle shop

■ Eateries/drinking spots

■ Event/festival/activity/tour

■ Top list

# Foreword

In 2006 my partners and I opened Port Brewing and The Lost Abbey in San Marcos, California. It was our stated goal to become a world-class brewery with beers people would travel across time zones to experience in situ drinking with us at our base of operations. Ultimately, we knew if we succeeded in making the very best beers we could brew, people would notice. It was our own "if you build it they will come" theory for the brewery we wanted to operate.

It was an ambitious opening goal to say the least. World-class breweries take time to build and cultivate. But we knew deep down that beer is one of the best social lubricants, and where great beers flow, better conversations follow.

It's also been 23 years since I stepped through my first brewery door as an employee. So many of those days have been filled trying to experience the very best breweries, festivals, and brewers on the planet which, needless to say, has been awesome because deep down inside, while I have been a professional brewer for more than half my life, I have been a passionate beer enthusiast for even longer.

Like many of you, my life revolves around seeking out incredible beer, people, and locations every time I head out the door. To say that beer is a big part of my life would be underestimating by a magnitude of no less than ten.

Imagine my surprise when I opened this book, which revealed hundreds of bars, restaurants, and events that I personally have made the pilgrimage to experience. Clearly, Justin and I share a love of great people and amazing beers. His choices and points of view were a fantastic "been there, done that" sort of reassuring wingman helping me relive so many positive memories.

But I was also very pleased to see so many places I hadn't considered before. I've spent the bulk of my international travels in Europe. Maybe you, too, have your preferred regions to visit. If so, like me, you're likely a bit under-versed as to where to point your compass in Thailand or China. How about in Estonia or Poland? No worries. You'll find plenty of opportunities presented here.

Like an intrepid explorer charting future journeys for us, Justin Kennedy has left trail markers behind to guide each of us on our way. If you're an avid lover of Belgian beers, he's here to affirm your decisions as you shuffle over the cobblestones in the Grand Place. Perhaps you've been wondering what you should do if you ever find yourself in Switzerland? Do yourself a favor and make sure you knock #500 off the list and become an acolyte at BFM. When you do, tell Jérôme that Justin and Tomme say hello.

I'm certain you're going to be captivated by the pictures and the stories each entry depicts. Each and every one of the 1,000 items presented is thoughtful and insightful. I can only imagine what had to be left out. Lists like this can be exhausting. Couple this with a world of beer evolving at a dizzying pace and it's impossible to imagine any book definitively collecting all of the bucket list beer experiences in one place. But let's give credit where it's due. As someone who has been to a large chunk of these places and whose friends are listed in these pages, I can assure you this is a damn good list that should reward novice and veteran travelers alike.

Safest travels, and hoping our paths cross out there.

*Tomme Arthur*
Co-founder and chief operating officer
Port Brewing and The Lost Abbey
*In Illa Brettanomyces Nos Fides*

# Introduction

Never has there been a better time to love beer than now. Literally tens of thousands of breweries—mostly small, independent, and family-run—are now in operation in all corners of the globe, from Australia and New Zealand to Africa, the Middle East, Asia Pacific, and particularly Europe and North America. In fact, as of this writing, here in the US alone more than 7,000 breweries both large and small are producing countless varieties of beer ranging from traditional European styles to cutting-edge, *avant-garde* brews filled with revolutionary ingredients.

But it's not just sheer numbers. There's no doubt that beer quality has never been better, either.

In light of such rapid expansion and growth, a question I hear asked quite often is: "Is the whole beer thing a bubble? And if so, when will it burst?" Call me overly optimistic, but my answer to those questions is summarily, "No," and "Probably no time soon." The reason I'm so confident that beer will continue to flourish is simple: the industry fosters community, creates many decent to well-paying jobs, and, most importantly, it makes its consumers endlessly happy. What's not to love?

Even though most beer styles are now brewed the world over, visiting local breweries, beer bars, museums, and beer festivals is still one of the best ways to get a feel for the local community. With that idea in mind, this book compiles 1,000 of the very best beer experiences around the world and tells you where to find them, why they're important, and what makes them unique.

As you set off on your beery adventures, do keep in mind that the things that make the industry so exciting and dynamic may cause unanticipated situations. Brewery closures do happen, and establishments like bars, restaurants, and bottle shops may change their hours, move locations, or even shut down with little notice. Even historic pubs like those in London and Dublin throw in the towel from time to time. Given modern beer lovers' fervent desire for all things new and different, breweries change recipes and discontinue brands increasingly often, meaning some of the beers mentioned in this book may no longer be available.

But don't let that stop you from getting out there, embracing your inner beer geek, and discovering the treasures and pleasures the world of beer has to offer.

Regarding terminology, I have tried to adhere to whatever the brewery uses in its name, for instance, Avery Brewing, Burial Beer, Jolly Pumpkin Artisan Ales, etc. For other parts of the world, the term "microbrewery" is still used, though it has fallen out of fashion in the US and in Europe. "Craft brewery" is nominally independent and small; and "brewpub" is a brewery within a restaurant.

*Justin Kennedy*

# Eastern US

For more than a century, the East Coast was the US's brewing capital, with hundreds of primarily German-style lager breweries dotting the seaboard from Boston to Jacksonville. Post-Prohibition, however, many of these nineteenth- and early-twentieth-century operations shuttered, resulting in a dearth of regional producers. Today, thanks to the American craft beer explosion, the East Coast is once again one of the most exciting regions for beer: literally thousands of small and independent craft breweries supply the region's urban, suburban, and rural locales.

The hills and farmlands of Vermont offer some of the most revered beers in the world, while urban centers like Portland, Maine; New York City; and Philadelphia have become hotbeds for hip, boundary-pushing brews. Further south, small cities like Asheville, North Carolina, and Nashville, Tennessee, continue to offer a range of styles from hoppy ales to funky barrel-aged beers. And in the many cities and towns in between, you'll find a plethora of high-quality suds.

FREEPORT, MAINE

## 1   Make a reservation for "Dinner" beer

One of American craft beer enthusiasts' favorite pastimes is waiting in line for a special beer release. Most of the time they're strong beers like imperial stouts, but occasionally, like this beer from Maine Beer, they are hoppy ales. Maine Beer creates a range of hoppy ales, but its most coveted is Dinner, released several times throughout the year, by reservation only through the brewery's website.

NEWCASTLE, MAINE

## 2   Party at an outdoors beer fest

One of the best developments in the American craft beer world is the evolution of beer festivals from massive, corporate-influenced gatherings to small, independent, niche festivals that cater to the fervent few. Goods from the Woods is one of the best, and takes place each fall at Oxbow Brewing. Festival-goers are free to explore the wooded areas surrounding the brewery, drinking from taps and bottles obscured deep within. In addition to plenty of Oxbow beers, guest brewers are invited to pour their wares. Graffiti artists, musicians, and local chefs are always on hand to create a lively community-like atmosphere that transcends your run-of-the-mill beer fest. There's no other beer experience like it.

**2**   *Below:* Oxbow Brewing's annual Goods from the Woods festival

### 3 Try a lobster brew

The cold waters of coastal Maine are prime territory for lobsters. In the summertime, they get boiled and stuffed into lobster rolls, eaten along the coast and at roadside shacks. Maine's Oxbow Brewing has another use for them: a beer called Saison Dell'Aragosta. Oxbow partnered with Birrificio del Ducato of Parma, Italy, to concoct this lobster-infused mixed-fermentation seaside saison brewed with real live lobsters and sea salt.

SAISON
DELL'ARAGOSTA

farmhouse ale brewed with lobster
1 pint .9 fl. oz (500ml)

**OXBOW BREWING CO.**

### 4 Get ghoulish with this spooooky brew

Allagash Brewing has been the anchor of the Maine beer scene for more than two decades. Founded in 1995 by owner Rob Tod, its flagship Allagash White beer is a textbook example of a Belgian-style wheat beer and an absolute classic in American craft beer lore. Brewed with oats and both malted and unmalted raw wheat for a hazy, "white" appearance, it's spiced with a blend of coriander and curaçao orange peel for a complex and extremely refreshing profile. Allagash does more than White, though. Some of its best beers are fermented with the wild yeast strain brettanomyces, and in the cooler months it creates spontaneously fermented beer in a coolship (a wide, shallow, bathtub-like open cooling vessel). Tours are available year-round.

PORTLAND, MAINE

## 5  Walk among half a dozen breweries

Allagash Brewing is located at 50 Industrial Way in Portland, but just steps away at 1 Industrial Way—a twelve-bay industrial warehouse—are a handful of other much smaller niche breweries that have incubated in this part of Portland. Previous tenants have included revered breweries like Maine Beer, Bissell Brothers, and Rising Tide Brewing. Current tenants include Foundation Brewing, Austin Street Brewery, and Battery Steele Brewing. On weekends, beer lovers can mosey from one brewery to the next, without walking more than one hundred yards between each tasting room. It's a magical slice of craft beer heaven located in one of the most exciting drinking cities in the US.

PORTLAND, MAINE

## 6  Drink in the craft beer "revolution"

Founded in 2008, Novare Res Bier Cafe is located off a hidden alleyway in Portland's downtown district. It features both indoor and outdoor spaces (the latter open only in warmer months) and an always-impressive selection of dozens of draft and bottled beers. The place is a destination unto itself—rather than dropping in for a single pint, it's the type of bar that warrants a night's worth of lingering and exploration. You're guaranteed to leave rosy-cheeked and happy.

PORTLAND, MAINE

## 7  Bend an elbow at this beer hub

The Great Lost Bear is a historical American beer bar that's been around for decades and shows no signs of slowing. Its more than seventy drafts means you'll always find something new and unusual on tap, ranging from local barleywines to imported Belgian saisons, and the gregarious, laid-back bartenders always create a welcome and inviting environment.

LOVELL, MAINE

## 8  Sip a rare vintage beer

Looking for a rare vintage bottle of Belgian Trappist beer or a long-out-of-production English barleywine? Chances are you'll find it at Ebenezer's Pub, a storied restaurant and beer bar in Lovell, a small town near the New Hampshire border. The bar's dedication to Belgian beer is so fierce it got co-owner Chris Lively knighted by the Belgian Brewers' Guild in 2014.

### 9  Visit a brewery in the middle of nowhere

Often casually cited as the best brewery in the world—an official designation it won twice from the beer-rating website RateBeer—Hill Farmstead Brewery is located in a rural section of Vermont known as the Northeast Kingdom. Owner Shaun Hill, once a brewer in Europe, moved home to Vermont in 2010 and took over his family's farmhouse to create Hill Farmstead. The brewery specializes in a range of styles from Belgian-inspired saisons to hoppy American ales, stouts, and porters. Its barrel-conditioned mixed-culture beers like Anna and Dorothy (each named for a member of Shaun's extended family) are some of the best in the world, and the addition of canned beers means you can take its expertly crafted Mary pilsner to go. The busy tasting room has a communal and cheerful vibe.

### 10  Savor a pint at this bustling brewhouse

The storied Three Penny Taproom in Vermont's capital is always an exciting, stimulating place to drink. Its tap list contains nearly twenty-five beers spanning all territory from local upstarts like River Roost Brewing to international standards like Saison Dupont. (It's also one of the few places you can get Backacre Sour Golden Ale, a local specialty.) For a quick bite, order from the stellar menu of hearty American fare like grilled cheese, burgers, and fried pork rinds.

6  *Above:* The outdoor area at Novare Res Bier Cafe

9  *Above:* Drinking in the sun at Hill Farmstead Brewery

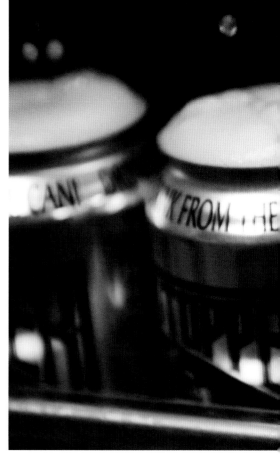

STOWE, VERMONT
## 11 Get "Heady" in this popular tasting room

Renowned as the creators of the famed Heady Topper double IPA, Alchemist Brewery and Visitor's Center is another of Vermont's revered breweries. Having had no official tasting room, beer trekkers used to follow its delivery truck around the state, snatching up cases of the famous beer stop by stop. But since the summer of 2016, the brewery has maintained a bricks-and-mortar outpost in Stowe, where fans can line up to buy cases and four-packs of Heady, as well as other offerings like Focal Banger, Crusher, Pappy's Porter, and Petit Mutant sour ale. A tasting room lets you sample more than half a dozen beers on draft and pick up some official Heady Topper merchandise. All in all, it's a much better experience than following a truck around the backroads of Vermont.

**11**  *Above:* Alchemist Brewery and Visitor's Center

WATERBURY, VERMONT
## 12 Go bar-hopping in a busy beer town

Waterbury is most famously the home to the Alchemist Brewery (with its visitor center based in Stowe), but it also contains an embarrassment of riches in terms of beer bars, bottle shops, and restaurants. Start with a pint at the cozy downtown Blackback Pub, where locals sip beers from Burlington's Foam Brewers and Zero Gravity Brewing. (There's typically a great selection of Hill Farmstead and Lawson's on as well.) Next, head to Craft Beer Cellar to stock up on bottles from small breweries like Off Color, Evil Twin, and local Frost Beer Works. You can also purchase edible goodies like mustard made with Heady Topper IPA. For an upscale dinner, settle in to Hen of the Wood, a farm-to-table restaurant with an eclectic menu of hearty Vermont fare. If a gastropub is more your speed, check out Prohibition Pig for Southern-style barbecue and smoked meats, as well as excellent house-brewed beers and handcrafted cocktails. Finally, take a nightcap next door at The Reservoir, a lively bar and restaurant with an awesome selection of local craft beers.

## 13 Quaff a sip of sunshine

The trifecta of Hill Farmstead, Alchemist, and Lawson's Finest Liquids makes the Green Mountain State one of the world's top destinations for world-class breweries. Like the Alchemist, Lawson's opened its doors to the public with an expanded tasting room and brewery. Here, you can sample nearly a dozen different creations from proprietor Sean Lawson and his merry band of brewers. The flagship Sip of Sunshine is a great place to start, backed by other hoppy offerings like Triple Sunshine, Hopzilla, and Chinooker'd. Don't leave without trying Fayston Maple, a rich, complex imperial maple stout brewed with huge doses of Vermont maple syrup. It's a boozy, sticky treat that's worth the trip alone.

## BURLINGTON, VERMONT
## 14  Take in views while knocking back suds

Considering its wealth of world-class brewers, it should come as no surprise that the Vermont Brewers Festival is one of the premier beer festivals in the world. It's also one of the most picturesque, held on the waterfront of Lake Champlain overlooking the Adirondack Mountains of New York State. The host, the Vermont Brewers Association, invites nearly fifty breweries from both Vermont and surrounding states to participate. The festival is typically held on the third weekend of July, and has been going for more than twenty-five years. It includes experiential tastings and pairing classes, as well as live music, food, and craft vendors. Afterward, hit up the burgeoning downtown Burlington, the largest city in Vermont, for more live music, hip restaurants, and local brews.

**14**  *Above:* Visitors at Vermont Brewers Festival have stunning views of Lake Champlain

## NEWMARKET, NEW HAMPSHIRE
## 15  Unearth the Granite State's hoppiest brews

One of the handsomest taprooms in the Northeast is found at Deciduous Brewing. Opened in 2015 by cofounders Frank and Maryann Zagami and Dave Sakolsky, the brewery focuses on New England-style IPAs (NEIPAs), robust porters, and simple sour ales like Auroral Berliner Weisse, brewed with lychee and blood orange. The loungey space encourages slow sipping and long conversation, but if you're in a hurry you can always grab a few bottles to go.

## BOSTON, MASSACHUSETTS
## 16  Taste the suburban beers of Boston

What started as a small brewery in a tiny warehouse in historic Fort Point has now expanded to multiple breweries, beer gardens, and tasting locations throughout greater Boston. The original space has shifted two blocks north and ballooned into a full-service restaurant and bottle shop with an expansive beer selection. Most of that is made in Canton, where Trillium Brewing's sprawling brewery, tasting room, and barrel-aging facility is located. In warm months, the brewery operates a downtown beer garden in the Rose Kennedy Greenway Conservancy.

## BOSTON, MASSACHUSETTS
### 17  Visit the second-largest craft brewery in the US

Samuel Adams is the second-largest "craft brewery" in the US, producing millions of barrels of beer each year. Much of that is made outside Massachusetts, but it has been making a small portion at its Boston-based Jamaica Plain brewery for more than thirty years. Grab a pint of the iconic Boston Lager—as well as experimental brews like its Brut IPA—at the tasting room where, in the evenings, it becomes something of a hangout for locals, complete with food trucks and karaoke nights.

## BOSTON, MASSACHUSETTS
### 18  Get extreme at a mind-expanding beer festival

Each February, extreme beer enthusiasts gather in Boston to celebrate some of the most extraordinary and palate-bending beers on the planet. Brothers Jason and Todd Alström of the beer website and publication *BeerAdvocate* partnered with Sam Calagione of Dogfish Head for the first Extreme Beer Fest in 2004 with just a handful of breweries. There are now hundreds of beers from dozens of breweries with a new focus on low-alcohol beers. In 2017, the festival expanded westward for its first West Coast gathering in Los Angeles.

BOSTON, MASSACHUSETTS
## 19  Drink where everybody knows your name

Ever wanted to bend an elbow with Norm and Sam? Established in 1969, the Bull & Finch Pub was the original inspiration for the TV show *Cheers*, which aired from 1982 to 1993. Over the years, it has become something of a tourist trap, but die-hard fans can still enjoy a pint among the memorabilia and trinkets commemorating the classic show. In 2002, the bar officially changed its name from the original Bull & Finch to Cheers Beacon Hill.

BOSTON, MASSACHUSETTS
## 20  Revel in real ale

The New England Real Ale eXhibition is the longest-running real ale celebration in the US, having served thousands of pours of rarely seen, award-winning cask ales for decades. As the drink's popularity has peaked in the US, it's no longer held every year, but every other year.

RHODE ISLAND
## 21  Go on a liquid Rhode trip

For the country's smallest state, Rhode Island has a commendable selection of craft breweries. One of the best is Proclamation Ales, known for its NEIPAs. Its Derivative series features a rotating hop brewed into a base IPA (try Derivative: Galaxy), available at its tasting room in Warwick. Another standout is Tilted Barn Brewery, where again the focus is on NEIPAs, with some solid English-style ales. Also look for beers from Grey Sail Brewing, Whalers Brewing, and Foolproof Brewing. No visit to the Ocean State would be complete without crushing a couple of Narragansetts.

CHARLTON, MASSACHUSETTS
## 22  Unearth the origins of NEIPA

Along with Trillium, Tree House Brewing was one of the originators of the widely celebrated NEIPA (hazy, low bitterness, and extremely heady with juicy hops). It quickly outgrew its original Monson, Massachusetts location and in 2017 opened an expansive, Disneyland-like brewery and taproom dedicated to can sales and a tasting room selling pints. A visit requires some planning—before heading out to wait in line (and you will have to wait in line!), check the brewery's website for opening hours, as it's only open for can sales and pints on some days, while on others only cans are available. Saturdays feature live music and food, but tend to be the busiest (and therefore craziest) days to visit.

## 23 Explore eccentric wild ale

Founded in 2014 by Ben Neidhart, in connection with its sister company international beer importer B United, OEC (Ordinem Ecentrici Coctores) Brewing is one of the few US breweries fully dedicated to sour beer production. There is no flagship beer *per se*, but a constantly rotating selection of ales aged in wood barrels, concrete vessels, and stainless steel tanks. Visit the tasting room or book a tour of the facility.

## 24 Visit a contract brewery

Contract brewing—making beer at other brewers' facilities—used to be viewed negatively by craft beer enthusiasts. That perception changed in the early 2010s, though, thanks largely to high-quality contract brewers like Two Roads Brewing. The facility, located in a historic manufacturing building, produces some of the best beers in the country from brands like Evil Twin, Stillwater, Carton, and Lawson's Finest. It also makes a killer lineup of its own beers, like Ol' Factory Pils and Igor's Dream Imperial Stout. In 2018, the brewery opened a 25,000 sq ft (2,323 sq m) barrel-aging facility called Area Two Experimental Brewing to focus on sour and funky beers.

## 25 Discover true farmhouse breweries

Two of the best breweries in Connecticut happen to be located on farms. Kent Falls Brewing, in Kent, and Fox Farm Brewery, in Salem, produce some of the state's best liquid, taking inspiration from a variety of sources, including their natural surroundings. Kent Falls, in the western part of the state near the New York border, sits on a fully functioning farm, complete with hop bines and acre upon acre of fallow land. The brewery produces farmhouse-inspired ales as well as lagers and IPAs, and has a small tasting room. On the southeastern portion of the state is Fox Farm. Housed in a 1960s-era barn, the brewery specializes in hazy NEIPAs, porters, and saisons.

**MANHATTAN, NEW YORK**

## 26  Experience old-time Irish New York

McSorley's Old Ale House is the oldest Irish tavern in New York City, dating back to the mid-nineteenth century. (The exact year is often disputed; the sign outside says "Established 1854," but public records show it sat vacant until at least 1861.) Inside, not much has changed in more than a hundred years. You'll notice it has just two beer selections: light or dark. Whichever beer you order, instead of being served in a proper pint glass, it comes in two 8 oz mugs. On the walls, you can see the history of New York, from when McSorley's first opened through to today. There's an odd food menu, but no better place to soak in the genuine atmosphere of centuries gone by.

## 27 Attend a firkin festival

Each spring, Long Island's Blue Point Brewing (a subsidiary of Anheuser-Busch) hosts one of the biggest cask festivals in the US: Blue Point Brewing Co. Cask Ales Festival. Cofounder Mark Burford started the fest in 2004 and quickly grew it into one of the area's premier beer festivals, with more than 200 cask ales from sixty-plus breweries. Until 2019, the festival was held at the original brewery on River Avenue in Patchogue, but subsequent fests will continue at Blue Point's new brewery in downtown Patchogue. In addition to beers, there are local food vendors and live music.

## 28 Go on an industrial canal tour

The best neighborhood to soak in Brooklyn's hip beer culture is along the Gowanus Canal. Start at Threes Brewing for house-brewed lagers and saisons before walking south to Strong Rope Brewery, dedicated to making beer with nearly 100% New York State ingredients. Afterward, head to Other Half Brewing, Brooklyn's hippest producer of hazy IPAs and imperial stouts. Unwind by strolling six blocks northwest to Folksbier Brauerei, a cozy German and Alpine-inspired brewery with a welcoming tasting room. (Be warned: the tasting room gets crowded on weekends.)

## 29 Drink where George Washington drank

Another piece of New York history is further downtown at Fraunces Tavern, where George Washington is said to have bid farewell to his officers of the Continental Army. Today, you can see a museum dedicated to the history of the building and knock back a pint at the pub next door. Beers from Ireland's Porterhouse Brewing are the main attraction, with several stouts and porters on offer (said to be Washington's favorite style).

## 30 Celebrate Christmas—in July

The popular Blind Tiger Ale House is one of New York's first and best craft beer pubs. Located in Manhattan's picturesque West Village neighborhood, it features twenty taps of domestic craft beer as well as cask and bottle pours. The bar often hosts entire tap takeovers from local and renowned breweries and VSK (very special keg) events where a bartender will tap a rare or vintage keg of specialty beer. In the summer, aged Christmas beers from the year before are served at its annual Christmas in July festival.

NEW YORK, NEW YORK

### 31 Sip your way across five boroughs

There are more than thirty breweries within the five boroughs of New York City. In Staten Island check out Flagship Brewing for its tasty beers and Kills Boro Brewing for modern takes on hoppy and fruited ales. In north Brooklyn, Grimm Artisanal Ales and Interboro Spirits & Ales make some forward-thinking beer. Also in Brooklyn, KCBC, Transmitter, Sixpoint, and Brooklyn Brewery lead the charge. In Queens you'll find BIG aLICe Brewing, Rockaway Brewing, and Fifth Hammer. Nearby LIC Beer Project makes heady IPAs and wild ale, while Mikkeller Brewing NYC crafts excellent ales and lagers. In Ridgewood, visit Evil Twin Brewing for boundary-pushing brews. In the Bronx, Gun Hill and Bronx Brewery lead the charge, while Torch & Crown crafts beers for its Manhattan outpost. Death Avenue produces Manhattan's only beer.

BROOKLYN, NEW YORK

### 32 Dive into the former brewing capital of the US

When people think of brewing in Brooklyn, they think of hazy IPAs, sour ales, and trendy brewpubs. But there's so much more to the history of beer making in the borough than meets the eye. For nearly a century, Brooklyn was the US's brewing hub, with large-scale German-style breweries dotting the northern part of the borough. Many buildings that once housed breweries are still standing, including the Nassau Brewing Company in Crown Heights (a mixed-use condo building) and Schaefer Brewing along Kent Avenue in Williamsburg (also condos). A small exhibit documenting Brooklyn's brewing past can be found inside the tasting room at Brooklyn Brewery in trendy Williamsburg, appropriately located on the stretch of North 11th Street called Brewers Row.

## 33  Visit the breweries of the Hudson Valley

The area along the Hudson River between New York City and Albany can roughly be defined as the Hudson Valley, and it contains some of the best breweries in the state. Starting north and moving south, Suarez Family Brewery in Livingston, just south of Hudson, is an absolute can't-miss spot for beer enthusiasts. Proprietor and brewer Dan Suarez brewed at Hill Farmstead for years before opening his lager and "country beer"-focused brewery in 2016. At its tasting room, you'll discover one of the calmest, most idyllic experiences in beer. Nearby, check out Sloop Brewing for hazy IPAs and sour ales. Further south, you'll want to stop in at Plan Bee Farm Brewery in Poughkeepsie, a true farm brewery where the gregarious Evan Watson makes innovative and poetic farmhouse ales all fermented with yeast harvested from his own beehives. Cross the river and try the delightful offerings at the riverfront Newburgh Brewing, where the brown ale is a classic. Continue south to Industrial Arts Brewing in Garnerville, where owner Jeff O'Neill makes all varieties of hop-centric ales and lagers. Finally, work your way back across the river to the famed Captain Lawrence Brewing in Elmsford, a multifaceted microbrewery that specializes in both clean and sour ales. Don't leave without trying the Clearwater Kölsch and the Cuvée De Castleton.

## 34  Tap into New York

Each spring since 1998, New York State brewers have taken over a Catskill Mountains ski resort town for the annual TAP New York Craft Beer & Food Festival. Join the weekend-long event and enjoy beer from hundreds of breweries. It's a good place to survey the state of New York craft beer in one place.

## 35  Don't get busted at this brewpub

Prison City Pub and Brewery, located in the heart of the Finger Lakes region, brews textbook examples of hazy IPAs and fruited simple sours like Cherry Poppins Berliner weisse. You'll also find more classic styles like brown ales and porters, and you can choose from a full menu of hearty American pub grub.

COOPERSTOWN, NEW YORK

## 36  Camp among the kegs

One of the coolest beer festival experiences is Belgium Comes to Cooperstown (BCTC) held in August. That's because you get to camp and mingle all weekend long among the brewers and beer enthusiasts pouring beer at the fest. It attracts breweries from around the country to the home base of Brewery Ommegang, a charming Belgian-focused brewery. Be sure to buy tickets and make camping reservations well in advance, as the festival routinely sells out.

ROCHESTER, NEW YORK

## 37  Taste ale made like lager

Perhaps New York's most famous beer, Genesee Cream Ale is an old-fashioned lager-ale hybrid beer that contains no cream at all. The beer was first introduced by the Genesee Brew House in 1960 and has since become a lowbrow classic. Though found mostly at dive bars, the Rochester brewery has recently invested in a pilot system catering to craft brewers, with some surprisingly good results. Check out Genesee Brew House for tours and tastings of the brewery's newfangled beers.

BUFFALO, NEW YORK

## 38  Experience a nanoscale brewery

Community Beer Works is a tiny nanobrewery that has multiple locations throughout Buffalo and Niagara Falls. It serves as a real gathering place for the working-class city's beer community. The focus is a range of American styles (IPAs, hoppy stouts, and brown ales) with a full-service food menu at the 7th Street taproom address.

NEW JERSEY

## 39  Discover the Jersey Shore breweries

Despite its dense population, New Jersey had relatively few breweries until 2012, when the Garden State finally came into its own as a destination-worthy beer state. The two leaders were Carton Brewing and Kane Brewing, both in Monmouth County. Carton's Boat Beer, a hoppy session ale that drinks like a double IPA, is worth the trip alone. Also check out its culinary-inspired beers like Regular Coffee, an imperial coffee cream ale, and Gilded Lily, a white truffle-infused Belgian-style tripel. Kane makes some of the best IPAs in the state, as well as a series of imperial stouts, such as A Night to End All Dawns. Also worth a visit are: Beach Haus Brewery, Icarus Brewing, Little Dog Brewing, and Dark City Brewing.

## PHILADELPHIA, PENNSYLVANIA

### 40 Head down a back alleyway

Fermentery Form is an exciting brewery in
Philadelphia, located down a back alleyway in
the uber-hip Kensington neighborhood. The trio
of founders are friends of nearly twenty-five
years who met while playing in punk rock bands
in Philly's underground music scene in the 1990s.
They began homebrewing together around 2008,
and decided to go professional, cobbling together
and outfitting a space on the cheap to avoid
taking on investors and potentially losing some
creative control. Rather than brewing their own
beer, Ethan Tripp, the head brewer, works with
nearby Saint Benjamin Brewing to create wort
(unfermented beer) based on his own recipes.
After the wort is made, he trucks it five blocks
back to Fermentery Form where it ferments for
several weeks. The beer is Belgian-inspired with
a focus on mixed-fermentation ales. The tasting
room is open just two days a week—with three
drafts and about half a dozen different bottles.
Nearly always available is the flagship Form to
Table, a table beer that is taut but nuanced,
bone-dry and delicate with a lively body and
a heady bouquet.

## PENNINGTON, NEW JERSEY

### 41 Get spiritual with spontaneous ales

A unique brewery in New Jersey is The Referend Bier Blendery, a sour brewery and blendery that
specializes in lambic-influenced beers. Proprietor James Priest focuses on blending rather than brewing,
obtaining unfermented wort from other breweries around the state and in nearby Pennsylvania. The
results are spectacular—complex, earthy, and tart without being cloying or over the top.

CARBON COUNTY, PENNSYLVANIA

## 42  Party naked at a nudist beer festival

The most—ahem—stripped-down beer festival
in the US is the clothing-optional Sunny Rest
Naked Beerfest. This "Bare Beach Beer Bash"
is held annually in summer at the Sunny Rest
Resort (a nudist resort). Revelers can bare it all
among a bevy of craft beer from across the state,
though truth be told, the beer selection isn't the
main draw here.

PHILADELPHIA, PENNSYLVANIA

## 43  Find rare Belgian brews in Philadelphia

The venerable Monk's Cafe is a beer lover's
dream. The pages-long bottle list offers dozens
of rare and obscure beers from Belgium and
Belgian-inspired breweries around the world.
Its impressive draft beer selection has rare drafts
from California's Russian River Brewing and
Belgium's 3 Fonteinen. Food-wise, try any
of the moules paired with a Flemish Sour Ale
brewed in Belgium especially for the restaurant.

AMBLER, PENNSYLVANIA

## 44  Discover a brewery inside a Victorian home

Forest & Main Brewing is a tiny pub and
brewery set in a transformed Victorian house.
Founders and brewers Daniel Endicott and
Gerard Olson make exquisite saisons, IPAs, and
British-style cask beers, and pair them with some
seriously delicious food. A taproom has opened
next door, with an open floor plan and a bigger
selection of beers.

PHILADELPHIA, PENNSYLVANIA

## 45  Drink a modern-day legend

A Philadelphia institution for decades, the
Yards Brewing taproom and brewpub in the
city-center neighborhood is a stunner. There's no
better place to taste the freshest classics Philly
Pale Ale or Brawler English mild. A rotating
selection of seasonals is always offered as well
as vintage beers and a menu of pretzels, wings,
and sandwiches.

DOWNINGTON, PENNSYLVANIA

## 46  Crush a can of this primo lager

Victory Brewing makes many great beers, but Prima Pils has always been its most classic. The base beer is a typical Bohemian pilsner, but to appeal to American palates, Victory hops it with a generous dose of German and Czech hops. The clean, crisp profile makes it great for summer day drinking—make sure you drink it quickly so that it doesn't warm up too much. *Prost!*

ADAMSTOWN, PENNSYLVANIA

## 47  Knock back a Kölsch

Stoudts Brewing was started in 1987 by Ed and Carol Stoudt and quickly became known for its clean, classic lagers. One of its best beers is a winter and spring seasonal called Karnival Kölsch, a classic Cologne-style beer made with two-row malt, a small amount of red wheat malt, and German hops for bittering and aroma. Look for it in bottle shops and bars around the East Coast or at the brewery's restaurant and taproom.

POTTSVILLE, PENNSYLVANIA

## 48  Sip an American classic or two

Yuengling Brewery is the oldest US beer producer, having been founded in Pottsville in 1829. The flagship Traditional Lager is a rich amber lager that goes down easy with a touch of sweetness on the finish. More recent additions include a seasonal Oktoberfest, Golden Pilsner, and Black & Tan. The brewery is open for free tours and tastings year-round with a well-appointed gift shop to boot.

HERSHEY, PENNSYLVANIA

## 49  Drink an elfish brew

Mad Elf from Tröegs Independent Brewing— a boozy winter warmer clocking in at 11% ABV— always signals the start of the holiday season along the East Coast. Brewed with chocolate and Munich malts, German and Czech hops, and a spicy Belgian yeast strain, it's a cheerful holiday treat. If you're visiting the brewery, look for Wild Elf, a tart foeder-fermented version of Mad Elf spiked with brettanomyces and Balaton cherries.

MILTON, DELAWARE

## 50  Explore the origins of extreme beer

The original American beer innovator is located in a small town in Delaware. Sam Calagione's Dogfish Head Brewery is known for off-centered ales and extreme beers. Drop in for a tour and tasting to try the range of brews. Classics include 60 Minute and 90 Minute IPA (try 120 Minute if you dare!), while newer beers like SeaQuench Ale (brewed with black lime and sea salt) will have you wanting to make repeat visits.

BERLIN, MARYLAND

### 51  Live the J.R.E.A.M. in rural Maryland

Burley Oak Brewing made a splash with its line of various sour ales spiked with fruit juices and spices called J.R.E.A.M. (Juice Rules Everything Around Me). This ongoing and ever-changing series includes beers like Banana Bread Jream (notes of vanilla, cinnamon, and banana) and Coquito Jream (coconut, vanilla, and nutmeg). Hokey? Sure. Delicious? Absolutely.

BALTIMORE, MARYLAND

### 53  Discover the art of brewing

Located in Fells Point, Max's Taphouse has a mind-bending selection of more than one hundred taps from local, domestic, and international breweries, while the beer menu includes over 1,000 bottles. Special tappings and events run throughout the season.

HALETHORPE, MARYLAND

### 54  See what else Guinness can brew

Guinness has been brewed in the US for years, but it now has a full-fledged experimental brewery dedicated to crafting new and exciting styles in addition to the classic Irish Stout. The Guinness Open Gate Brewery & Barrel House is just outside Baltimore and you can visit the full bar with exclusive taproom-only beers, as well as tours and tastings.

BALTIMORE, MARYLAND

### 52  Dine and drink ale in a Baltimore rowhouse

A brewery and upscale restaurant tucked into a former townhouse in downtown Baltimore, The Brewer's Art is one of the classiest places to sample a house-made beer. The focus is on Belgian-style beers like Resurrection Abbey dubbel and Beazly Belgian strong ale. A full menu ranging from steaks and chops to pastas and mussels is available in a white tablecloth adorned dining room.

*Right:* Guinness in the US brews new styles of beer

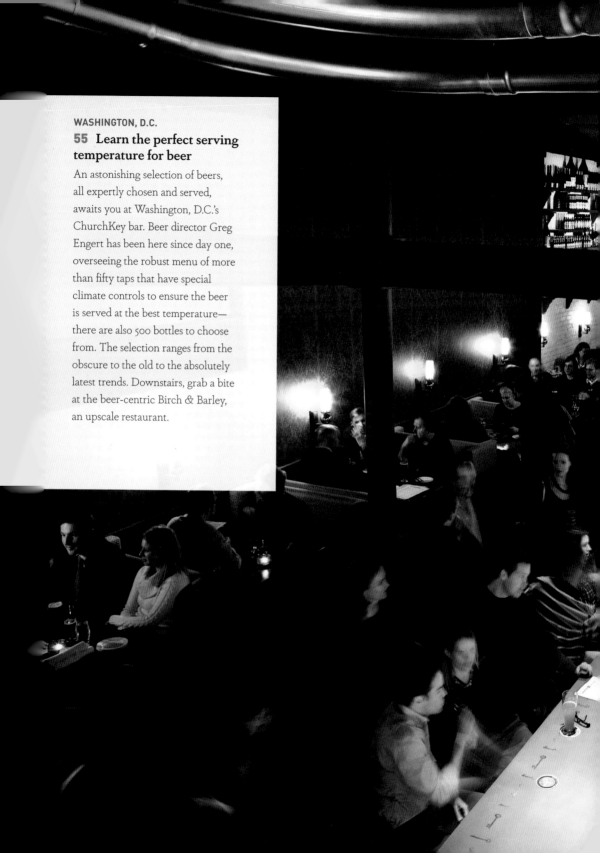

WASHINGTON, D.C.

## 55 Learn the perfect serving temperature for beer

An astonishing selection of beers, all expertly chosen and served, awaits you at Washington, D.C.'s ChurchKey bar. Beer director Greg Engert has been here since day one, overseeing the robust menu of more than fifty taps that have special climate controls to ensure the beer is served at the best temperature— there are also 500 bottles to choose from. The selection ranges from the obscure to the old to the absolutely latest trends. Downstairs, grab a bite at the beer-centric Birch & Barley, an upscale restaurant.

## 56  Sample artisanal eats and handmade ales

Visit one of two locations of Right Proper Brewing, which opened in D.C.'s historic Shaw neighborhood in 2013. The original location features draft beers and bites, while a larger production outpost in the Brookland section features a spacious outdoor area and plenty of amazing beers.

## 57  Discover the history of brewing

In 2017, the Smithsonian hired its very own beer historian to curate historical beer artifacts at its National Museum of American History. The archives now include various memorabilia, but the main draw is its series of events focusing on the craft beer industry.

## 58  Wallow in the past with wood-fired ales

Prior to establishing Pen Druid Brewing in rural Rappahannock County, brothers Jennings, Van, and Lain Carney churned out psychedelic riffage in their proto-metal band Pontiak. The trio now dabbles in mixed-fermentation and barrel blending. That means everything from Diamond Jim, a farmhouse ale fermented in Hungarian oak with brettanomyces, to Mild Child, an English-style dark mild. Other beers, like Wheels of Confusion (a "pilsner pale ale") and Paranoia (a dark sour fermented in red wine barrels), take their names from classic metal songs. Don't miss the special releases, festivals, and live music on weekends.

## 59  Mend your broken heart with this bitter

Are you the owner of a lonely or broken heart? Each January, Alewerks produces the special Bitter Valentine beer to mend broken hearts on the loneliest of lonely holidays, Valentine's Day. With its brilliant orange color and huge aromas of grapefruit, pine, and resin, this double IPA is one of the best beers made on the East Coast. Once available only in 22 oz (625 ml) bottles, it now comes in tallboy cans for even more consolation.

## 60  Sweat it out with the country's top brewers

Every August, Richmond's The Veil invites dozens of the best brewers in the country to participate in the sun-soaked Forever Summer Fest. Each year has a different theme, from IPAs to sour ales, and all proceeds go toward a local charity. Ticket sales are limited, which keeps lines short and the beer flowing—so make sure you buy yours in advance.

## 61 Knock back Richmond's best IPAs

Richmond has quickly become one of the top-tier beer destinations in the US. It started in 2011 with Hardywood Park Craft Brewery, just the second brewery in town, and quickly expanded to include a roster of quality breweries. The current hotspot is the Scott's Addition neighborhood where you'll find breweries like The Veil, Ardent, and Väsen. Start at Ardent, a small collective that grew out of a weekend garage homebrewers' club. It specializes in clean, crisp pilsners and IPAs with a focus on drinkability. (Pro tip: be sure to hit up ZZQ Texas Craft Barbeque next door.) Next, visit The Veil, known for hazy IPAs, fruited sours, rich stouts, and mixed-fermentation ales—the taproom is one of the sleekest in town. Then drop in at Väsen, a sprawling brewery focusing on saisons. Breweries to seek out outside of the Scott's Addition area include Final Gravity Brewing, Triple Crossing Brewing, The Answer Brewpub (and its sister restaurant Mekong), Stone Brewing Tap Room (an outpost of the San Diego stalwart), and Strangeways Brewing.

**61** *Above:* Quality brews from the small Ardent collective

ABINGDON, VIRGINIA

## 62 Catch a pint and a bluegrass show

The small Wolf Hills Brewing in rural southwest Virginia is located along the Crooked Road, Virginia's bluegrass music trail, which winds through almost 300 miles of scenic, mountainous terrain. Drop in on a weekend and you're likely to find live bluegrass or country from local musicians, or an impromptu jam session. On tap, try Troopers Alley IPA or Creeper Trail Amber, a nod to a local rail trail that traverses a nearby mountain range.

RALEIGH, NORTH CAROLINA

## 63 Eat as well as you'll drink at this brewpub

Brewery Bhavana is an odd duck. Under a single roof it contains four distinct businesses: a flower shop, brewery, bookstore, and dim sum restaurant—that coalesce to form more than the sum of their parts. The beer program focuses on saisons and sour ales, often brewed with culinary ingredients like peppercorns, mango, and honey, and is rounded out by textbook-clean beers like IPAs and pilsners. Don't leave without trying the innovative modern dim sum menu.

**63** *Right:* The multiple spaces of Brewery Bhavana

**FARMVILLE, NORTH CAROLINA**

## 64  Discover dark ales in the Tar Heel State

The sultry, sticky, humid environs of eastern North Carolina might sound like a strange place to open a dark beer-focused brewery, but Duck-Rabbit Craft Brewery proves that these beers are actually perfectly suited for the climate. Owner and brewer Paul Philippon focuses on stouts, rich porters, and black ales. His bestselling beer year-round is the frothy Milk Stout; Baltic Porter is one of the best examples of the style outside of Poland; and his Doppelbock is a malty German-style lager. The dark beers work in such a humid environment because they pair with summery foods—burgers, barbecued meats, and charred vegetables. Dark beers actually benefit from the hot weather—as the beers warm, their complex, smoky undertones begin to unfurl and open.

**MILLS RIVER, NORTH CAROLINA**

## 65  Visit "Malt Disney World"

Sierra Nevada Brewing's sprawling, copper-adorned facility is far and away the largest, most impressive brewery in the Asheville region. Make your way there to find tours, an on-site restaurant and brewpub, an outdoor music venue, and miles of trails and recreational areas. Inside, you can sample dozens of beers brewed on-site, including the iconic Sierra Nevada Pale Ale and Torpedo Extra IPA, as well as small-batch brews made on the pilot system. The full-service restaurant has your grub needs covered and you can work off all that beer hiking the adventure trails.

**ASHEVILLE, NORTH CAROLINA**

## 66  Celebrate the harvest

Held annually in the fall, Burnpile Harvest Festival is the premier event from one of Asheville's best breweries, Burial Beer.
The festival brings together brewers, artists, musicians, winemakers, and chefs for a day-long celebration of their craft. In addition to numerous Burial beers—namely, saisons, IPAs, lagers, and stouts—the celebration brings in some of the most talented brewers from around the country. Entry includes commemorative glassware and tokens for beer pours (additional tokens can be purchased on-site), and food from several of Asheville's best chefs is always available.

**MORGANTON, NORTH CAROLINA**

## 67  Immerse yourself in beer *terroir*

The driving force behind Fonta Flora Brewery's annual summer State of Origin festival is for each of the dozens of participating breweries to pour a beer that's reflective of their respective locale's *terroir*. That can mean beer brewed with a certain type of regional malt, for instance, or one infused with a native fruit, herb, or vegetable. Fonta Flora specializes in this style of beer making, incorporating adjuncts like North Carolina-native Bloody Butcher corn into its saison and locally grown pawpaw fruit (native to the Appalachian region) into its Carolina Custard mixed-fermentation ale.

## 68 Learn to pair beer and cheese

The Funkatorium is Wicked Weed Brewing's outpost for its funky and sour beer program. Located in the South Slope neighborhood, it features dozens of varieties of Wicked Weed's sour ales on draft and in bottles, with a small plates menu of dishes to pair with the beer (think cheese plates, charcuterie, and duck confit salad). A recent expansion now includes an outdoor beer garden open on weekends as well as a venue for live music. It's one of the country's few taprooms dedicated exclusively to funky and sour beers.

# Visit Asheville's top nine breweries

Asheville has more than thirty breweries in the metropolitan area. Here are nine of the best to visit in this idyllic town surrounded by the Blue Ridge Mountains.

### 69 Green Man Brewery

This pioneering brewery opened in 1997. Don't leave town without trying its Green Man ESB or the highly sought-after Snozzberry sour wheat ale.

69

### 70 Highland Brewing

Asheville's original craft brewery, Highland dispenses an array of old-school and new-school beer styles, like the flagship Gaelic amber ale and the hoppy AVL IPA, a West Coast iteration of the style.

### 71 Wedge Brewing

A picturesque, family-friendly location near the banks of the French Broad River makes this one of Asheville's buzziest and most active breweries, particularly in the warmer months.

### 72 Zillicoah Beer

This relative newcomer to the Asheville scene made a big splash in 2017 with a focus on lagers and other traditional styles.

73

### 73 Asheville Brewing

The perennially packed North Asheville brewpub and movie theater offers a range of house-brewed ales and lagers beside a lengthy menu of pizzas and hearty sandwiches. Movies are just $3 and in summertime are often shown al fresco.

### 74 Wicked Weed Brewing

Acquired by Anheuser-Busch InBev in 2017, Wicked Weed is a reliable—and extremely crowded!—place to taste beer. There are dozens of unique brews on draft, while the nearby Funkatorium spin-off offers barrel-aged sours and high-gravity beers.

77

### 75 Burial Beer

This tiny brewery in Asheville's downtown South Slope neighborhood has quickly burgeoned into one of the South's premier producers. Try a wide range of styles from saisons and stouts to IPAs and pilsners.

### 76 Bhramari Brewing

What happens when you take familiar beer styles and add unexpected twists? Bhramari Brewing answers that with odd styles like black gose, sour pale ale, and California common brewed with local organic corn. Check out the equally eclectic food menu.

### 77 Hi-Wire Brewing

This circus- and sideshow-themed brewery has two locations: a small tasting room downtown and a larger production facility in Biltmore Village. Styles range from crisp lagers and dank IPAs to robust oak-fermented sours and porters.

### ASHEVILLE, NORTH CAROLINA

## 78  Earn your beer on a cycle tour

Pubcycle tours are a unique way to experience a city while burning calories and drinking some beer. The idea is that about a dozen riders sit around a cycle-like bar-on-wheels drinking and pedaling their way through town. One of the best is the Amazing Pubcycle in Asheville. The company offers two options: one is an hour and a half pub tour that makes two fifteen-minute stops for beer. The other is a forty-minute "nomad" tour without the pub stops. Both tours encourage pedalers to bring their own beers to drink during the pedaling. With many places to grab beer to go in downtown Asheville (check out Bruisin' Ales and Tasty Beverage for killer beer selections), you shouldn't have trouble finding high-quality local suds.

## 79  Savor the fresh flavors of gose

Gose, a tart, salty simple sour ale native to Leipzig, Germany, is now one of the most common sour beers in the US. That wasn't always the case. When South Carolina's Westbrook Brewing released its Gose several years ago, it was one of the first examples of the style brewed in the US. Now it's become the standard. Why is it so popular? It comes in tastefully designed, outdoor-friendly cans, it clocks in at just 4% ABV, and its flavors echo the salty scents of summer: fresh aromas of stone fruit upfront, crisp pear and citrus on the palate, and a gentle oceany brine to finish. It's an overall super-fun beer to drink.

## 80  Pair your favorite beers with fine food

Charleston, South Carolina, is known as a culinary hotspot, with many new, hip, and historical restaurants located throughout the small city. Edmund's Oast Brewing is the most beer-focused of these, with an on-site brewery making some stellar beer, and a full-service restaurant that's head and shoulders above your typical brewpub. Start with a charcuterie and cheese plate paired with a house-brewed saison before moving on to a main course of spicy greens and fish paired with a dry-hopped sour wheat ale.

## 81  Chill out with an urban farmhouse brew

Birds Fly South Ale Project dabbles in "urban farmhouse" brewing, which includes all manner of saisons, mixed-culture ales, and rustic wild beers. The small tasting room includes two separate bars, live music, an outdoor patio, a large lawn space, and a beer garden. It's one of the most chilled spots in town for sipping a beer.

## 82  Sample a "weedy" drink

SweetWater Brewing's 420 Strain G13 is an uber-dank American IPA (named for the brewery owners' favorite weed strain), which incorporates marijuana terpenes, but no actual THC. The terpenes—organic compounds responsible for lending plants their unique aromas—give this beer an over-the-top whiff akin to the stickiest dime bag you've ever opened. Within months of its initial release in 2018, G13 became SweetWater's second bestselling beer.

ATHENS, GEORGIA

## 83  Crush it at Creature Comforts

Founded in 2014, the nationally renowned Creature Comforts Brewing is known for making some of the best beers in the South. Its most well-known offering is Tropicália, an insanely fruity American-style IPA. Other year-round beers include the supremely clean Bibo pilsner and the pleasantly tart Athena Berliner weisse. Special releases from the brewery's extensive barrel-aging program occur throughout the year and it holds other beer- and arts-centric events.

ATLANTA, GEORGIA

## 84  Treat your taste buds

Wrecking Bar Brewpub is located inside a twentieth-century Victorian-style house that was previously used as a Methodist Protestant church, dance school, and architectural antiques store. It serves some of the best beer in the ATL, like Berry White Berliner Weisse and Breaking Bob Kölsch. Meanwhile, local specialties, like boiled peanuts and wild striped bass, dot the Southern-accented menu.

ATLANTA, GEORGIA

## 85  Ride a beer bus

Jump aboard the Atlanta Beer Bus party shuttle bus that offers a hop-on/hop-off tour of Atlanta's most delicious breweries. Fifteen bucks gets you an all-day pass to sampling the finest local brewing establishments like Atlanta Brewing, SweetWater Brewing, Orpheus Brewing, Wrecking Bar Brewpub, and Scofflaw Brewing. Buy your tickets in advance.

ATLANTA, GEORGIA

## 86  Discover a new realm

Former Stone Brewing brewmaster Mitch Steele decamped from Southern California to Atlanta to open New Realm Brewing, a brewery and restaurant in the Poncey-Highland neighborhood. Fans of Steele's previous work will recognize much of what's on draft: hop-forward pale ales and IPAs rounded out by classic clean lagers and rich stouts.

### 87 Find good beer in Alabama

Alabama isn't known for great craft beer, but Birmingham's Good People Brewing is hoping to change that. With a wide range of standards like IPA, pale ale, and brown ale, as well as specialty sours, one-offs, and the Funk Farm series, it's changing the face of beer in the Deep South. The brewery is outfitted with a hip tasting room, including an outdoor area with games, and tours are offered on Saturdays for a fee, which includes a take-home glass and draft pour.

### 88 Sip a fruity beer style

Try this "Florida weisse,"—a fruited-up version of the classic Berliner weisse—one of the few regionally specific beers in the US. The creator of that style, Jonathan Wakefield, makes one of the best in the country with his Dragon Fruit Passion Fruit (DFPF for short). Its deep magenta hue is simply stunning, as are its big notes of tropical fruity goodness.

**TOP 3**

JACKSONVILLE, FLORIDA

# Drop in on Jacksonville's top three breweries

Jacksonville doesn't have the glitz and glamour of other Florida cities like Tampa or Miami, but it maintains a robust craft beer and brewing scene. Try these top three places:

### 89 Aardwolf Brewing

This uber-hip brewery is located in a raw space with exposed brick and rough-hewn tabletops. Nearly two dozen beers are available on draft, including pilot and experimental batches, and nearly as many bottles, mostly barrel-aged variants and mixed-fermentation ales.

### 90 Intuition Ale Works

Located in the heart of Jacksonville's entertainment district, Intuition focuses on hoppy IPAs, simple sours, and strong stouts served in a spacious industrial-chic tasting room. Check out the rooftop bar for sweeping views of the city.

### 91 Wicked Barley Brewing

This waterfront brewery compound features a full-service restaurant and taproom with TVs for sports viewing, a covered patio, a pet-friendly waterfront beer garden, and a boat dock. Beers include an all-American selection of hoppy styles and European-influenced classics.

TAMPA, FLORIDA

## 92 Soak up some sun and beer

Held each March, Cigar City Brewing's Hunahpu's Day festival gathers hundreds of breweries from the Sunshine State and around the country to pour beer in sunny Tampa. The occasion is the release of Hunahpu's Imperial Stout from Cigar City Brewing, made with chocolate and chile powder. Tickets to the festival, a beer lover's dream, include unlimited pours from every brewery, as well as bottles of the coveted (and highly tradable) stout. Buy tickets in advance, as they typically sell out quickly.

TARPON SPRINGS, FLORIDA

## 93 Add these beers to your bucket list

Bob Sylvester, owner and brewer of Saint Somewhere Brewing, is something of an unsung hero in the US beer industry. He nearly single-handedly introduced Belgian-style saison brewing to the US market with beers like Athene and Lectio Divina. Notoriously stubborn, Sylvester doesn't follow trends and he doesn't brew anything that he himself doesn't want to drink. That means mostly saisons and farmhouse-style ales, as well as a smattering of Belgian-style strong ales. Besides Saint Somewhere drafts and bottles, Sylvester offers a selection of Belgian bottles to drink on-premise, including Orval, Sylvester's favorite.

GRAND RAPIDS, MICHIGAN

## 94 Join the line for strong stout

Each April, Michigan's Founders Brewing releases its Kentucky Breakfast Stout, a bourbon barrel-aged version of its regular coffee-and-chocolate-infused Breakfast Stout. The beer is in such high demand that fans begin lining up the night before just to sample the current year's release. The brewery hosts events all week long at dedicated bars and restaurants around the city.

UPPER PENINSULA, MICHIGAN

## 95 Enjoy brews beside Michigan's Great Lakes

Upper Hand Brewery—a tiny offshoot of Bell's Brewery—caters to the Upper Peninsula (UP), a forested region of Michigan surrounded on three sides by the Great Lakes and jutting off from mainland Wisconsin. The brewery produces its own brands (not Bell's clones) like Yooper Ale, made with UP-grown oats, and Upper Hand IPA, a punchy, tropically aromatic IPA that's like a gentler cousin of Bell's Two Hearted. Although tours are not offered, you can bend an elbow in the brewery's on-site taproom.

**GRAND RAPIDS, MICHIGAN**

# Visit Grand Rapids' top three breweries

### 96 The Mitten Brewing

Set inside a Victorian-era firehouse, The Mitten offers American-style craft beers paired with specialty pizzas and sandwiches.

### 97 Speciation Artisan Ales

Speciation focuses on mixed-fermentation and wild beers. But rather than brewing its own wort, the Ermatingers source from Grand Rapids-area breweries and spruce it up with house cultures, culinary flourishes, and barrel treatments.

### 98 Brewery Vivant

Housed in a refurbished historic funeral home in the East Hills neighborhood, this brewery offers pub food alongside its selection of Belgian-inspired farmhouse ales.

97

---

**WARREN, MICHIGAN**

## 99 Taste this super-strong beer

Kuhnhenn Brewing's Raspberry Eisbock is an extremely strong German-style beer that undergoes a freezing process in order to concentrate the alcohol. It's worth seeking out for its rich, toasty notes of bread crust, dark chocolate, and raspberry jam. At 15.5% ABV, it's extremely boozy, but mellows with age. A true bucket-list beer!

**KALAMAZOO, MICHIGAN**

## 100 Savor the flavors of Bell's Two Hearted IPA

Bell's Two Hearted IPA is a benchmark for the American IPA style, a classic that helped define an entire generation of beers. It has a refreshing but complex profile from a balance of malts and bitter, but highly aromatic Centennial hops. It has huge notes of grapefruit and pine.

DEXTER, MICHIGAN

**101** Find the funk at Jolly Pumpkin

Jolly Pumpkin Artisan Ales was a founder of, and continues to be a leader in, the American sour beer movement, producing complex, funky, oak-aged beers fermented and conditioned with a mix of yeast and bacteria. The brewery itself features a restaurant and taproom, and a series of brewpubs and café outposts in the greater Ann Arbor and Detroit areas, meaning opportunities to try the beer are in no short supply. Start with Bam Bière, an effervescent, thirst-quenching saison, or Oro de Calabaza, a heftier, but equally complex sour ale. Other beers include La Roja, a sour red ale, and Madrugada Obscura, a dark stout-like sour ale with notes of cocoa and pine.

CLEVELAND, OHIO
## 102 Treat yourself to some Christmas cheer

Most Christmas beers tend to be overly spiced, but Christmas Ale from Cleveland's Great Lakes Brewing hits all the merry notes without going over the top. A blend of fresh honey, cinnamon, and ginger flavors, it pairs well with hearty winter fare like roast duck and spiced desserts. Check it out at the brewery's West Side restaurant and tasting room or in six-packs throughout the East Coast.

ATHENS, OHIO
## 103 Indulge in barrel-aged beers

One of the best places to try a range of high-gravity barrel-aged beers is at Jackie O's production taproom. Start with a 4 oz (114 ml) pour of Bourbon Barrel Brick Kiln, an English-style barleywine aged in bourbon barrels, before moving on to Oil of Aphrodite, an imperial stout with black walnuts and Belgian candi syrup. Vintage bottles are also available for on-premise only. These beers are astonishing in their depth and complexity—not to mention their merrymaking.

COLUMBUS, OHIO
## 104 Go on, slay a beer!

Join the music and beer celebration of Dragonsaddle Day, which takes place in late summer at Hoof Hearted Brewing's suburban location. Festival-goers can buy music-only tickets (past bands include Dinosaur Jr.) or beer-and-music tickets, which let you sample beers from renowned breweries from around the country like Oxbow, Other Half, and Horus Aged Ales. The main attraction is the brewery's Dragonsaddle Triple IPA.

**103** *Right:* Sampling Jackie O's robust barrel-aged strong beers

### LEXINGTON, KENTUCKY
## 105 Get into the community spirit

The community-focused West Sixth Brewing makes a range of beers from its hoppy flagship IPA to taproom exclusives like Strawberry Kölsch. One of the best is Pennyrile Pale Ale, a classically mellow American pale ale made with Mosaic and Citra hops. The brewery supports community endeavors like a walk/run club, yoga classes, and a monthly science lecture series. Tours are available on the weekends.

### LOUISVILLE, KENTUCKY
## 106 Drink in a "holy" gastropub

Holy Grale is a former church-turned-craft beer altar, and is one of the holiest places to drink beer in the US. Opened in 2011, it features twenty-plus beers on draft and a wide selection of bottles and cans. The restaurant features gussied-up Southern classics like Scotch Kentucky quail eggs and heirloom tomato and peach salad.

### LOUISVILLE, KENTUCKY
## 107 Whet your palate with a range of brews

Highbrow and lowbrow come together at Nachbar, a dive bar dedicated to high-quality craft and imported beer, and locally made whiskies and bourbon. From the outside it looks like a run-of-the-mill neighborhood bar, but the draft and bottle list contains some real gems. An outdoor dog-friendly area makes it popular with a young, hipster crowd.

### MADISON, WISCONSIN
## 108 Savor the great tastes at this festival

The Great Taste of the Midwest festival, which has run for more than thirty years, takes place each August and features more than 190 of the Midwest's best independent brewers pouring beer at picturesque Olin Park overlooking Lake Monona. Notable return brewers include Jolly Pumpkin Artisan Ales, Off Color, Urban Chestnut, and Perennial Artisan Ales.

### CHIPPEWA FALLS, WISCONSIN
## 109 Sip a shandy in summer

Summertime in the Midwest calls for a Leinenkugel's® Summer Shandy® or two. This blend of German-style wheat ale and lemonade flavors makes it a crisp, refreshing, low-alcohol crusher. Other varieties are available, too, including orange, berry, and grapefruit. The lemon remains the standard, though.

**110**   *Right:* Wisconson's Old Milwaukee is best drunk in Milwaukee

### MILWAUKEE, WISCONSIN
**110** Drink an
Old Milwaukee

Old Milwaukee certainly isn't the best beer in the world— far from it—but knocking back a couple in a historic Milwaukee dive bar like George's Pub or while tailgating before a Brewers game at Miller Park is an event unto itself. There's no better match for a real Wisconsin brat.

### INDIANAPOLIS, INDIANA
**111** Try a house beer
called Table

The Koelschip is a handsome bar and tasting room, and an outpost for Central State Brewing. It features draft and packaged beers from the house brewery, as well as packaged beer and wine from other producers. Table Beer is a good place to start—it's a slightly rustic, low-alcohol saison-like ale with notes of white grape and clove.

### INDIANAPOLIS, INDIANA
**112** Race to Speedway
for a special beer

Located in the appropriately named Speedway neighborhood, Daredevil Brewing crafts the easy-drinking Race Day lager every May just in time for the annual Indianapolis 500 held every Memorial Day weekend. It's a smooth, crisp beer meant for long sessions at the racetrack. It's available on tap at the tasting room and in cans throughout the greater Indianapolis area.

## 113 Drink beers available only in Wisconsin

Wisconsin's New Glarus Brewing is known for its extreme dedication to the
Badger State. The brewery doesn't distribute outside state lines, but within
the state its beer is available nearly anywhere that serves beer. A visit to the
brewery itself, perched atop a steep hill, is a treat. You can do a self-guided
tour or pay a nominal fee for a more structured tour. Tastings and pints are
available as well as beers to go. Be sure to snag one of the limited bottles like
Serendipity, a sour ale aged on apples, cranberries, and cherries.

MUNSTER, INDIANA

## 114 Rock on at an epic beer fest

One of the most epic beer and metal festivals is the annual Dark Lord Day from Three Floyds Brewing in Munster. What started as a small party in celebration of Dark Lord imperial stout has blossomed into a full day-long beer and music festival with some of the biggest names in modern heavy metal and American craft beer. Thousands turn out every spring to sip the rich, robust ale and hear bands like Dying Fetus and Pig Destroyer play the main stage. Various VIP packages are available and include mixed variants of the Dark Lord stout.

CHICAGO, ILLINOIS

## 115 Join the revolution against insipid ales

Revolution Brewing has several outposts in the greater Chicagoland area, which include a couple of brewpubs and large production brewery with spacious tasting room. The flagship Anti-Hero IPA is a great beer to start, piney and citrusy with a heady kick. Other standouts include Sun Crusher hoppy wheat ale, a summer seasonal, and Straight Jacket barleywine, one of the best examples of the traditional English strong ale brewed in the US.

CHICAGO, ILLINOIS

## 116 Taste colorful esoteric styles in a funky tasting room

The Mousetrap taproom outpost of Chicago's quirky Off Color Brewing features an array of draft and bottled beers from the idiosyncratic brewery. Start with Troublesome, its take on a German-style gose, with notes of coriander and salt. Then move on to seasonals like Coffee DinoS'mores imperial stout or a vintage bottle from the cellar. Tours are offered on Sundays (reserve online in advance) and you're welcome to bring your own food into the taproom.

CHICAGO, ILLINOIS

## 117 Grab a Black Friday beer release

Each year on the Friday after Thanksgiving, hordes of dedicated Goose Island fans wait in the cold for the first taste of the year's Bourbon County Brand Stout (BCBS). Fans also line up for Proprietor's Bourbon County Brand Stout, a rotating variant—only available in the greater Chicago area. Past editions include a double-chocolate version and one with bananas, roasted almonds, and cassia bark.

CHICAGO, ILLINOIS

## 118 Check out the award-winning beer at FoBAB

Chicago is home to the Festival of Wood & Barrel-Aged Beer (FoBAB) dedicated to wood-fermented and barrel-aged beers. It attracts more than 200 breweries every year in November, pouring close to 400 different strong beers.

CHICAGO, ILLINOIS

## 119 Ask for cellared ales at this gastropub

The beverage directors at The Publican, a gastropub from chef Paul Kahan, purchase many cases of Orval every year and allocate several to a temperature-controlled beer cellar for long-term storage. Some are reserved for special events and tastings, but you can ask the bartender if any older, cellared versions are currently available.

**CHICAGO, ILLINOIS**

## 120 Sip a hoppy ale on the north side

Some of the best beer in the Midwest comes from Chicago's Half Acre Beer. Its Daisy Cutter pale ale sets the standard for low-alcohol hoppy ales and its IPAs and pilsners continue making even the most fatigued beer drinkers come back for more. The brewery has two locations in Chicago—both offer tours and full-service tasting rooms. One is in the Lincoln Ave area and the other in Bowmanville.

scratch brewing company

<u>familiar</u>  $1 SAMPLE · $4 PINT
   MUNICH ALT                              Soda
                                          $1 sample
                                          $4 gal

<u>forest 'foraged fire</u>  $1.50 · $5    HEARTH
BASIL · BIÈRE         STOUT/RED HEFE· gruit  BREAD
        de GARDE                            $6
<u>fancy</u>  $2 · $6       take away GROWLER  $6
                        $5 Refillable bottle
   GOTLAND · 9 HOUR      see menu for fill price.
              BARLEYWINE  LOTUS
                        SEED BIERE
                         de GARDE

## 121 Go back to nature with these brews

Scratch Brewing in rural southern Illinois crafts a range of
botanical and nature-inspired beers with ingredients grown
on the farm or foraged from the surrounding wilderness. Its
Single Tree series includes beers called Birch, Cedar, Hickory,
Maple, and Oak, each one incorporating leaves, nuts,
branches, berries, hulls, and bark from their respective trees.
Meanwhile, its Spring Tonic, a 4.4% ABV gruit brewed
without hops, gets its bitterness from dandelion, carrot tops,
and clover, all grown in the brewery's garden. There is also an
on-site tasting room and bottle shop.

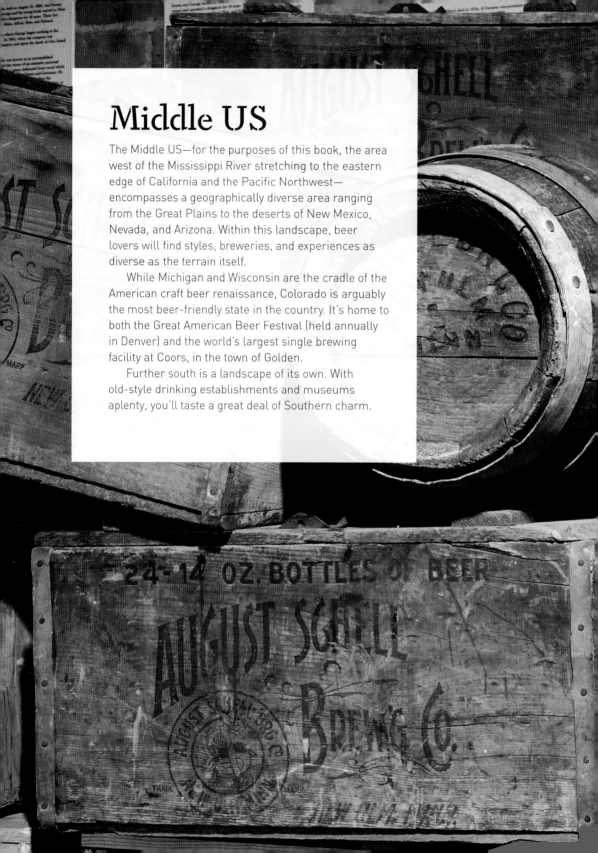

# Middle US

The Middle US—for the purposes of this book, the area west of the Mississippi River stretching to the eastern edge of California and the Pacific Northwest—encompasses a geographically diverse area ranging from the Great Plains to the deserts of New Mexico, Nevada, and Arizona. Within this landscape, beer lovers will find styles, breweries, and experiences as diverse as the terrain itself.

While Michigan and Wisconsin are the cradle of the American craft beer renaissance, Colorado is arguably the most beer-friendly state in the country. It's home to both the Great American Beer Festival (held annually in Denver) and the world's largest single brewing facility at Coors, in the town of Golden.

Further south is a landscape of its own. With old-style drinking establishments and museums aplenty, you'll taste a great deal of Southern charm.

AUGUST SCHELL
BREWING CO.
NEW ULM, MINN.

AUGUST SCHELL
BREWING CO.
NEW ULM, MINN.

Schell's
DEER BRAND
BEER
IN STEINIE BOTTLES
NEW ULM, MINN.

MINNESOTA/WISCONSIN

## 122 Drink a dose of darkness

Surly Brewing's Darkness Day is a fall weekend festival similar to Three Floyds' Dark Lord Day or Cigar City's Hunahpu's Day. It is full of big beers, thrashing hardcore metal music, and an armada of food trucks from around the Minneapolis region. Tickets are tiered and include a selection of Darkness bottles (the namesake Russian Imperial Stout), including variants, as well as access to campgrounds and general admission to the "party." Past headliners have included English extreme metal band Carcass and NYC hardcore legends Sick Of It All. In 2018, the festival moved east of the Minnesota state line into Wisconsin. Keep an eye on the brewery's website for details about locations and dates.

LINO LAKES, MINNESOTA

## 123 Quaff Nordic-inspired ales in the Land of 10,000 Lakes

HammerHeart Brewing in the northern suburbs of Minneapolis was founded in 2013 by Austin Lunn—a black metal musician best known for his band Panopticon—and his brother-in-law, Nathaniel Chapman. Lunn takes care of the brewing and finds inspiration in Nordic and Celtic cultures as well as the heavy metal scene (the brewery is named for an album by Swedish metal legend Bathory). Drop in to the brewery's tasting room, which is decked out in a wooden cabin with a Nordic feel.

NEW ULM, MINNESOTA

## 124 Grab a Grain Belt beer

This storied Minnesota classic, produced by August Schell Brewing since 2002, has been made in a number of varieties by a handful of different breweries since the late nineteenth century. The original iteration, Golden Grain Belt, was introduced in 1893, and current offerings include Grain Belt Premium, Grain Belt Premium Light, and Grain Belt Nordeast.

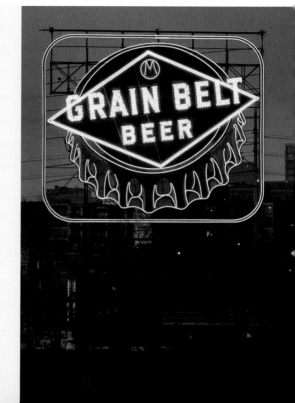

MINNEAPOLIS, MINNESOTA

# Discover the Twin Cities' best drinking places

### 125 Fair State Brewing Cooperative

This brewery makes some of the best craft beer in Minneapolis, with a focus on hoppy IPAs and clean, classic lagers. Drop in to the tasting room and, in warmer months, knock back a pint in the outdoor beer garden.

### 126 The Happy Gnome

This neighborhood bar and grill features around ninety draft lines dedicated to local, domestic, and imported specialty and craft beer. It also has a deep selection of American whiskies, Canadian ryes, and single-malt scotches.

### 127 Red Cow

With four locations throughout the Twin Cities, the Red Cow is a local powerhouse of craft beers and burgers. Each location offers around forty drafts from local and regional breweries.

### 128 New Bohemia

This beer and sausage chain with five locations in St. Paul and Minneapolis is a US take on a German-style bier and wurst hall. More than thirty local and domestic beers are available on draft rounded out by a sausage-heavy menu with vegan and vegetarian options.

ST. PAUL, MINNESOTA
## 129 Dabble in a winter beer festival

The Winter Beer Dabbler festival features more than 160 breweries pouring 500-plus beers. It's one of the few winter beer fests held outdoors—snow or shine!—and features live music, a silent disco, and a homebrew competition where local homebrewers compete for top honors. It's a true celebration of hearty Midwestern winters.

ROCHESTER, MINNESOTA
## 130 Tantalize your taste buds

The stylish Forager Brewery is a restaurant that features foraged ingredients—wild mushrooms, herbs, flowers, and spices—both on its menu and in its beer. The draft list includes a selection of fruited sours, hoppy beers, experimental brews, and malt-forward boozy tipples. Pair them with hearty dishes like cast-iron mac and cheese, wood-fired pizzas, and nachos. Weekends often feature live music and an outdoor area is open in warmer months.

### NEW ULM, MINNESOTA

## 131 Delve into the brewing past

Behind Yuengling, August Schell Brewing is the second-oldest family-owned brewery in the US. Founded in 1860 by August Schell, the brewery survived Prohibition by crafting a variety of non-alcoholic beverages, and in 2002, it purchased the famed Grain Belt beer and became the sole producer of that label. Today, the brewery has a variety of craft and regional American brands. The core craft beers are German- and European-influenced styles, including Firebrick Vienna lager, a Bavarian-style pilsner, and a dark lager, while seasonals include a gose and a grapefruit radler. Schell's legacy series is made up pre-Prohibition American lager and lite beer. There is also an on-site brewery dedicated to wood-aged sour beers sold under the Noble Star Collection. Join a tour at the New Ulm brewery, which includes a visit to the Schell Museum of Brewing. Here, you can learn about the history of the founding family. The tour ends at the Rathskeller Tap Room where you can sample beer and non-alcoholic beverages. The brewery holds several festivals throughout the year, including Bock Fest and Oktoberfest celebrations.

## 132 Jump on the hype train at the Midwest's hottest brewery

One of the hottest breweries in the US is Toppling Goliath Brewing, a hop-centric operation focusing on IPAs and big American-style stouts. The bi-level taproom features around twenty beers on draft like Pseudo Sue, a pale ale hopped with Citra hops, and Zeelander IPA brewed with New Zealand Nelson Sauvin hops. Book yourself on a brewery tour and you'll receive a 10 oz (295 ml) commemorative glass, a 10 oz pour of a flagship beer, and a thirty-minute tour of the brewing and packaging facility. The brewery also hosts specialty bottle releases, including Assassin, SR-71, and Kentucky Brunch Brand Stout, an imperial stout brewed with coffee aged in bourbon barrels.

## 133 Sip state-specific suds in the summer

Small, state-specific beer festivals are some of the best ways to try what a region has to offer without being tempted by big-name regional and national brands. Take Festival of Iowa Beers, for instance, the state's longest-running beer festival. The annual event (held on the Sunday before Labor Day) first started in 2005 with 300 attendees sampling beers from just eight Iowa breweries. Today, it's blossomed into one of the biggest festivals in the state with 1,400 attendees sampling beer from more than forty Iowa-only breweries. Tickets include unlimited sampling—live music and food are also available.

## 134 Be educated about beer

With fifty beers on draft and another 300-plus in bottles and cans, The Cellar Peanut Pub is the best beer bar in the Hawkeye State. Located in a former train depot circa 1875, the bar focuses not just on serving beer, but also on educating imbibers about the beer itself. Each bartender must pass the Certified Beer Server exam administered by the Cicerone Program and is always happy to chat about the geekiest details of every pint served.

## 135 Pop in to Perennial Artisan Ales

This brewery, located in the South Carondelet neighborhood, was founded in 2011 and specializes in Belgian-style saisons and American-style ales. The tasting room features Perennial's core beers, as well as taproom-only releases. Join a brewer-led tour of the expansive establishment, which includes a fifteen-barrel brewhouse and a robust barrel-aging facility. A short food menu is available on-site as well. In addition to the stellar saisons, be sure to check out Abraxas, an imperial stout brewed with cocoa, ancho chiles, cinnamon, and vanilla beans. It's one of the best examples of the spicy-chocolatey dessert beer style.

ST. LOUIS, MISSOURI
## 136 Say *Prost!* in Middle America

The German-style Urban Chestnut Brewing
was founded by several Anheuser-Busch alumni
in 2011. Brewmaster Florian Kuplent crafts
exquisitely clean, classic lagers like Zwickel
and Stammtisch as well as Belgian-style ales,
including Pierre's Wit and Winged Nut brewed
with chestnuts. You can take a self-guided tour at
the Grove Brewery & Bierhall location free of
charge, along with less-frequent guided tours.

KANSAS CITY, MISSOURI
## 137 Swig from the smokestack series in Kansas City

Established way back in 1989, Boulevard
Brewing is one of Kansas City's premier craft
breweries. Now owned by Duvel Moortgat USA,
the brewery features a beer hall, a gift shop, and
event spaces. Tours last forty-five minutes and
conclude with a tasting in the taproom. On draft,
you'll find classics like 80 Acre hoppy wheat ale
and Boulevard pale ale, plus more recent additions
like Hazy IPA (a collaboration with Colorado's
WeldWerks Brewing) and Changeling dark sour
ale. Boulevard's Smokestack series features big
and bold beers, including the famous Tank 7
saison and Bourbon Barrel Quad aged in oak.

ST. LOUIS, MISSOURI
## 138 Visit one of the country's original craft breweries

St. Louis's original craft brewery, Schlafly
Brewing was founded in 1991 in a city dominated
by Budweiser and Bud Light. Thomas Schlafly
founded the brewery, known as Saint Louis
Brewery, and began making beer under the
Schlafly brand. The original lineup of beers was
made up of Schlafly Pale Ale, Hefeweizen, and
Oatmeal Stout, while experimental beers include
the Ibex Cellar Series of barrel-aged saisons,
sours, and high-gravity beers. The brewery now
makes more than fifty different beers annually
and the tasting room is the best place to sample
them. Book a tour of the brewery, which is
housed in a restored wood and brick building
that's listed on the National Historic Register.

MAPLEWOOD, MISSOURI
## 139 Saddle up to the bar at this side-gig spot

As the name suggests, Side Project Brewing
began as a side project for former Perennial
Artisan Ales brewer Cory King. King and his
wife Karen have grown the brewery from a labor
of love into one of the top-rated breweries in the
world, according to Untappd and RateBeer. King
focuses on mixed-culture fermentations roughly
based around the saison style. The beers are
conditioned in wood, often with fruits added,
and are released in 25 fl oz (750 ml) bottles. The
tasting room, called The Side Project Cellar,
offers many Side Project beers on draft, as well as
some from other breweries. A bottle list includes
deep cuts from the brewery's robust portfolio, as
well as lambics and Trappist ales from some of
the best Belgian producers.

## 140 Go all weekend long at Boulevardia

The two-day Boulevardia festival is one of the best beer-focused summer events in the country. It features two days of craft beer, food, and live music with a makers' market, charity bike ride, and other family-friendly experiences. Boulevard Brewing brings it all together with a killer lineup of breweries from all around the US and as far away as Europe. Local restaurants, including members of Kansas City's world-renowned barbecue scene, supply the food. The music is an equally important component and past headliners include Tech N9ne, Bleachers, Guster, George Clinton and Parliament Funkadelic, and Catfish and the Bottlemen.

### ROGERS, ARKANSAS

### 141 Tromp the Ozarks to find this brewery

Located in northwest Arkansas, the small Ozark Beer produces some of the best beer in the state. Onyx Coffee Stout is a collaboration stout with roaster Onyx Coffee Lab and is fortified with Red Queen and Mexico Zongozota cold brew. Other beers include American standards like IPA and Pale Ale as well as a Belgian Style Golden Strong and a Cream Stout. Visit the brewery's tasting room in downtown Rogers.

### LITTLE ROCK, ARKANSAS

### 142 Fly into this draft emporium

Knock back a cold one at the Flying Saucer draft emporium chain location on President Clinton Avenue. Dozens of beers are available on draft from both local Arkansas breweries as well as regional and national names like Stone, Bell's, Oskar Blues, and Ballast Point. For less than $20, you can join the UFO Club and receive a members-only T-shirt and a magnetic swipe card, which keeps track of all the different beers consumed.

### NEW ORLEANS, LOUISIANA

### 143 Party in New Orleans on Paddy's Day

Forget Mardi Gras. New Orleans' best celebration is the weeklong festivities in March that lead up to the Irish-themed St. Patrick's Day Parade, which snakes through many of the city's historic neighborhoods. A great place to catch it is at Parasol's Bar in the Irish Channel, an area originally named for its heavy concentration of Irish families, and is just a short cab ride from the French Quarter. The entire block gets packed with people overflowing out of this tiny neighborhood dive bar, which serves plenty of ice-cold beer and amazing po'boy sandwiches. Partying here on Paddy's Day is one of the most fun experiences in a city replete with good vibes.

**NEW ORLEANS, LOUISIANA**

## 144 Catch a cold one at this corner pub

The twenty-four-hour Avenue Pub near the Garden District features a fireplace, tin ceilings, an ornate balcony, and the best beer selection in town. American cult producers are often featured on the bar's forty-plus draft list, including Tennessee's Blackberry Farm, Texas's Saint Arnold Brewing, and Louisiana's own Parish Brewing, while a lengthy bottle list encourages sampling some of Belgium's best beers. It often attracts brewers from around the country with special monthly events and tastings.

**145 Explore a brewery museum**

Home to stores, bars, and restaurants, New Orleans' French Quarter also contains a small museum dedicated to the history of Jax Brewery that is free and open to the public. Stroll through the stores, grab a bite to eat, and be sure to check out the view of the Mississippi River from the museum.

**147** *Above:* Parish Brewing's Ghost in the Machine DIPA is a Southern classic

**NEW ORLEANS, LOUISIANA**

### 146 Wander the streets with a beer in hand

New Orleans' drinking laws allow you to walk around nearly anywhere in public with a pint or two if you so choose—so long as your drink is in a plastic cup. Most bars offer plastic cups, so if you don't finish your drink, you're usually welcome to take it out the door with you. The French Quarter is crowded and touristy, yes, but it's a great place to wander with a drink in hand and do some stellar people watching with tens of thousands of other visitors.

**BROUSSARD, LOUISIANA**

### 147 Relax with a ghostly brew

The small Parish Brewing just outside Lafayette brews one of the best IPAs in the state. Ghost in the Machine is a hopped-up double IPA made with an obscene quantity of Citra hops from Washington State's Yakima Valley. Hazy, juicy, and citrusy, it's almost always available in the brewery's taproom, either in bottles or on draft, along with variants like the double dry-hopped (DDH) Ghost in the Machine. While you're there, also try classics like Canebrake wheat ale and Rêve coffee stout.

## 148 Cause a commotion in Shreveport

Great Raft Brewing produces modern American-style pale ales and lagers as well as Belgian-influenced saisons. Stop by for a tour and tasting—try the flagship Commotion pale ale or Southern Drawl pilsner, or go for something more experimental like Farmhouse Slang, a Belgian-style mixed-fermentation saison with notes of peaches, pineapple, and funk. Food trucks are always on hand in the parking lot to satisfy your food cravings.

## 149 Go for grog in Fargo

With two locations in Fargo, Würst Bier Hall is one of the best places to check out beer in the largest city in North Dakota. The drawn-out tap list is made up of locals like Fargo Brewing and Drekker Brewing as well as German imports, American regional and national brands, and a small selection of ciders and meads. Food is German-influenced American pub grub.

## 150 Drink under "brew" skies

The annual Under Brew Skies Beer Festival, hosted by the North Dakota Brewers Guild, is a summer celebration of North Dakota brewers. It also features breweries from bordering states and is one of the best opportunities to try a selection of beers from all over the region.

## 151 Cackle and catch a live show at a brewery

Laughing Sun Brewing is a brewery, restaurant, and live music venue in North Dakota's capital city—and it is a great place to check out locally made brews while catching a live show. The taproom features a dozen house-brewed beers as well as guest taps, wine, cider, and non-alcoholic beverages like kombucha. Try the flagship Great Plains pale ale or an experimental brew like a tart Sour Radler infused with grapefruit.

## 152 Surrender to offbeat pizza with beer

Specializing in local craft beers and pizza, Independent Ale House features forty drafts from the Midwest region as well as imports and dozens of other beers available by the bottle. Pizzas are the focus of the food menu with offbeat toppings like Thai peanut sauce with coconut, and garlic mashed potatoes with bacon and sour cream.

## 153 Pair beer with yoga at this fest

Held at Rushmore Plaza Civic Center, the annual Mountain West Beer Fest features beer yoga, a human foosball tournament, a college football sports bar, and more than fifty regional and national craft breweries. Grab yourself early-bird VIP tickets, which guarantee early entrance and a catered lunch service.

SIOUX FALLS, SOUTH DAKOTA

## 154  Take a sip of the Great Plains

Fernson Brewing features a core lineup of classic styles including the crisp, refreshing Lion's Paw lager; a complex but approachable saison called Farmhouse Ale; and the bold Shy Giant IPA. The brewery has two taprooms: one at its production brewery and another in historic downtown Sioux Falls. Find out more on a brewery tour at the production facility.

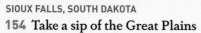

### 155 Get cozy in this hunting lodge-inspired brewery

Crow Peak Brewing, located in the Black Hills region, features a cozy log cabin vibe with twelve beers on draft. Start with 11th Hour, a bitter but balanced West Coast-style IPA, or—if it's in season—a 605 Harvest Ale brewed with fresh South Dakota hops. Perhaps its most famous beer is the robust Pile O'Dirt Porter, but the brewery also crafts more experimental batches like Mjöllnir, a spruce tip-laced ale.

### 156 Jump aboard this boozy bus tour

One of the best ways to explore Omaha's burgeoning beer scene is via the Omaha Brew Bus. The four-hour tour includes stops at two local breweries, a flight of four 4 oz (118 ml) pours at each location, and a behind-the-scenes peek at at least one stop. You'll begin and end the tour at The Casual Pint, a craft beer market and pub.

### 157 Admire the oak-aged ales of Nebraska

Nebraska's highest-rated brewery is the eponymous Nebraska Brewing. The brewery has two locations where you can try its flagship beers (IPA, pils, hefeweizen), but the main attraction here is the barrel-aged beer in its Reserve Series. Try Mélange À Trois, a Belgian-style strong ale aged in Chardonnay barrels, or HopAnomaly, a big, bold, Belgian-style IPA conditioned in oak.

### 158 Learn a thing or two about beer at this educational festival

The Great Nebraska Beer Fest held in August is one of the Midwest's best beer events. It attracts dozens of breweries and cideries from around the country, pouring hundreds of different beverages. Brewers host seminars throughout the day and an official after-party happens at nearby Nebraska Brewing. Tickets often sell out, so buy yours well in advance.

### 159 Conquer the crafts of the Cornhusker State

The Happy Raven bar features seventeen drafts and dozens of bottles and cans. The list highlights local breweries like Scratchtown Brewing, Nebraska Brewing, and Lincoln's own Code Beer. You'll find craft brewery memorabilia decking the walls and TV screens behind the bar listing the current draft list—including information about when the particular keg was tapped.

### 160 Try a gose aged in a tequila barrel

Drop into the GABF medal-winning Zipline Brewing to sample its year-round offerings, seasonal, and barrel-aged beers. Adventurous drinkers will enjoy the tequila barrel-aged lime gose, while more modest palates can go for a German-style Kölsch or a traditional nut brown ale. The brewery's GABF award went to its Copper Alt, a bronze-hued ale-lager hybrid style.

### LAWRENCE, KANSAS
### 161 Kick back at an original Kansas craft brewery

Founded in 1989, Free State Brewing is Kansas's original craft brewery. Core beers include Copperhead Pale Ale and the crowd-pleasing Wheat State Golden, while seasonals comprise the bold Stormchaser IPA. The brewery also experiments with small-batch modern styles such as Cloud Hopper Imperial IPA.

### WICHITA, KANSAS
### 162 Drop anchor amid local brews

Grab a brew and bite at The Anchor bar and grill. Choose from close to sixty draft beers from breweries like Dogfish Head, Wichita's own Hopping Gnome, and Rahr & Sons from Texas. On Sundays, a DIY Bloody Mary bar is available for the brunch crowd. Wings, nachos, and tacos round out the food menu.

### HAYS, KANSAS
### 163 Gulp a Gutch in small-town America

The small-town Defiance Brewing has some interesting takes on classic styles. Grab a pint of Gutch, a 5% English-style mild ale with notes of hazelnut, chocolate, and toffee, or opt for an amped-up Fuzzy Knuckles imperial stout with cocoa nibs and coffee. Visit the tasting room and pick up six- and four-packs to go.

**162** *Above:* The Anchor Bar serves up local and national craft brews

TULSA, OKLAHOMA

### 164 Sample a beer Bomb!

Bomb! is an American-style imperial stout from Prairie Artisan Ales modeled off the dessert beer category. After it's brewed, it's aged for months with coffee, chocolate, vanilla beans, and ancho chile peppers, which lend it an intoxicating but subtle kick. The peppers' heat complements the intense coffee and chocolate flavors for a balanced but boozy beer. Bomb! is widely regarded as one of the best imperial stouts in the world by beer aficionados.

TULSA, OKLAHOMA

### 165 Explore a fictitious family tree in Tulsa

The awesomely irreverent Willows Family Ales located in the Pearl District of Tulsa is helmed by brewer Heath Glover and known for its grotesque but amusing label illustrations featuring the fictitious "Willows" family. The beers are equally amusing with clever, pun-based names like I'm Sour Ms. Jackson (a sour ale with passion fruit) and When Doves Rye (a rye ale with tart cherries). The taproom features weekly events like karaoke and live music with overall fun vibes and an artsy, anything-may-happen feel.

TULSA, OKLAHOMA

### 166 Find foeders and Flanders-inspired ales in the Sooner State

Chase Healey, founder of Prairie Artisan Ales, detached from his successful brewery at its prime to open this experimental endeavor in 2016. Located in West Tulsa, American Solera Brewing is loaded with oak fermenters—including barrels, casks, and a flock of foeders—and focuses on long-fermented, mixed-culture wild ales. Healey also installed a coolship inside an open-at-both-ends shipping container out the back for spontaneous ale production. The brewery focuses on multistage fermented beers like Foeder Cerise, a sour golden ale aged on tart cherries for six months in Italian oak foeders, and Man-Made Earthquake, a 15% tripel aged in whiskey and Cognac barrels and bottle-conditioned for a year. Not all the beers are oak aged, however. Hazy double IPAs are often on draft and available in cans as well as imperial stouts and the occasional pilsner. The beer lineup is constantly changing as are the number of locations; i.e. a downtown outpost called American Solera SoBo opened in 2017.

### 167 Drop into the original Ginger Man

This mini-chain of craft beer pubs has locations throughout the country, but the original, located in Houston's Rice Village area, is a classic. Opened in 1985, it was one of the country's very first beer bars dedicated to craft beer, helping to introduce a generation of Texans to a world of beer outside of Bud, Coors, and Miller. With dozens of draft lines, it poured a wide array of new and interesting beers (Sierra Nevada Pale Ale and Celis White) and was years ahead of its time. Today, it still offers a plethora of beers in several locations in Texas.

### 168 Sip a Shiner Bock beer

Founded in 1909, Spoetzl Brewery is the oldest independent brewing operation in Texas, and one of the oldest in the entire US. It produces a diverse line of Shiner brand beers, including the flagship Shiner Bock, a dark German-style lager. Besides Lone Star beer, it's one of the iconic Texas regional specialty beers. From barbecue joints to roadside honky tonks, you can find it nearly anywhere in the Lone Star State.

**TOP 3**

**TULSA, OKLAHOMA**

# Drink in these three great Tulsa places

### 169 American Solera SoBo

This neon-lit outpost of Tulsa's best brewery features around a dozen drafts served in a stylish, minimalist tasting room. Canned and bottled beers are available to go.

### 170 James E. McNellie's Public House

A local chain of traditional pubs, McNellie's features dozens of beers on draft and in bottles paired with traditional American pub food.

### 171 Valkyrie

This industrial-chic downtown bar and lounge features craft cocktails, a carefully curated selection of American craft beers, and distinctive brews from around the world.

**AUSTIN, TEXAS**

## 172 Imbibe in some "German" bier

Texas's Hill Country has a long history as a haven for German immigrants, and the German brewing traditions in this part of the state date back centuries. Live Oak Brewing, located a stone's throw from the Austin–Bergstrom International Airport, doesn't have quite that long a history—it was founded in 1997—but it continues the Bavarian and German brewing tradition better than practically any other brewery in the region. Founder Chip McElroy is something of a legend in the beer scene, known for his sense of humor, strong opinions, and affable personality. He founded the brewery in a small industrial space on East 5th Street in central Austin before moving to its current location in late 2015. The new brewery features a large taproom, a German-style sausage cart, and an expansive outdoor area complete with a disc golf course. You can taste Live Oak's core lineup of beers including HefeWeizen, Pilz, Big Bark, and Gold, as well as specialty German-style smoked beers like Grodziskie and Schwarzer Rauch, and even some non-German styles (IPA, etc.). The tasting room often offers events like trivia nights, beer-release parties, and other happenings. Packaged beer is available to purchase and a gift shop has a selection of Live Oak T-shirts, hats, and other merchandise.

**TOP 4**

**HOUSTON, TEXAS**

# Try these tasty hazy IPAs

Despite being nearly 2,000 miles from New England, several breweries in Houston make some of the best NEIPAs in the country. Here are the best of the best.

### 173 SpindleTap Brewery

SpindleTap's Houston Haze IPA is brewed with Citra and is absolutely bursting with grapefruit and orange flavors. A double dry-hopped delight.

### 174 B52 Brewing

Located about 40 miles north of Houston, this brewery makes Wheez the Juice, the city's first beer to be explicitly labeled a "hazy IPA." It hits all the juicy, fruity, dank notes of a textbook NEIPA.

### 175 Baa Baa Brewhouse

When this brewery released Cow Jumped Over the Moon, it was the first beer in the greater Houston area labeled NEIPA. Since then, it has shifted focus to brew more beers in the same style.

### 176 Ingenious Brewing

Ingenious quickly amassed a following for beers like the bold, hazy Infinity Hopped triple NEIPA as well as Haze Race, a more modest beer.

## 177 Learn the meaning of *terroir* at this true farmhouse brewery

The bucolic Jester King Brewing, located on a sprawling farm, is an inspiring and life-affirming place to drink. The specialty is mixed-fermentation, saison-style ales, many of which are brewed with farm-grown or foraged ingredients and reflect the *terroir* of the surrounding land. Proprietor Jeffrey Stuffings founded the brewery in 2010 with his brother, Michael Steffing. In 2016, Jester King purchased 58 acres (24 ha) of land surrounding its facility and installed a farm-to-table restaurant. Beer highlights include Le Petit Prince, a low-ABV table beer; Snörkel, a saison brewed with oyster mushrooms from neighboring Logro Farms; and Spon, a series of blended spontaneous ales.

AUSTIN, TEXAS
## 178 Say "Hell Yes" to Helles

Austin Beer Garden Brewing—or ABGB as it's locally known—is a brewery specializing in German-style beers, though there's much more on offer, too. Founder Brian Peters cofounded Live Oak with Chip McElroy, but left in 2001 to go to The Bitter End. He eventually went on to found ABGB where he continues making award-winning lagers and ales. The flagship Hell Yes helles is a great place to start—it's light and refreshing to keep you coming back for sip after sip. Industry and Rocket 100 are two exemplar pilsners that please even the pickiest lager heads. American-style IPAs are also part of ABGB's portfolio as are one-off sours, saisons, and single-hop pale ales. The kitchen cranks out world-class pizzas and the environment—communal tables and a large outdoor area—encourage lingering and socializing.

AUSTIN, TEXAS
## 179 Brunch at Banger's

Located in the Rainey Street Historic District, Banger's Sausage House & Beer Garden is a cottage-like restaurant featuring a large bar and spacious beer garden where weekend brunchers line up early to snag a table. All ordering is done at the bar from a menu that features a plethora of house-made sausages. Traditional German-style brats and smoked hot dogs are available as well as more experimental links made from rabbit, bacon, antelope, and wild boar. The beer menu is overwhelming—it's one of the largest draft lists in Austin—but bartenders are always happy to help guide you to a particular beer based on your preferences. The list skews local with plenty of Texas breweries as well as national brands.

CANYON, TEXAS
## 180 Pair Texas-size rib-eyes with craft beer

The Imperial Taproom features more than twenty rotating drafts of local, regional, and national craft beer ranging from light to dark, mild to hoppy, funky to sour. There are also dozens of rotating can, bottle, and big-bottle format beers as well as an upscale menu of Texas-style dishes.

HELENA, MONTANA
## 181 Become an ale explorer

The explorer-themed Lewis & Clark Brewing features a range of American-style craft beers—Selway Stout, Tumbleweed IPA—as well as German-influenced lagers and ales. Stop by the taproom to sample six core beers and six rotating seasonal ales. Packaged beers are available in cans as well as growlers.

MISSOULA, MONTANA
## 182 Fill up at The Dram Shop

Dozens of taps at this growler-filling station, bottle shop, and beer bar pour a range of beer from imports to domestic craft brands as well as ciders and cask ales. Most are available to go in growler pours and there is a deep list of bottled and canned beers. Try Shadow Caster Amber from Missoula's own Draught Works Brewing.

## 183 Drain a barleywine under the big sky

Big Sky Brewing opened in 1995 and is the largest in Montana. It features a core lineup of eight beers including Big Sky IPA and the roasty Moose Drool brown ale. One specialty bottle is Olde Bluehair, reputed to be one of the best barleywines in the US. The taproom features a dozen beers on draft as well as one cask ale. Note that Montana law only allows 48 oz (1,364 ml) of beer per person per day, so if you want to try a range of styles, be sure to order the 8 oz (227 ml) sampler size.

SHERIDAN, WYOMING

## 184 Booze it up in the Bighorns

Situated at the base of the majestic Bighorn Mountains, Black Tooth is Wyoming's most-awarded craft brewery. Opened in 2010, it offers a core lineup of amber ale, cream ale with lime, West Coast-style IPA, and brown ale. The tasting room is relaxed and low-key with limited and seasonal releases.

JACKSON HOLE, WYOMING

## 185 Wind down with an après-ski beer

Located in a ski resort town, Snake River Brewing is the oldest brewery in the state. It features nine drafts of mostly American-style beers in a cozy, après-ski environment. Craving something sweet? Try the I Just Pecan't pecan pie porter. Or if bitter is more your speed, an Alpha Prime IPA should do the trick. Canned beers are available to go and a small selection of daily specials will keep you full.

COLORADO

## 186 Explore nature-inspired brews

Beers Made by Walking is an interactive program that invites brewers to make beers inspired by nature hikes and urban walks. The idea is for brewers to go on a short to moderate hike in nature and then take their experience back to their respective brewery and craft a beer based on it. The beer is then served at a later date, often with other beers made from a similar experience. Anyone can register for the walks for a behind-the-scenes peek at how brewers find inspiration for beers. You can also attend tasting events, which are often ticketed and held in a handful of cities each year. Colorado typically hosts at least one event each year.

GREELEY, COLORADO

## 187 Home in on the haze

Located about an hour north of Denver in a small cattle town, the small WeldWerks Brewing attracts a fervent following for its hazy IPAs and big imperial dessert stouts. The taproom offers nearly thirty beers on draft, in taster and pint sizes, and you'll often find a local food truck parked outside. Try Juicy Bits, a soft hazy IPA bursting with huge hop aromas, or Eggnog Barleywine, a blonde high-octane barleywine conditioned on charred oak spirals and pasteurized egg yolks.

## 188 Marry tantalizing hops with Thai food

What started in the back of a Thai restaurant in Jackson in 2010 has now grown into one of the largest regional breweries in the country, with outposts in Alpine and Jackson, as well as Bellingham and San Diego. Melvin Brewing owner Jeremy Tofte began on a nanoscale 20-gallon (76 L) brewhouse making the flagship Melvin IPA, 2x4 Double IPA (two of the best IPAs in the country), and Ch Ch Cherry Bomb. After winning the Brewpub of the Year award at GABF in 2015, the brewery quickly expanded to a thirty-barrel production facility and now distributes beer all around the country. Don't miss the rotating series of imperial IPAs (dubbed RIIPA for Rotational Imperial IPA), which includes Asterisk*, Chuck Morris, Citradamus, and Drunken Master.

FORT COLLINS, COLORADO
## 189 Trek through a foeder forest

New Belgium Brewing is home of the iconic Fat Tire Amber Ale—but New Belgium makes a lot more than just Fat Tire. Its Voodoo Ranger series of IPAs, for instance, includes half a dozen variants like Juicy Haze, Imperial, and Atomic Pumpkin, and its line of oak-aged sour ales are some of the best in the world. They're aged in vessels called foeders—tall, upright wooden fermentation and conditioning tanks typically used in wine production. The brewery uses them for an array of beers like La Folie, Transatlantique Kriek, and Le Terroir. Book a tour and discover the brewery's "foeder forest"—a sprawling room filled with these tanks. The tour concludes at the taproom where you can try the entire range of New Belgium beers, including many taproom-only exclusives.

DENVER, COLORADO
## 190 Drink a Blue Moon inside a baseball stadium

The copper-clad Sandlot Brewery, which opened in 1995 within the walls of the Colorado Rockies' baseball stadium, is the birthplace of Blue Moon, the iconic "crafty" beer brand from MillerCoors (it was originally known as Belly Slide Wit). It was also the very first brewery located inside a baseball stadium. The taproom is only open to the public during baseball season (March–October), and usually only on game days when the Rockies play at home, though it sometimes holds expanded hours for private events. The brewery makes an entire range of American- and German-style beers, including Vienna Lager, Where the Helles Bill, Smalls Pils, Naptime Stout, and Wicked Hop IPA. Fans can also get Right Field Red, one of the original beers Sandlot made in 1995.

DENVER, COLORADO
## 191 Take a walk on the wild side

Opened in 2017, the US's first all-sour taproom, Goed Zuur (the name translates to "Good Acid" in Dutch) features an array of tart, funky, and barnyard-y draft and bottle pours from spontaneous and wild ale producers like Jester King, Casey Brewing, and Denver's own Black Project. The menu ranges from simple, quick-fermented sour ales (think: goses and Berliner weisses) to long-aged, oak-conditioned beers, some of which sit in barrels for multiple years. There's always a good selection of local, regional, and international beers and a wide range of food to pair them with. Start with the duck fat and Parmesan popcorn or a selection of charcuterie and cheeses before settling on a main course like pork chops with roasted potatoes, little neck clams, or the vegetarian *entrée du jour*.

# Visit Fort Collins' top five breweries

In addition to New Belgium Brewing, here are five breweries to check out in Fort Collins.

### 192 Funkwerks

As the name suggests, this brewery focuses on funky saisons and sour beers. The flagship Saison is one of the best in the country, while others include dry-hopped versions like Nelson Sauvin, named for a New Zealand hop.

**194**

### 194 Jessup Farm Barrel House

This collaboration with Funkwerks is located inside a 130-year-old barn that sits on a 13-acre (5 ha) farm. The taproom offers a sixteen-tap selection of various blends of barrel-aged beers brewed on-site.

### 193 Odell Brewing

This is a regional powerhouse with an outpost in Denver. The original location features a large tasting room and bar where drinkers can try flagships like 90 Shilling Ale and Myrcenary double IPA as well as specialty seasonals.

### 195 Zwei Brewing

An old-world German brewery, Zwei features the spectrum of lager beers (from light pilsners to black schwarzbiers) as well as an outdoor, dog-friendly patio, which often features live music.

**195**

### 196 Black Bottle Brewery

This brewery offers forty-plus drafts of house-brewed beers and guest taps, a wide selection of bottled beers, and a full-service gastropub-inspired restaurant.

**DENVER, COLORADO**

## 197 Let loose at the colossal GABF

The Great American Beer Festival, better known by its acronym GABF, is an annual fall festival that attracts more than 60,000 attendees over the course of three beer-fueled days. It all started in 1982 when the American Homebrewers Association invited twenty-four breweries to pour beer in Boulder, Colorado. Eight hundred attendees showed up that first year, and the festival has grown seemingly exponentially ever since. These days, more than 800 breweries participate in the festival itself, while well over 8,000 beers are entered into the competition, which awards gold, silver, and bronze medals in more than 102 categories. To avoid massive crowds, the best time to attend is Thursday night. For an industry-insider glimpse of the festival, check out the Saturday afternoon session, which is open to Brewers Association and American Homebrewers Association members only (anyone can join the latter). GABF also features the PAIRED festival, which matches a handful of exclusive beers with upscale food from highly acclaimed chefs. In addition to the festival, many beer events take place throughout Denver the week of GABF.

DENVER, COLORADO

## 198 Bang your head to heavy metal brews

If you're in the mood for pairing your beer with blaring heavy metal, look no further than TRVE
Brewing (pronounced "True"). The taproom, conveniently located near several other breweries south of
Denver's downtown area, features a range of both clean and funky styles. Start with Cold, a Czech-style
Keller pilsner before moving on to Seven Doors hoppy saison or Cosmic Crypt farmhouse pale ale.
Mixed-culture (funky) beers are also available on draft and in bottles (try This Day Anything Goes,
a Halloween-inspired blended mixed-culture ale brewed with pumpkin and honey). Also ask about
Wavering Radiant, the brewery's first 100% spontaneous ale. The taproom itself is quite a scene, with
a custom-built satanic altar behind the bar. It's all done in good jest, though, so there's no need to be
intimidated by the occult themes.

DENVER, COLORADO
## 199 Join a secretive beer club

What began as a typical US brewery called Former Future has morphed into one of the most exciting and experimental outfits in the country. Black Project Spontaneous & Wild Ales, located in the Platt Park neighborhood, creates complex, barrel-aged beers, most of which are spontaneously fermented (meaning no laboratory yeast is added to the beer for fermentation). Instead, the brewery relies on ambient yeast present in the air to inoculate the beer and produce it from unfermented wort. The results are tart, complex, and rustic, unlike nearly any other beer in the world. You can try six draft beers brewed on-site as well as bottles and a selection of non-sour guest taps for the sour-averse drinker. The brewery also offers a "secret" bottle club, which allows members early access to special bottle releases as well as other perks.

DENVER, COLORADO
## 200 Sip a slow-pour pilsner

Lagerbier lovers will be in heaven at the Bierstadt Lagerhaus, located in the hip River North Art District (RiNo). The brewery makes just three core beers—a dunkel, helles, and pilsner—with one or two seasonals occasionally available. Settle in with a Slow Pour Pils. As the menu notes, the beer takes longer than usual to arrive due to the exquisitely nurturing technique used to pour it. The northern German-inspired beer is pale, crisp, and bitter with an inch of foamy head peaking above the rim of the glass. Next, order a mug of Bierstadt Helles, a light but complex 5% ABV lager that represents the purest expression of the pale malts used to make it. Finally, dig in to a half-liter of dunkel, or "dark" beer. This Munich-style beer is often considered liquid bread due to its flavors of dark bread crust and chocolate, and is one of the most nutritious-tasting beers in the world.

DENVER, COLORADO
## 201 See red at an all-red ale brewery

Black shirts are a symbol of rebellion and it's that rebellious spirit that led Black Shirt Brewing to initially focus on a single color of beer: red. The Red Ale Project, as it was known, is still going strong as part of the brewery's core lineup, but brewer David Sakolsky has branched out to include more than just copper-hued ales. The tasting room, located in the RiNo section of Denver, features nearly a dozen beers on draft, pizzas, and an outdoor beer garden with free live music, vinyl listening parties, acoustic shows, and pub quiz trivia.

DENVER, COLORADO
## 202 Seek out the elusive urban Yeti

Yeti Imperial Stout from Great Divide Brewing is a roasty, toasty party in a glass. Clocking in at 9.5% ABV, it's a heavy hitter, but balanced and smooth with a mix of toffee and rich caramel notes. You can find it at Great Divide's Ballpark-adjacent brewery and taproom, or barrel-aged variants at its Barrel Bar in the RiNo district.

## 203 Sip suds and sample sausages

Euclid Hall, perhaps the best gastropub in the country, is a perennial favorite for visiting brewers and casual beer enthusiasts alike. The main attraction here are the house-made sausages, which come in a variety of styles like beef short ribs, lamb merguez, and blood sausage. Other offal dots the menu (pig ears, chicken livers) as well as hearty dishes like poutine and fried cheese curds. About a dozen, mostly local, beers are available on draft and there's a lengthy bottle and canned beer list to boot.

## 204 Locate a brew at The Source

One of the highlights of The Source—a creators and retail collective in the RiNo area—is this taproom from the funky players at Crooked Stave Artisan Beer Project. The beer isn't brewed on-site, but the taproom is the best place to sample the brettanomyces-fermented ales. Try WildSage brett saison, a tart little number brewed with all Colorado ingredients, including sage and lemongrass, or St. Bretta, a citrus-forward saison with citrus and coriander. Not everything is on the wild side, however. The Von Pilsner is a textbook German-style Keller pils, while the Trellis Buster is a bold classic American double IPA dry-hopped with Azacca, Citra, Motueka, and Simcoe hops.

DENVER, COLORADO

## 205 Relish rare brews for a worthy cause

The Denver Rare Beer Tasting is a charity event supporting Pints for Prostates, which takes place annually in fall, on the Friday afternoon of GABF weekend. Think of it as a highly curated version of GABF, a smaller, more intimate beer festival with some of the absolute best—and rarest—beers from around the US. The festival attracts the geekiest of geek beer fans who get to rub elbows with many of the brewers themselves. You'll often find Brooklyn Brewery's Garrett Oliver pouring his Black Ops stout, for instance, or Sam Calagione of Dogfish Head serving vintage bottles of 120 Minute IPA. The festival also attracts cult up-and-coming breweries like North Carolina's Fonta Flora and The Alchemist.

GLENWOOD SPRINGS, COLORADO

## 206 Book a blending session

After spending years as an experimental brewer with Coors' AC Golden Brewery, Troy Casey opened Casey Brewing & Blending in 2013 with his wife, Emily. Casey focuses solely on 100% wild-oak fermentations using saccharomyces, brettanomyces, and lactic acid bacteria in conjunction with local Colorado ingredients. The resulting beers are complex and funky, but ultimately balanced and approachable. Due to the small nature of the brewery, the tasting room is not open regular hours. However, you can purchase tickets in advance for guided tours and tasting sessions. The brewery offers a large selection of vintage bottles and fresh blends to drink on-site or to go.

GOLDEN, COLORADO

## 207 Radiate the gold in Golden

Opened in 1873, the current Coors Brewery is the largest single-site brewery in the world where it churns out brands like Coors Banquet Beer and Coors Light. Book a self-paced tour and see the malting, brewing, and packaging processes as well as enjoying samples along the way. At the end, view historic photos, beer cans and bottles, and other memorabilia. A gift shop has all your T-shirt, glassware, and bottle-opener needs. The brewery encourages you to soak in Golden's scenery and outdoor spirit, with dozens of hiking, kayaking, and other adventure opportunities nearby.

BOULDER, COLORADO

## 208 Discover one of the US's first sour beer producers

Founded in 1993, Avery Brewing has long been one of the best craft breweries in the US. It opened its Boulder location in 2015, a sprawling, shiny building that includes an expansive barrel-aging facility and a taproom with thirty of its own beers on draft. Try a sour ale like Raspberry or Apricot Sour, or one of the boozy stouts (Uncle Jacob's, Tweak) for which the brewery has become known.

**207** *Right:* Coors Brewery in Golden encourages you to get involved in local outdoor activities

**TAOS, NEW MEXICO**

### 209 Try a Taos Green Chile Beer

Eske's Brewpub in the artsy, meditation retreat town of Taos makes a green chile-laced beer with freshly roasted Sandia chiles added to a blonde ale base beer. The roasty, vegetal, and spicy flavors come through, though they're restrained and balanced. It's a unique beer that reflects the local flavors of this scenic region.

**SANTA FE, NEW MEXICO**

### 210 Discover desert farm-to-table beers

Rowley Farmhouse Ales, a small brewery and farm-to-table gastropub, focuses on rustic farmhouse and sour ales. In addition to house-made beers, the taproom features an extensive draft and bottle list of some of the best beers from New Mexico and around the world.

**ALBUQUERQUE, NEW MEXICO**

### 211 Hop into Marble Brewery

The hop-focused Marble Brewery has three locations throughout Albuquerque where visitors and locals can knock back a pint—you can book a tour at the downtown location. Top beers include the Marble IPA and double IPA as well as Red Ale and Imperial Stout. Cans and bottles are available to go.

**ALBUQUERQUE, NEW MEXICO**

### 212 Climb to the top of the hops

Another hop-centric brewery in Albuquerque, La Cumbre Brewing has two locations featuring a hopped-up lineup of year-round and seasonal brews. The brewery's best-known offering is Elevated IPA, a 2011 GABF gold medal-winning 7.2% ABV West Coast-style IPA brewed with eight different hops. Each location has food trucks, TVs, and an outdoor space.

### 213 Imbibe indigenous ales

Shyla Sheppard and Missy Begay, two Native American women who grew up on reservations, opened Bow & Arrow Brewing in Albuquerque in 2016. The focus is American Southwest-inspired wild, sour, and barrel-aged beers. Step into the on-site beer hall and enjoy a warm, inviting atmosphere with more than fifteen beers available on draft.

### 214 Get groggy in the Grand Tetons

Founded in 1988, Grand Teton Brewing (named for a local mountain range) brews old-school American craft ales and a Brewers' Series of more experimental styles. Visit for tastings and tours, and refuel from the food trucks that are often stationed in the parking lot.

### 215 Explore two world-renowned National Parks near this brewery

Located near both Arches National Park and Canyonlands National Park, the small Moab Brewery offers nine house-made beers, including stouts, pilsners, and IPAs. It also features hearty fare in huge portions—think prime rib with roasted potatoes and a barbecue plate with sausage, ribs, and onion rings.

### 216 Buzz into the Beerhive

The cozy Beerhive Pub near the Salt Palace Convention Center features elegant, vintage décor, a wide range of craft beers, and upscale pub grub. Pick from sixteen taps featuring local and regional brands or the long list of bottled and canned beers. You're bound to find something great to pair with exemplary hand-cut fries, nachos, burgers, and pizzas.

### 217 Consume an Epic brew

Founded in 2008, Epic Brewing produces an array of ales and lagers in its Classic, Elevated, and Exponential Series. The latter features experimental brews like Smoked & Oaked Belgian-style ale and Sour Apple Saison, made with tart apples and spiced with coriander, grains of paradise, anise, nutmeg, cloves, cinnamon, cardamom, and ginger. Book a tour or visit the taproom to sample core beers Escape to Colorado IPA, Hop Syndrome pilsner, and Los Locos Mexican-style lager.

### 218 Devour a Big Bad Baptist imperial stout

Epic Brewing makes this bold chocolate-and-coffee-infused stout. Each year's batch features a new dark roast coffee bean. Variants are available some years, like the Double Barrel Big Bad Baptist, featuring coffee beans from Colorado's HotBox Roasters that were themselves aged in whiskey barrels.

SALT LAKE CITY, UTAH
### 219 Sip a pour of Polygamy Porter

Founded in 2000, Wasatch Beers and Squatters Pub Brewery came together to form this unique company of two breweries under one roof. Utah Brewers Cooperative's portfolio comprises more than twenty-five beers, including the famous Wasatch Polygamy Porter, Wasatch Summerbrau Lager, Squatters Hell's Keep, and Squatters Provo Girl Pilsner.

SALT LAKE CITY, UTAH
### 220 Taste Utah brewing history

Founded in 1993, Uinta Brewing produces a range of beers named after cultural and natural icons. It's consistently one of the top fifty largest breweries in the country, producing Cutthroat Pale Ale, King's Peak Porter, and Golden Spike Hefeweizen. Stop at the tasting room and pub to try Hop Nosh IPA, a modern West Coast-style beer, and Rise & Pine, a dark IPA with notes of pine and juniper.

SALT LAKE CITY, UTAH
### 221 Discover a touch of Bavaria in SLC

Beer Bar is a sprawling beer hall co-owned by TV star Duncan Burrell of *Modern Family* fame. It offers more than one hundred beers—thirty on draft and a hundred more in bottles—paired with German-influenced food like pretzels and sausages.

**220** *Left:* Uinta Brewing is one of the country's top fifty largest breweries

CHANDLER, ARIZONA

## 222 Taste Kiwi-hopped beers

Founded in 2007, SanTan Brewing produces craft hop-forward ales and the occasional lager. Brewer Anthony Canecchia was one of the US's earliest production-scale users of New Zealand hops, which are now some of the most in-demand varieties among American brewers. The brewery's flagship HopShock IPA is brewed with Nelson Sauvin hops, known for their white wine-like character. Canecchia also uses other Kiwi varieties like Motueka, Green Bullet, and Riwaka in several other beers. When you visit, also check out the distillery, which makes spirits like craft vodka infused with lime and American single-malt whiskey.

**222** *Above:* SanTan Brewing uses a variety of New Zealand hops in its beers

### TUCSON, ARIZONA
### 223 Seek thirst-quenching suds in the desert sun

Two locations of the bottle shop-cum-taproom Tap & Bottle keep Tucsonians hydrated with plenty of local and regional craft beers. Try Frosty Friends from the in-town Dragoon Brewing or Phantom Bride IPA from San Diego's Belching Beaver. Both locations host live music, trivia, and other events.

### PHOENIX, ARIZONA
### 224 Enjoy pizza and a pint

The pizza is the main draw at Pizzeria Bianco from chef-owner Chris Bianco, and beer is secondary to wine when it comes to beverages on offer. But stop in and take delight in one of a handful of craft beers paired with the famed Margherita, Sonny Boy (with salami and olives), or Wiseguy (smoked mozzarella and sausage). Small plates and salads are also offered. It's one of the best pizzerias in the country.

PHOENIX, ARIZONA

### 225 Drink with like-minded beer geeks

The small Wren House Brewing produces everything from light lagers and sticky IPAs to robust imperial stouts and porters. Start with the Kölsch, brewed with traditional German ingredients and a touch of honey malt, and finish with a Pom Czar Russian imperial stout, brewed with pomegranate molasses. The tasting room is small, communal, and simple, but offers a friendly environment to taste beers and chat with brewers and other industry insiders.

GILBERT, ARIZONA

### 226 Explore the wilderness—and wild beers— of Arizona

This Kickstarter-funded grassroots brewery opened in 2013. Arizona Wilderness Brewing quickly blossomed into one of the most exciting new breweries in the American Southwest, producing a mind-boggling variety of beers. The current brewpub pours more than fifteen draft beers, including experimental IPAs, funky saisons, and bold imperial stouts, and offers a menu of burgers, tacos, and fresh salads. Pick up a four-pack of cans to go, like Refuge IPA, Brutal Nature: Canyon X brut IPA, or the Abundansea imperial stout.

PHOENIX, TEMPE, AND SCOTTSDALE, ARIZONA

### 227 Savor a Scottish ale in the suburbs

Opened in 1996 and acquired by Anheuser-Busch in 2015, Four Peaks Brewing has locations in Tempe and Scottsdale. The flagship beer is Kilt Lifter, a 6% ABV Scottish-style ale. Seasonals include Kühl Beans, Pumpkin Porter, and the dry Brut IPA. Book a free tour at the 8th Street location in Tempe. It features a variety of taps as well as a full-service restaurant and kitchen.

**227**  *Right:* Four Peaks Brewing has two locations in which to sample its beverages

**LAS VEGAS, NEVADA**

## 228 Seek glitz, glamour, and glitter off the Strip

CraftHaus Brewery is a Kickstarter-funded brewery and tasting room opened by a husband-and-wife duo inspired by the craft beer culture in Europe. Kick back in the modern tasting room that has couches, benches, and pops of bright colors. The house-brewed beers are fun and adventurous and include a super-wonky, glitter-dosed beer, which is sometimes on draft.

### 229 Take in a beer and a view

Visiting the Las Vegas strip? Stop into Beer Park—the glass-enclosed rooftop beer garden across from the Bellagio Fountains. Though it's owned by Budweiser, the lengthy beer list includes many beers from Anheuser-Busch's High End division of acquired craft breweries—10 Barrel Brewing, Elysian, and Goose Island, for instance.

### 230 Indulge in beers, burgers, and desserts

Founded in the renovated Palace Station Hotel & Casino in 2018, b.B.d.'s (Beers, Burgers, Desserts) is an outpost of a Long Island-based bar. Chef-owner Ralph Perrazzo crafts unique burgers, sandwiches, and desserts, including vegan options. He brought on beverage director Mike Amidei, formerly of Brooklyn's famed Tørst bar, to lead the beer program. Dozens of drafts and many more bottles round out the best beer selection in Sin City.

**229** *Above:* The Bellagio Fountains can be seen when visiting Beer Park in Las Vegas

**LAS VEGAS, NEVADA**

### 231 Become an ace at discovering local brews

Two locations of the Aces & Ales mini-chain offer several dozen draft beers from local breweries and regional and national players. Join in the weekly events that include the beer-centric trivia night Geeks Who Drink.

**RENO, NEVADA**

### 232 Drink in the biggest little city

Reno, affectionately dubbed "the biggest little city in the world," is a rapidly expanding city with a booming tech industry, a mountain-town feel, and much of the charm of old downtown Vegas. It's also a good place to get a great beer. Check out Chapel Tavern for local brews and whiskies, the Ole Bridge Pub for beers and shuffleboard, and The Brewer's Cabinet for house-brewed blonde ales, IPAs, and stouts.

**234** *Above:* Hop-forward beers are the order of the day at Revision Brewing

**RENO, NEVADA**

## 233 Savor saisons in a former icehouse

Brasserie Saint James, set on the site of an old icehouse—complete with its own water source—concocts Belgian-influenced saisons, farmhouse ales, and other styles. Most of the beers are conditioned in one of the brewery's hundred-plus barrels, which help mature the beer into complex but delicate ales. Newer styles include lagers like Santiago Mexican lager and Black Gate schwarzbier.

**SPARKS, NEVADA**

## 234 Scour the desert for hoppy ales

Former Knee Deep Brewing brewmaster Jeremy Warren founded Revision Brewing in 2017, quickly becoming known for hop-forward beers. The lineup includes a core series of IPAs, a line of hazies and triple IPAs, a dark beer program, and a collection of one-off and experimental beers called the Skunkwerks Experimentals. The taproom drafts are divided by style including about a dozen NEIPAs, and an equal number of West Coast varieties, and a handful of experimental beers. Beer is also available to go.

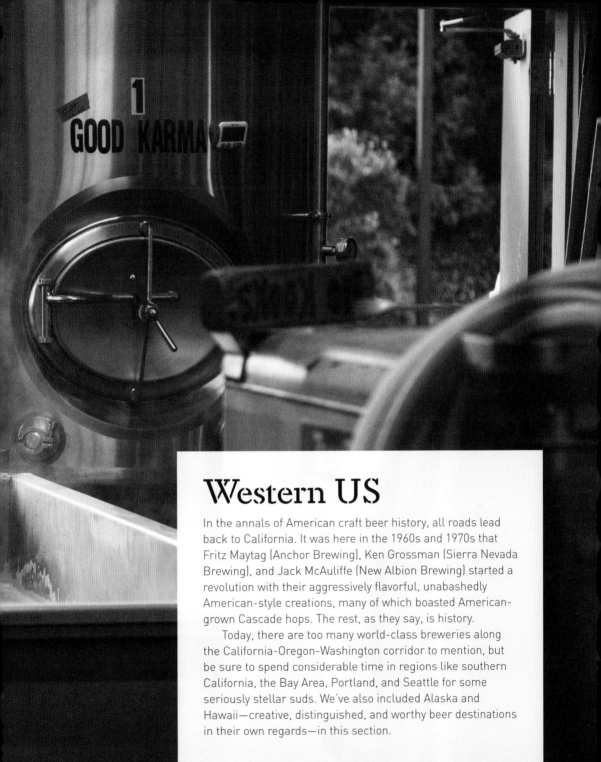

# Western US

In the annals of American craft beer history, all roads lead back to California. It was here in the 1960s and 1970s that Fritz Maytag (Anchor Brewing), Ken Grossman (Sierra Nevada Brewing), and Jack McAuliffe (New Albion Brewing) started a revolution with their aggressively flavorful, unabashedly American-style creations, many of which boasted American-grown Cascade hops. The rest, as they say, is history.

Today, there are too many world-class breweries along the California-Oregon-Washington corridor to mention, but be sure to spend considerable time in regions like southern California, the Bay Area, Portland, and Seattle for some seriously stellar suds. We've also included Alaska and Hawaii—creative, distinguished, and worthy beer destinations in their own regards—in this section.

WASHINGTON AND THROUGHOUT THE US

## 235  Tour a hop farm

The practice of agricultural tourism is more common in Europe, especially in Italy where many farms run an *agriturismo*. In the US you can also visit farms and enjoy seeing where your raw ingredients come from. It just might take a little more work. If you're a beer lover, visiting an operational hop farm should be on your list of things to do. Most in the Yakima Valley of Washington are extremely busy during harvest and wouldn't likely allow visitors outside of industry guests and workers. But with hop farms popping up in states like New York, Michigan, and Idaho, it should be relatively easy to find one that will allow you to drop by. You can contact a hop farm directly or try asking the local tourist office. If you do make it to Yakima, check out the Yakima Hops Trail, visit the American Hop Museum in Toppenish, or close out harvest season at the Fresh Hop Ale Festival typically held in early October.

YAKIMA VALLEY, WASHINGTON
## 236 Be surrounded by hops
Yakima Valley is the largest hop-growing region in the US with more than 32,000 acres (13,000 ha) producing around 75% of the total commercial hop production in the country. Though yield varies farm by farm, Yakima averages about 2,000 lb (907 kg) of dried hop cones per acre on mature hop yards.

SEATTLE, WASHINGTON
## 237 Taste beers bursting with hop flavor
Opened in 2016—and founded by Elysian Brewing veteran Steve Luke (who left Elysian following its sale to Anheuser-Busch)—the small Cloudburst Brewing focuses on all varieties of IPAs and hoppy beers. Look for the teal and red neon sign above the taproom entrance. Inside you'll find a tiny, no-frills tasting lounge.

SEATTLE, WASHINGTON
## 238 Reach the saison summit at this "holiest" of breweries
Founded by two homebrewing friends and former hardcore musicians, Holy Mountain Brewing blends funky saisons with a shared love for doom metal and the occult. Many of the brewery's beers are first fermented in 17,598 oz (500 L) oak puncheons, which promote a gentler, more complex fermentation than stainless steel, resulting in tart, peachy flavors. Others are conditioned in tall oak foudres with a blend of mixed cultures like brettanomyces, lactobacillus, and pediococcus. At first sip, the beers can come across as simple, if highly crushable, saisons. But underneath the easy magnetism, there's a heady mix of crisscrossing flavors. The co-mingling of fruity Belgian esters with citrusy hops, layered over a crisp but frothy body, is at times nothing short of fermentation alchemy. Holy Mountain also makes a top-notch pilsner called Three Fates. You can visit the brewery and, once a week, bartenders drop a special cellar reserve list of rare and aged bottles for on-premise consumption.

**TOP 3**

SEATTLE, WASHINGTON

# Visit these three beer bars in Seattle

**239**

**239  No Anchor**

This hip nautical-themed bar offers close to twenty drafts at two serving temperatures: 42°F (5.6°C) and 52°F (11.1°C) delineated on a chart by Modern vs. Traditional and Approachable vs. Esoteric.

**240  Toronado**

The outpost of this San Francisco classic features forty taps, a deep list of whiskies and spirits, and comfy digs with burgers and other hearty American grub.

**241  The Noble Fir**

This nature-themed beer, cider, and wine bar pours dozens of beers on draft and from bottles, and features a small library nook in the back where you can browse over a pint.

SEATTLE, WASHINGTON

## 242 Sample some strong ales

The long-running Fremont Brewing makes dozens of great beers, but the forte is strong ales, which are often aged in barrels and packaged in wax-capped bottles. Be sure to try the most popular: B-Bomb, a bourbon barrel version of Abominable Winter Ale with rich caramelly notes of bourbon, wood, and vanilla. Also seek out barrel-aged Dark Star stout and The Rusty Nail imperial stout.

TACOMA, WASHINGTON

## 243 Find wild ales in a former firehouse

Built in 1907, the former fire station that now houses the unique E9 Brewing is a Tacoma landmark that appears on the National Register of Historic Places. E9, founded in 1995, was the city's first craft brewery, but you'd never know it by the modern, forward-thinking beer styles it makes. Try the line of wild American-style sours and hoppy farmhouse ales.

## 244 Partake in this brew celebration
The eleven-day PDX Beer Week typically held in June features educational panels and lectures, beer and food pairing events, plus art, film, and design aspects unlike any other beer festival in the US. Although local brewers are the focus, the best of the beer world descends to party. The event is organized by local beer writers, bottle shop owners, and craft beer entrepreneurs whose aim is beer education and brewery promotion.

## 245 Celebrate cherry beer at Kriekfest
Organized by beer writer Brian Yaeger, this annual festival is a celebration of cherry-infused beers. With Mount Hood as your striking backdrop, sample dozens of Belgian-inspired cherry beers, mostly from the Pacific Northwest and West Coast. Cherry ciders, wines, and meads are also offered.

**HOOD RIVER, OREGON**

## 246 Soak in views of two rivers at this upscale brewpub

Nestled in a gorge where the White Salmon River empties into the Columbia, the handsome, industrial-chic pFriem Family Brewers takes inspiration from Belgium, Germany, and the Pacific Northwest for its exemplary line of clean, classic beers and wood-aged sours. The tasting room sits adjacent to Hood River's Waterfront Park, offering spectacular views. Order from a menu crafted from locally sourced ingredients—kale and farro salad, burgers made from local grass-fed beef—while sampling pFriem classics like Blonde IPA, Helles Lager, and Pilsner. For those with a funky palate, try the range of fruited long-aged sour ales like Peche, Fraise, and Frambozen. Boozy barrel-aged beers (Bourbon Barrel Imperial Stout, Cognac Barrel Aged Belgian Style Dark) are also available.

**BEND, OREGON**

## 247 Sample beer brewed in a hollowed-out tree trunk

Located up a rural ridge, the small Ale Apothecary from former Deschutes brewer Paul Arney is a "vintage-batch oak barrel brewery." Everything here goes through some kind of wood fermentation and often Arney looks to the past to make beers like Sahati, a Finnish-style filtered through spruce branches and hopped with Cascade hops from local Goschie Farms.

**BEND, OREGON**

## 248 Sip beers from one of the US's original craft breweries

Bend's original brewery, the one that started it all, is the Deschutes Brewery and pub. Head there for classics like Black Butte Porter, Inversion IPA, and Fresh Squeezed IPA. While you're at it, try some experimental and limited-release beers like The Abyss and Black Butte 30th Birthday Reserve.

# Drop into Bend's top three breweries

Per capita, Bend likely has more breweries per person than anywhere else in the country. These are our favorites.

### 249  Boneyard Beer

Opened since 2010, this hop-focused brewery pours pints and tasters of its iconic West Coast styles in sleek digs at a pub in downtown Bend. Bottles and crowlers are available to go.

### 250  10 Barrel Brewing

The original outpost of this brewpub (now owned by Anheuser-Busch InBev) features dozens of West Coast-style ales and lagers with American bar food served in generous portions.

### 251  Bend Brewing

One of Bend's oldest breweries is this laid-back brewpub featuring an outdoor patio where you can knock back surprisingly modern styles. Think: juicy IPAs and dry-hopped pilsners.

251

**252 Enjoy the ephemeral nature of fresh hop beers**

Wet hop IPAs are seasonal fall brews made with uber-green hops that have been plucked from the fields and used in a beer within twenty-four hours (i.e., unkilned). The technique captures many volatile oils and sticky resins that almost instantly begin to fade after harvest. (Think of the difference between using fresh and dried herbs when cooking.) Although made around the country, these beers are popular in the Pacific Northwest due to their proximity to the hop-growing regions of the Yakima and Willamette Valleys. Some of the best come from Astoria Brewing, Fort George Brewery, Fremont Brewing, and Bale Breaker Brewing. Enjoy these while they last because once they're gone, they're done until next season.

PORTLAND, OREGON

# Look out for these three IPAs in Portland

PDX is flush with great hoppy ales. Here are three to go out of your way to try.

**253**

### 253 Great Notion Ripe IPA

Portland's darlings of the hazy IPA boom, Great Notion's Ripe IPA brings a bit of Vermont and New England to the Pacific Northwest.

### 254 Laurelwood Workhorse IPA

This West Coast-style IPA features multiple dry hoppings for an assertive bitterness to balance the slightly sweet finish.

### 255 Breakside IPA

A stalwart of Portland's beer scene, Breakside's flagship IPA is a textbook American-style GABF-medal winner.

PORTLAND, OREGON

### 256 Savor high-gravity ales with Hair of the Dog

A PDX institution since 1993, Hair of the Dog Brewing is one of the best specialty breweries in Portland. Brewer and owner Alan Sprints has been making beer here for more than twenty-five years, specializing in high-gravity, bottle-conditioned beers that are unlike anything else in the city. His most famous beers are barleywine- and stock ale-style beers with huge aromas of dark fruit and chocolate with yeasty, beguiling esters. Sprints also specializes in historic European brews, reviving the German Adambier style (a strong variation of altbier) for his flagship Adam ale. You can taste all of these and more (including a lengthy vintage beer list) in the wood-adorned, lodge-style tasting room and restaurant. A selection of beer-friendly bites—charcuterie and cheeseboards, hearty brisket—is served. Though the beers are often boozy (the average ABV hovers at around 8-9%), pours are short and several lower-alcohol beers are often available, like the "Little Dog's" Adam (3.5%) and Lila, a 6% maibock.

PORTLAND, OREGON
## 257 Quaff a blueberry pancake-inspired beer

Great Notion Brewing is most famous for dank IPAs, but one of its most fun beers is the Double Stack breakfast stout, an imperial stout aged with Vermont maple syrup and locally roasted coffee beans. At the taproom, pair it with a bite from the comfort food-heavy menu.

PORTLAND, OREGON
## 258 Discover "beervana" at this long-running bottle shop and bar

Since its founding in 1997, Belmont Station bottle shop and bar has been a local gathering place for craft beer locals and visitors alike. Located in a quaint residential neighborhood, the front features a draft bar and more than a thousand packaged beers. Grab a local or imported draft and post up in the backyard beer garden.

PORTLAND, OREGON
## 259 Learn to love lagers in PDX

Think Portland's beer scene is oversaturated? Think again. Wayfinder Beer, opened in 2017 from Double Mountain cofounder Charlie Devereux, Relapse Records' Matthew Jacobson, and restaurateur Rodney Muirhead, quickly became one of the hottest breweries in this perennially white-hot market. The focus is on clean, classic, low-ABV lagers. The flagship Czech Pils is an exemplary bitter and spicy Czech-style pilsner, while Hell is a crushable helles-style lagerbier. The tasting room is decked out in dark, handsome wood tones and exposed brick.

PORTLAND, OREGON
## 260 Sample the best brews of the Beaver State

Each July, around 70,000 attendees descend on Waterfront Park for this five-day extravaganza of Oregon-made brews. Oregon Brewers Fest started in 1988 and is now one of the most popular beer festivals in the US, with each participating brewery bringing one beer to pour (there are often more than a hundred different beers available). Admission is free, but you must purchase a plastic tasting mug as well as $1 beer tokens, which can be exchanged for tasting pours or full pints. Live music and food are also featured.

PORTLAND, OREGON
## 261 Jump on a brewery tour

For even the most versed beer geeks, mapping out Portland's beer scene can be an intimidating prospect. There are literally hundreds of breweries in the region, most of which are worth a visit. So, where to begin? One option is the slick BREWVANA Brewery Tours, a play on the city's nickname Beervana. The company offers a range of tour options, from preplanned book-it-on-the-website tours to fully curated private beer experiences. There are also out-of-town options to regional breweries and festival trips (round-trip transportation to and from PDX) as well as tours that incorporate delicacies beyond beer (coffee, beer, and doughnuts). No matter which option you choose, you're guaranteed to get a personalized perspective of one of the world's true great beer cities.

PORTLAND, OREGON

## 262 Drink a Dead Guy Ale

Founded in 1988, Rogue Ales is one of the Pacific Northwest's OG craft breweries. Its flagship beer, Dead Guy Ale, is a legend among old-school beer enthusiasts. Based on the German maibock style, Dead Guy is a rich and robust ale with notes of toffee and honey, and it has a smooth finish. One of the coolest things is that it's made with a high percentage of ingredients grown right on the Rogue Ales farm, including Rogue Farms' proprietary Dare and Risk malts.

PORTLAND, OREGON

### 263 Meet the "little beasts"

Named for the "little beasts" that convert wort into beer—yeast, bacteria, microflora, and other microscopic critters—the small Little Beast Brewing from veteran Portland brewers Charles Porter and Brenda Crow produces bottle-conditioned wild farmhouse ales. Visit the taproom for a pour of the flagship Fera brettanomyces ale and seasonals like Tree Spirit Beer with tart cherries.

PORTLAND, OREGON

### 264 Sip San Diego brews in the Pacific Northwest

Located in the former Commons Brewery space on SE Belmont Ave, Modern Times' Belmont Fermentorium is a welcome addition to the Portland beer scene. The spacious, sun-drenched tasting room showcases a handsome brewhouse with close to thirty beers on draft, growler fills, and a merch shop. The brewery plans to add an on-site coffee roastery and café.

**TOP 5**

PORTLAND, OREGON

# Find the five best funky brewers in Portland

Hops are the focus here, but so are complex sours. Here are five funky options.

### 265 Upright Brewing

With a small, intimate basement tasting room, this brewery crafts a range of saison-based tart and funky beers. Try Pathways Saison blended from a series of barrels.

**UPRIGHT BREWING**

### 266 Cascade Brewing

A pioneer in the Pacific Northwest sour beer scene, Cascade focuses on blended ales spiked with all varieties of fruit like apricot, peach, cherries, and raspberries.

### 267 Culmination Brewing

This hip spot in northeast Portland crafts a range of beers, including funky beers like Foed for Thought farmhouse ale and Native Oregonism, a collab with Ale Apothecary.

### 268 Modern Times Belmont Fermentorium

Housed in the former Commons Brewery space, this San Diego transplant brings some seriously funky beers to the table.

### 269 LABrewatory

This nanobrewery specializes in experimental one-off beers, meaning you'll never have to drink the same beer twice. Many are sours amped up with fruits, vegetables, and other adjuncts.

NEWBERG, OREGON
## 270 Discover a brewery located on an active hazelnut farm

Former beer writer and journalist Christian DeBenedetti founded Wolves & People Farmhouse Brewery in 2016 on his family's active hazelnut farm (just outside Portland). DeBenedetti grew up on the farm and now makes a range of beers like mixed-culture pale ales, low-ABV stouts and crisp lagers in a barn the family once used to process filberts. His farmhouse-style saisons and grisettes, which often incorporate fruits, nuts, and wild yeast—all sourced right from the farm—have quickly catapulted the brewery into the national spotlight. You can relax in the tasting room located inside a circa-1912 Craftsman-style barn, which also houses the brewery. With the use of local ingredients and native yeast, DeBenedetti's is one of a handful of US breweries aiming to impart their beer with a true sense of place—still a novel idea in today's ever-expanding world of practically indistinguishable hazy double IPAs and dessert-flavored stouts. Try his Zester Queen, a sour spiked with Douglas fir tips from the farm, or La Truffe, a table stout with local truffles brewed in collaboration with the Oregon Truffle Fest.

ASTORIA, OREGON
## 271 Crack a cold one in coastal Oregon

Opened for more than a decade, the well-regarded Fort George Brewery in coastal Astoria produces clean, classic West Coast-style beers shaped by the surrounding Pacific Northwest environment. The brewery features multiple venues in a single spot, including its original pub and brewery, an upstairs pizza pub with sweeping views of the Columbia River, and a courtyard-adjacent taproom.

TILLAMOOK, OREGON
## 272 Savor spontaneous ales

The tiny de Garde Brewing is located in a town known more for cheese than beer. The brewery makes spontaneously fermented beers inoculated in a coolship and then transferred to oak barrels for aging. Fruit additions are often added, and the tasting room offers bottles to go, and drafts and vintage bottles to stay.

MCMINNVILLE, OREGON
## 273 Sip German-inspired brews from a father-and-daughter team

Founder Rick Allen started Heater Allen Brewing in 2007 on what was essentially a glorified homebrew system, after working for years as an investment banker. The brewery is located in the heart of Oregon's wine country and is surrounded by wine-tasting rooms, about an hour's drive southwest of Portland. In 2009, Allen's daughter Lisa joined the brewery and is currently the head brewer. The concentration is on German- and Czech-style lagers like Pils, Schwarz, and Dunkel as well as seasonal lagers and even some ales. A small taproom is open for visits.

### PACIFIC CITY, OREGON
## 274 Take a sip by the seaside

A beachside outpost of this Oregon coastal brewpub chain, Pelican Brewing's Pacific City location offers one of the world's best views for sampling beer. Grab a table on the sand-dusted patio overlooking the sea and sample a flight of Kiwanda cream ale (named for the state preserve just feet from where you're sitting), Beak Breaker double IPA, and Tsunami export stout.

### CHICO, CALIFORNIA
## 275 Sling back a Sierra Nevada Oktoberfest or two

Held over two weekends in late September, the iconic Sierra Nevada Brewing throws one epic Bavarian-style party. At the core is Sierra Nevada's annual Oktoberfest beer collaboration with a German brewery. During the festivities you can knock back liters of the beer alongside German-style fare, games, and activities. A similar celebration was introduced at the brewery's North Carolina facility.

### BERKELEY, CALIFORNIA
## 276 Pick up a pilsner

In 2004, Austria-based brewery Trumer built Trumer Brauerei in California in order to supply beer for its US market. Trumer Pils has now become one of the most-loved locally brewed beers in the Bay Area. All ingredients are shipped from Austria (except the water, which comes from the High Sierras), including Czech Saaz and German Spalt Select hops.

### TRUCKEE, CALIFORNIA
## 277 Get stuck into this stout series

FiftyFifty Brewing composes one of the best imperial stouts in the world with its Eclipse series. The variant bottles, which change from year to year, are packaged in waxed color-coded bottles and feature different whiskey barrel treatments (Elijah Craig 12-year, Willett Bourbon) as well as adjuncts (maple coffee, salted caramel).

### PETALUMA, CALIFORNIA
## 278 Visit the birthplace of Lagunitas IPA

Though now owned by Heineken, Lagunitas Brewing was one of the pioneers of American craft beer in the 2000s. The original taproom has a lively atmosphere that still captures the reckless devil-may-care attitude of the brewery's earlier days. Tuck into a bar stool or a picnic table in the beer garden and order a pint of Lagunitas IPA, a piney and grapefruity classic. Then go for one of many newer rotating beers like Strawberry White Pale Ale or Willettized Coffee Stout aged in rye oak barrels from the Willett Distillery. During hop season, Born Yesterday is one of the best large-production fresh hop IPAs you'll find. Live music often includes local acts and jam bands.

SANTA ROSA, CALIFORNIA

**279 Don't miss Pliny the Younger**

The year 2019 marked the fifteenth anniversary of this beer's release. The triple IPA—a bigger, bolder nephew and adopted son of Russian River Brewing's year-round Pliny the Elder double IPA—is loaded with bitter, floral, and fruity hop flavors. Expect long lines and massive crowds as this beer is released just once a year on the first Friday in February, and is usually available for two weeks.

SAN FRANCISCO, CALIFORNIA

**280 Imbibe barleywine by the Bay**

After canceling the long-running Toronado Barleywine Festival in 2016, storied craft beer pub Toronado brought it back with a bang in 2017 and it shows no signs of slowing. Pouring perhaps the largest collection of barleywines in the country, look for perennial favorites from Lost Abbey, Sierra Nevada, Midnight Sun, and Firestone Walker, plus newer beers from Oregon's Alesong and Orange County's Beachwood.

**279**  *Below:* Russian River Brewing's downtown taproom

## 281 Discover why California Common is not typical

San Francisco's oldest brewery, Anchor, was founded here in 1896, and in 1965, it was purchased by Fritz Maytag, who saved the financially struggling microbrewery from closing. Maytag turned it into the US's first "craft" brewery and moved it to its current location in 1979 where you can take a walking tour of the historic building followed by a tasting. Anchor is one of the few US breweries still producing the historic California Common under its Anchor Steam label. Other specialties include Liberty Ale—one of the first examples of American pale ale, made with iconic Cascade hops—and Old Foghorn, a boozed-up elixir that was the first American-style barleywine ever produced. More recent offerings include Brewers' Pale Ale hopped with Citra and dry-hopped Anchor Steam. While you're there, check out the Anchor Distilling Company, which produces a wide range of products from gins and vodkas to *eau de vie* and liqueurs.

SAN FRANCISCO, CALIFORNIA
## 282 Drink beer at the proper temperature

One of the city's only beer-centric restaurants, Belgian-style The Monk's Kettle offers traditional US and Belgian-influenced pub grub alongside a massive book-length list of bottled and draft beers. The place prides itself on "proper beer service" and refrigerators are set to 40°F (4.4°C), 50°F (10°C), and 55 °F (12.8°C) to ensure all beer is served at proper temperatures.

HALF MOON BAY, CALIFORNIA
## 283 Hang out in Half Moon Bay

Surfboards and fish adorn the wooden walls at the eccentric brewpub Half Moon Bay Brewing. Knock back a dozen oysters on the half-shell paired with a crisp Kölsch or a properly bitter IPA. Post up next to the patio fireplace for the best seats in the house.

283  *Below:* The patio fireplace at Half Moon Bay Brewing

# Discover the best of the Bay Area

284

### 284 Drake's Brewing

A stalwart in the Bay Area craft beer scene since 1989, this brewery's original outpost in San Leandro features hop-forward ales and a robust barrel-aging program with drafts and flights served in a spacious taproom with plenty of outdoor space.

### 285 Cellarmaker Brewing

This hip, young brewery is focused on small batches of hop-forward American-style IPAs and pale ales. The handsome tasting room is the perfect spot for sampling short-pour flights of the brewery's ever-rotating selection of ales.

### 286 The Rare Barrel

This all-sour brewery specializes in blending mixed-fermentation barrel-aged beers, many with additions of fruits and spices. The rustic tasting room serves the brewery's own draft and bottled beers as well as guest taps of non-sour beers.

### 287 Fieldwork Brewing

Founded in Berkeley, this brewery now has taprooms throughout California. The original features twenty drafts of hoppy American styles with tamales and snacks by local eatery Comal.

### 288 Temescal Brewing

This cool Oakland brewery makes light and refreshing beers like New Kolsch and Temescal Pils as well as bold porters and dessert-flavored imperial stouts.

CAPITOLA AND SANTA CRUZ, CALIFORNIA

## 289 Worship at the altar of Adairius

What began as a quirky little brewery in Capitola has become one of the most recognized, revered, and award-winning operations in the world. The beer production at Sante Adairius Rustic Ales, or SARA—how the brewery is colloquially known in the industry, especially on the West Coast—is still small by any standards, but the quality of beer is off the charts. Founded in 2012 by Adair Paterno and Tim Clifford, SARA's primary focus is mixed-culture, bottle-conditioned saisons and farmhouse-style ales, though the portfolio has expanded to include other styles like hoppy IPAs, robust stouts, and porters. The original location, in an industrial park-like area off a busy highway, features a tasting room where you can see the original brewing operation, sip drafts, and order bottles. A newer tasting room in downtown Santa Cruz offers a more robust experience with more drafts, a full kitchen, and an expansive bottle list. Some of the best are classics like Saison Bernice, a dry, effervescent farmhouse ale, or Appreciation, a barrel-aged farmhouse ale with boysenberries. SARA's Cellar, a members-only club, offers access to special releases.

## 290 Catch the Firestone Walker Invitational Beer Fest

Held in early June (typically on the weekend after Memorial Day), this festival features the best brewers from around the world. Held at the old-timey Western-themed Paso Robles fairgrounds, it includes unlimited beers from California locals like Alvarado Street, Moonlight, and Hollister as well as esoteric and big-name breweries from around the US (Oxbow Brewing, Fonta Flora, Allagash, etc.). A host of international breweries like Omnipollo, Mahr's Braü, and New Zealand's Garage Project round out the list. Inside the festival grounds, you'll find a sun-soaked party-like atmosphere with live bands on a main stage and gratis samples from local restaurants located throughout. The festival smartphone app helps you tick off and keep track of every beer you sample and serves as your ballot for voting for your favorite breweries. The winners are announced at the culmination of the fest. Tickets sell out fast, so purchase yours early.

LOS ANGELES, CALIFORNIA

### 291 Fill your belly

Comfort food is the name of the game at this Koreatown outpost of LA's Beer Belly. Start with duck fat fries (tossed in duck fat, duck cracklings, and raspberry mustard) and a side of Jidori chicken wings (a breed of free-range chicken known for its robust flavor) to pair with more than a dozen local brews.

KERNVILLE, CALIFORNIA

### 292 Try a tangy double IPA

The aggressive but balanced seasonal Citra Double IPA from Kern River Brewing packs a lemony punch thanks to an abundance of Citra hops. It's rounded out by notes of mango and pineapple from a dry-hopping of Amarillo hops. It's a beer worth going out of your way to try, and is available late November until whenever it sells out.

---

**TOP 4**　LOS ANGELES, CALIFORNIA

# Enjoy the offerings of DTLA and environs

293

### 293 Highland Park Brewing

This second location of LA's smoking-hot Highland Park in Chinatown features a spacious taproom and bar pouring classics like Refresh House Lager and Going Global hazy IPA. Mexican-style snacks are also offered.

### 294 Mumford Brewing

A colorful, cartoonish mural covers the outside of this Skid Row-adjacent brewery featuring tasting flights of West Coast and NE-style IPAs, dry-hopped lagers, and rich imperial stouts. Cans are often available to go.

### 295 The Dankness Dojo

This slim outpost of San Diego's Modern Times features a long bar along one side and drafts in the back. Sling back an Ice pilsner or go for something funkier like Transit of Venus, a rye grisette.

296

### 296 Arts District Brewing

Featuring a fifteen-barrel brewhouse and vintage arcade games like Skee-ball, this downtown brewery is a fun place to gather. Check out beers like Flores Minimæ, a low-ABV farmhouse ale.

# Take in San Diego's top five breweries

### 297 Modern Times Beer

With two locations in San
Diego—and outposts in
Los Angeles, Encinitas, and
Portland—this brewery is one
of the fastest growing in the
country. From hazy IPAs and
clean lagers to funky sours and saisons, Modern Times does it
all—and does them well. Be sure to check out the cheeky Michael
Jackson-and-his-monkey mural at the Point Loma location
rendered entirely in Post-it notes.

### 298 AleSmith Brewing

This classic San Diego
brewery opened its shiny
brewery and tasting room in
2015 with dozens of year-
round and specialty beers
on draft. Try .394 Pale Ale
(brewed with famed Padres
player Tony Gwynn) or the
classic Nut Brown ale.

### 299 Stone Brewing

One of the original SoCal
breweries, Stone is widely
regarded for popularizing
the West Coast style of IPA with huge fruity aromas
and heavy bitterness. Several locations throughout
the city mean multiple opportunities for crushing
a Ruination or Delicious IPA.

### 300 Port Brewing

Check out the taproom of
this legendary surf-themed
brewery for textbook
examples of West Coast-style
hoppy ales. (See entry 302 for
The Lost Abbey and The Hop
Concept for more about its
spin-off breweries.)

### 301 Pure Project

This charitable and
community-focused brewery
blends the best of SoCal with
a global perspective. Drop
by the taproom for special
can and bottle releases (all
varieties of IPAs and sours)
or a pint from one of sixteen
draft lines.

301

SAN MARCOS, CALIFORNIA
## 302 Explore the conceptual side of a San Diego legend

Spin-offs of Port Brewing, The Lost Abbey and The Hop Concept each focus on a narrow range of styles. For The Lost Abbey, that means Belgian-style farmhouse ales, sours, and Trappist-influenced beers, and for The Hop Concept, exclusively hop-forward offerings. Both pour beers at Port's central San Marcos tasting room, and The Lost Abbey operates a second seaside facility in Cardiff-by-the-Sea (which also pours Port and The Hop Concept beers). The Lost Abbey is revered for complex wood-aged beers like Red Poppy, a Flanders-style brown ale aged on oak for more than twelve months, while The Hop Concept creates a rotating series of IPAs based around flavor profiles like "dank and sticky" or "tropical and juicy."

SAN DIEGO, CALIFORNIA
## 303 Spring for a Speedway Stout

AleSmith Brewing Speedway Stout is an ominous, pitch-black mother of an imperial stout and is the brewery's best-known beer. Replete with flavors and aromas of chocolate, dark dried fruit, toffee, and caramel, a dosing of coffee, and the beer's fine carbonation make it supremely drinkable. Seek out rare variants like Vietnamese Coffee infused with a blend of four beans known as cà phê sa đá.

SAN DIEGO, CALIFORNIA
## 304 Celebrate the dankness

Enjoy great beer with waterfront views of downtown San Diego. Held annually in August at the Waterfront Park, Festival of Dankness celebrates the hop-centric brews of producers from around the country. Past invitees have included Bottle Logic, Burial Beer, Creature Comforts, Green Cheek, and Monkish Brewing as well as international breweries like the UK's Cloudwater. Each year the festival donates profits to a local charity or non-profit.

ANCHORAGE, ALASKA
## 305 Get wise to Alaska's barrel-aging and blending master

In 2010, former Midnight Sun head brewer Gabe Fletcher left the company he had worked at for more than a decade to pursue a solo career, founding Anchorage Brewing. The focus is funky wood-aged beers akin to Jolly Pumpkin, Crooked Stave, and Holy Mountain, with a dash of clean IPAs and a boozy barleywine called A Deal with the Devil. Visit the wood-paneled tasting room and you'll sit in the shadows of the tall foeders used for conditioning, which surround one side of the bar, and sip from one of ten draft beers. Fletcher's forte is creating a blend of funk, wood, and hops with beers like Love Buzz Saison, Bitter Monk Citra, and Galaxy White IPA, showcasing his deft hand at perfectly melding delicate, beguiling flavors. The draft room also offers bottles to go and to stay, and a small selection of meats and cheeses, including local charcuterie and imported cheese. Be sure to check out the collection of metal fish and wildlife sculptures adorning the brewery walls and equipment—Fletcher, a well-known outdoorsman and angler, commissioned the works from a local father-and-daughter artist team known as the Big Ass Fish Company (BAFCO).

### TALKEETNA, ALASKA
**306 Visit a brewery in the shadow of Denali**

Situated in the shadow of the tallest mountain in North America, the small Denali Brewing is one of Alaska's oldest breweries. Try a variety of old-school American-style ales either at the bar or in the outdoor beer garden. Seasonal hours apply in winter, so be sure to call before you go.

### ANCHORAGE, ALASKA
**307 Drink beer under the midnight sun**

Founded in 1995, Midnight Sun Brewing creates bold beers for the American palate. Stop by for a tour and taste through the lineup of seasonal releases and flagship standards. The Loft tasting room offers sixteen beers on draft in a hip, apartment-like space above the brewery.

### JUNEAU, ALASKA
**308 Sample one of the US's first smoked beers**

One of the best beers in The Last Frontier state is Alaskan Brewing's Smoked Porter. The dark, rich ale has a pronounced smoked flavor from the use of smoked malt and packs a punch despite being just 6.5% ABV. It's produced in limited vintages once a year, on the first of November.

### ANCHORAGE, ALASKA
**309 Chill out at this cold beer fest**

Traveling to the coldest state in the Union in the middle of January may seem like madness, but when your reward is an array of big, flavorful beers, it's a risk you'd be willing to take. The annual Great Alaska Beer & Barley Wine Festival features over 200 beers from more than fifty breweries.

**303** *Above:* Speedway Stout is probably AleSmith Brewing's best-known beer

# Don't miss Honolulu's best three beer bars

### 310  Brew'd Craft Pub

This rustic but hip locale in the Kaimuki neighborhood features a wide selection of craft brews plus cocktails and a creative menu of tapas-like plates.

### 311  Growler USA

Located near Waikiki, this spot features numerous American craft beers with modern gastropub fare, plenty of TV tuned to sports, plus live music in the evenings.

### 312  Square Barrels

This is downtown Honolulu's outpost for gourmet burgers made from grass-fed beef plus more than a dozen craft beers—some rare—on draft and many more in bottles.

OAHU, HAWAII

### 313  Drink a beer while watching surfers

Ehukai Beach Park, also known as the Banzai Pipeline, on Oahu's north shore is a great place to sunbathe and stroll the shore—just leave surfing the huge waves to the pros. Pack a local picnic beer and set up along the shore for some great viewing.

OAHU, HAWAII

### 314  Pair beer with fish tacos

Fish tacos aren't indigenous to Hawaii (thank Baja California for that), but the islands are now replete with food trucks slinging them and other local fusion foods. Stop by North Shore Tacos in Pupukea or Hau'ula for a plate of fish tacos with rice and beans, and be sure to BYO favorite local beer.

THE BIG ISLAND AND OAHU, HAWAII

### 315  Catch island fever with these beers

With two locations, the island-themed Kona Brewing features plenty of opportunities for relaxing Hawaiian-style. Knock back a pint of Big Wave golden ale or Longboard lager, or a seasonal release like Castaway IPA. The Big Island location features a spacious 2,000 sq ft (186 sq m) outdoor lanai.

KIHEI, MAUI, HAWAII

### 316  Catch a coconut wave of beer

Founded in 2005 brewing just 300 barrels a year, the rapidly expanding Maui Brewing is now Hawaii's largest brewery, producing more than 50,000 barrels annually. Its line of flagship beers include Bikini Blonde, Big Swell IPA, and the favorite Coconut Hiwa porter, a dark ale brewed with toasted coconut. Four locations are now open—two in Maui and two in Oahu—and tours are offered at the original Kihei Tasting Room, a gorgeously landscaped facility near the shores of Maalaea Bay. Meanwhile, visitors to Waikiki can sample the beers just steps from Kuhio Beach in the brewery's expansive, open-air facility in the Waikiki Beachcomber by Outrigger.

# Canada, Mexico, and South America

Canadian beer culture—more so than that of nearly anywhere else—feels like a natural extension of the US's, particularly in its urban and suburban areas. The hotbeds are cities like Montreal, Toronto, and Vancouver, while other areas offer more limited experiences. The same is true in Mexico, to an extent: the majority of its craft beer (i.e. non-lager) is found in border cities like Tijuana, and urban expanses like Mexico City.

The beer scenes of Central and South America are nascent, but exciting ventures with many up-and-coming brewers utilizing local and native fruits and flora to create ales and lagers unlike any others in the world. Brazil in particular offers a range of robust beer experiences, from the boisterous German-themed Oktoberfest in Blumenau to the avant-garde brews of Way Beer and Cerveja Tupiniquim.

SHAWINIGAN, QUEBEC, CANADA

### 317 Make a deal with the devil at this brewpub

Meaning "the devil's hole," Le Trou du diable—Brewpub &
Restaurant—about 93 miles (150 km) northeast of Montreal—offers
some of the best beer in Canada. The styles run the gamut from
American-style IPAs to German-style pilsners to red ales, stouts,
and wheat beers. The menu skews heavy toward Quebecois
classics (pork rillettes, chicken liver mousse). A short walk away
is Le Trou du diable—Microbrewery, Boutique & Salon, which
offers beer to go, merchandise, and tours (book ahead). The
brewery partners with several local hotels to offer fixed-price
dinner, beer, and accommodation packages. Be sure to try
the barrel-aged beer selection and, if you're there around
Christmastime, La Grivoise de Noël, a complex, fruity brown
beer with notes of candy and berries that's perfect for the season.

**TOP 3**

MONTREAL, QUEBEC, CANADA

# Drop into Montreal's three best pubs

**318 Le Saint-Bock**

This laid-back spot offers an expansive array of house-made beers and local ales and lagers. A small beer garden in the front offers pleasant seating during warm weather.

**319 Broue Pub Brouhaha**

This Belgian-inspired brewpub-bar with two locations (Rosemont and Ahuntsic) serves twenty-four house-brewed beers on draft with many imports available in bottles.

319

**320 Vices & Versa**

Tuck into this bistro serving poutine, local cheeses, and other Quebecois specialties alongside mostly Belgian-inspired beers from the region.

320

# Check out Toronto's top three beer bars

321

### 321 Birreria Volo

The Morana brothers serve rare and imported beers (plus Canadian and US specialties) alongside rustic Italian-influenced snacks in a narrow, exposed brick space.

### 322 C'est What

This wine and craft beer bar focuses on Canadian-brewed ales and lagers served from drafts and bottles in a subterranean space. The food menu offers hearty North American grub.

### 323 Bar Hop

Each of the three locations of this local spot offers dozens of local drafts and a handful of cask ales with more than a hundred bottled beers.

MONTREAL, QUEBEC, CANADA
### 324 Try a beer built for the end of the world

Brewed since 1994, Unibroue's La Fin du Monde strong ale, whose name means "the end of the world," is one of the best-known Canadian beers among nascent beer enthusiasts. Nominally a Belgian-style tripel, its robust body, fruity esters, and warming finish make it Unibroue's international flagship beer.

MONTREAL, QUEBEC, CANADA
### 325 Reach for the heavens in Montreal

*Dieu du Ciel!* is the French version of the expression "Oh my God!" Dieu du Ciel! the brewery, meanwhile, is a tiny brewpub in Montreal's Mile End, opened since 1998. In 2008, a second location opened in Saint-Jérôme. Both locations serve exciting beers like Aphrodisiaque cocoa and vanilla stout.

BROSSARD, QUEBEC, CANADA
### 326 Sip a slice of Belgium in Quebec

Les Trois Mousquetaires microbrewery focuses on high-quality European-influenced ales, including saisons with brettanomyces, an Oud Bruin-inspired sour brown ale, and gose brewed with salt and spices. The tasting room, located in a suburb across the St. Lawrence River from Montreal, features drafts to stay and crowlers to go.

TORONTO, ONTARIO, CANADA
## 327 Quaff a cask ale at Cask Days Beer Festival

What began in 2005 with fifteen breweries serving twenty-two casks to a meager 150 attendees has evolved into one of the largest cask beer festivals in the world. Founded by the folks behind Bar Volo (now known as Birreria Volo), Cask Days Beer Festival in fall celebrates the love for unpasteurized, unfiltered, and naturally carbonated beer. Each of the beers is served direct from a cask barrel, and breweries travel from all over the world to attend. Past highlights include Modern Times and Beachwood BBQ from California, Cascade and Hair of the Dog from Oregon, Thin Man and Finback from New York State, and Allagash and Oxbow from Maine. Canadian breweries include Hopfenstark, Les Trois Mousquetaires, and Brasserie Dunham, as well as breweries from British Columbia and Nova Scotia. One section is even dedicated to homebrewers. A food component features some of Toronto's best chefs pairing "real food with real ale," and a music and art section highlights local DJs and beer-inspired artworks.

TORONTO, ONTARIO, CANADA
## 328 Be spellbound at Witchstock Festival

Bellwoods Brewery brings together dozens of breweries from Canada, the US, and Europe for this annual fall festival featuring some of the most exclusive beers and breweries in the world. Admission is steep—north of $100—but it's all-you-can-drink from breweries like Cantillon, Bissell Brothers, Dieu du Ciel!, and Cloudwater.

**327**  *Right:* Cask Days is one of the largest cask ale festivals in the world

CALGARY, CANADA
## 329 Drink at this 1980s-inspired brewery

The four founders of Calgary's Eighty-Eight Brewing really wanted to do something that would resonate with the people of their city. They thought that the 1988 Winter Olympic Games was a sort of coming-of-age moment for Calgary, and this was something to celebrate in beer form. The brewery also drew a lot of inspiration from the 1980s writ large, a feature readily noticeable in the brand and taproom. You'll find nostalgic elements both from the decade and the 1988 Olympics everywhere. Beers such as Cassette Table Beer, Duotang Dry-hopped Sour, and the Tiffany Rosé Saison attest to the obsession with the year-round selections and this trend continues with the seasonal selections such as the Eddie the ESB Extra Special Bitter, Hans Gruber Hopped Hef, and Fruity Pebbles Milkshake sour.

### 330 Drink Molson Canadian at a hockey game

There's no disputing that Canadians love ice hockey, and there's even littler doubt that hockey fans love beer. So next time you're in Canada during the hockey season (October–April), seek out a game from one of the country's seven professional hockey teams—only two are part of the National Hockey League's "original six"—the Montreal Canadiens and the Toronto Maple Leafs—and knock back a classic Molson Canadian or two.

---

**TOP 3**

VANCOUVER, BRITISH COLUMBIA, CANADA

# Kick back at Vancouver's three best pubs

### 331 St. Augustine's

This craft beer house and restaurant offers mostly local beers on its sixty-plus taps served with burgers and pizzas in a handsome tavern-like setting.

### 332 Craft Beer Market

Located in an airy, sprawling, barn-like structure, this beer-centric minichain features more than a hundred beers on draft ranging from basic ales and lagers to more obscure offerings.

### 333 Alibi Room

A hip bar located in a refurbished historic building, the Alibi Room serves upscale small plates (charcuterie boards, mezze plates) paired with more than fifty local and imported beers.

---

### 334 Try the local pulque

Though not technically beer (or brewed for that matter), this cloudy fermented beverage is a regional specialty that beer lovers will find worth seeking out. The milky, viscous liquid is made by fermenting the fresh sap of certain types of agave plants. It clocks in at around 4–6% ABV and is sold in *pulquerias* throughout Mexico.

## TIJUANA, BAJA CALIFORNIA, MEXICO
### 335 Take in Tijuana's highlights

Given Tijuana's proximity to San Diego, it should come as no surprise that this border city is Mexico's best beer destination. Many breweries focus on hoppy ales that originated just a few dozen miles to the north, but others are experimenting with native Mexican ingredients and brewing techniques. One of the city's best-known breweries is Border Psycho, a gritty tasting room with just over half a dozen drafts. Try the Cream Ale (infused with amaranth and orange peel) and La Perversa, a heady, hoppy double IPA. (Be sure to check out the—ahem—unorthodox glass tap handles.) Next, check out Cervecería Insurgente, one of Mexico's most famous craft brewers. One popular beer is Xocoveza, a collaboration with Stone Brewing made with cacao, coffee, chile, pasilla, cinnamon, and nutmeg. If you're searching for a spot to purchase bottles, check out the Beer Box. Opened since 2009, it's Tijuana's original craft beer shop for Baja-brewed beers. Pints are also available to drink at the bar. Finally, check out the cost-saving brewery Mamut, dedicated to making craft beer affordable to everyone, where you can knock back a classic Czech pilsner or petite saison.

**335** *Right:* Cervecería Insurgente is a renowned Mexican craft brewery

**TOP 3**

### MEXICO CITY, MEXICO

# Meet Mexico City's top beer locations

#### 336 El Depósito

This bottle shop and bar in the Roma neighborhood offers a huge array of bottles from Mexican craft brewers as well as imports. There's a small bar with a handful of taps and TVs tuned to sports.

#### 337 Hop the Beer Experience

Two locations offer a hoppy Mexico City experience with flights and tasters from breweries from around the country paired with pizza and other grub.

#### 338 Biergarten Roma

True to its name, this sun-soaked beer garden is a relaxing spot to knock back pints of German and Mexican craft beer, and nosh on Mexican-inspired barbecue and hot dogs.

### SAN JUAN, PUERTO RICO

### 339 Sip the best of San Juan

Puerto Rico might not be the top craft beer destination in the world, but it does offer some interesting options from a burgeoning scene. Start at the island's premier craft beer bar, La Taberna Lúpulo (the Hops Tavern), located on historic Calle San Sebastian in an open-air colonial building. The taps and bottle list skew heavy toward the US—Bell's, Founders, Stone—but often include at least a handful of local brews among the fifty-plus drafts. Then, check out Rincón Beer Company, a small tasting room and brewery that reopened after Hurricane Maria destroyed much of the island in 2017. The house-brewed beers are paired with *empanadas* and other Puerto Rican fare in a bright but cozy tasting room.

### DOMINICAN REPUBLIC

### 340 Partake in a Presidente on its home turf

First brewed as a dark lager in 1935 in Santiago, the classic Caribbean Presidente pilsner was transformed to its current pale lager formula in the 1960s. Clean and crisp, it's the perfect foil for sunny beaches and hearty Dominican stews, snacks, and sandwiches.

### BLUMENAU, BRAZIL

### 341 Explore an exceptional Brazilian beer fest

With more than 35,000 attendees, the spring Festival Brasileiro da Cerveja is a gathering of beer lovers, music fans, and food enthusiasts. More than 800 different breweries participate, pouring nearly 3,000 unique beers. A concurrent contest dispenses awards for the best beers in a variety of styles.

**RIO DE JANEIRO, BRAZIL**

## 342 Take a taste of "two heads"

2cabeças—two heads—is a small brewery with a taproom in the heart of Botafogo. Choose from ten drafts like MaracujIPA, an IPA fruited with passion fruit pulp. Colorful artwork and collages adorn the walls with small tables and low-slung chairs for lounging.

**PINHAIS, PARANÁ, BRAZIL**

## 343 Find your "Way" to this exciting Brazilian brewery

Brazil's premier craft brewery is Way Beer (Cervejaria Way) on the outskirts of Curitiba. The brewery creates dozens of different styles packaged in bright, neon-accented cans and bottles. Start with Die Fizzy Yellow IPA, a pale American-style IPA made with Columbus, Citra, and Galaxy hops. Then dig into an Avelã Porter, a creamy, slightly smoky porter brewed with peated malt and oats. Try the fruity Sour Me Not series of sour ales, which feature native Brazilian fruits like the high-acid Acerola or Graviola (also known as soursop). A no-frills tasting room offers beers to stay and to go.

**PORTO ALEGRE, BRAZIL**

## 344 Taste the indigenous flavors of Brazil in beer form

Tupiniquim Cerveja Artesanal Brasileira was founded in 2013 by a group of friends who, three years earlier, had formed a beer-importing company. The importing company still exists, bringing more than 150 different beers into Brazil from all over the world. With the expansion of breweries throughout the country, the group decided to build their own brewery to make uniquely Brazilian beers. The range of styles includes classics like pilsner and IPAs, but also experimental beers made with cashews, polenta flour, and mango. The brewery's most famous beer is Monjolo Imperial Porter, named for an ancient artifact used to crush grains. Tupiniquim has also collaborated with US nomadic brewers Evil Twin and Stillwater Artisanal.

*Above:* German-style Oktoberfest in Blumenau, Brazil

## 345 Experience Oktoberfest in Blumenau

This weeklong festival takes place in October in the Parque Vila Germânica (Germanic Village Park) section of Blumenau, a town founded in the mid-nineteenth century by the German scientist Hermann Blumenau. In 1984, the town decided to host an Oktoberfest to honor its German heritage and it has now evolved into one of the largest German-style fall beer celebrations in the world. Revelers dress in traditional German dirndl and lederhosen, sing traditional German folk tunes, and drink beer by the meter (literally). One of the most entertaining aspects is the National Competition of Chopp in Meter Drinkers, where competitors drink one meter of beer from a long 600 ml tulip glass. The fastest drinker (without spilling or spitting) is the winner.

## 346 Savor classic beers in Colombia

Bogotá Beer Company, founded in 2002 and acquired by Anheuser-Busch InBev in 2015, has multiple locations throughout the Colombian capital city. Each features spacious seating and a handsome, smartly appointed atmosphere to sip the house-made classics like Monserrate Roja red ale and Chapinero Porter, an English-style porter.

# Discover ten great craft breweries and bars in Buenos Aires

### 347  Bierlife

This pub in Buenos Aires' hipster San Telmo area serves forty-plus beers on draft from dozens of domestic and international breweries.

### 348  Buena Birra Social Club

With locations in Palermo and Colegiales, this social club and brewery offers a dozen beers on draft, more than half of which are brewed on-site.

### 349  Strange Brewing

This brewpub pours house-made hoppy beers (think: American-style hazy IPAs) alongside a selection of Mexican-inspired dishes.

### 350  Antares

One of Argentina's original craft breweries is still one of its best. Now with multiple locations, check out the original San Telmo spot for eight beers on tap and a good atmosphere.

### 351  Berlina Patagonia Brewery

Though originally founded in Patagonia, Berlina now has a home in Buenos Aires, too. Expect English-style IPAs and other pan-European styles. Don't miss its Foreign Stout.

### 352  Patagonia

This stalwart of the Argentine craft beer scene has multiple locations throughout Buenos Aires for trying its classics like Bohemian Pilsener and Patagonia Amber Lager.

### 353  Bélgica Caballito

This bar from the owners of Argentina's hottest brewery, Juguetes Perdidos, is centrally located in Buenos Aires' Caballito neighborhood. Expect plenty of beer from the host brewery, among others.

### 354  BlueDog

Founded by one of the owners of the local Grunge Brewing, BlueDog is a cozy, wood-paneled space where you can try a range of beers from Grunge and other Argentine breweries.

### 355  The Prancing Pony

Decked out in dark woods with a medieval Viking motif, this bar is one of the darker spots for enjoying beer in Buenos Aires. Domestic Argentine craft beer is the focus of the draft list (be sure to check out the custom tap handles).

### 356  Blest

Another import from an outside region (in this case Bariloche), Cerveceria Blest is one of Argentina's hottest breweries. Look for its taproom in the Palermo neighborhood serving Hop Shot IPA and its Wee Heavy Scotch ale, among others.

# Visit these five craft breweries in Uruguay

### 357 Montevideo Brew House

MBH, as it's colloquially known, produces a range of Belgian- and British-inspired ales, as well as some American styles. Visit its taproom in the capital city of Montevideo.

### 358 Oso Pardo

Looking for hazy IPAs in Uruguay? Oso Pardo is all you need. Its tiny Montevideo taproom (a hole in the wall, really) is one of the most exciting places to find innovative beer in the country.

### 359 Birra Bizarra

Bucking the current trend of brewing a new beer every week, Birra Bizarra sticks to the tried-and-true route of flagship ales and lagers. Luckily, they're all examples of solid craft beers.

359

### 360 Cabesas Bier

Opened in 2007, this small brewery quickly expanded through a government grant to increase its production more than a hundred-fold. Expect porters, blonde ales, and American-style IPAs.

### 361 Cerveza Mastra

Seek out Cerveza Mastra for classic offerings like wheat ale infused with orange peel and coriander, and stouts amped up with coffee and chocolate.

---

CANELONES, URUGUAY

## 362 Catch a Belgian ale in Uruguay

Belgian-style ales are the conceit at Volcánica. The Belgian IPA is the highlight, using a special yeast strain to impart fruity notes on the nose and a citrusy kick on the finish. You can tour the brewery and the owners will give brewing tips to burgeoning homebrewers.

PARAGUAY

## 363 Get to know Paraguay's best nanobrewery

Herken Paraguayan Ale is a nanobrewery that produces Paraguay's best craft beer. Seek out Paraguayan Ale, where 40% of the barley is replaced with cassava starch, and native herbs like lemon verbena and mint are added.

ANDEAN HIGHLANDS, PERU

**364 Pursue the Peruvian chicha**

Though it's tough to find traditional versions of this fermented maize beverage without a local guide, it isn't impossible. You just have to know where and what to look for. If you find yourself near Machu Picchu in Peru's Sacred Valley, seek out houses with red flags hanging outside or flowers lining the road. These are chicha bars (or *chichería*), essentially homes where chicha is made and served. The beverage is made from ground maize that is chewed and then spat into small balls that are collected in a vat and then fermented. (An enzyme in human saliva helps break down the maize into fermentable sugars.) How does it taste? Most reports indicate it's more akin to drinking chilled corn soup than any ale or lager.

CURACAVÍ AND SANTIAGO, CHILE

**365 Indulge in ales made from Chilean hops**

Cerveceria Kross operates three brewpubs (called KrossBars) in Santiago and a production facility in Curacaví making standard craft-inspired beers like Golden Pale Ale, Pilsner, and Stout as well as experimental ales like a wet-hopped IPA dosed with fresh Chilean hops. The pubs are lively spots to drink, while the production brewery offers tours and tastings.

**364** *Left:* Chicha is an ancient Peruvian fermented beverage made from maize

# Europe—North & East

Pub culture was born in the British Isles. From the Guinness-soaked literary pubs of Dublin to London's centuries-old waterholes, you'll find an abundance of history and liquid enjoyment within the walls of these storied establishments. The UK and Ireland boast renowned modern craft breweries, too, primarily found in the region's urban centers.

Scandinavia and Eastern Europe also offer bucket list-worthy beer destinations. Copenhagen, with its esoteric craft beer bars and uber-stylish pubs, is perhaps the center of modern European craft brewing, while Sweden, Norway, and Finland offer an excess of creative and progressive beers. And of course the Czech Republic, birthplace of the world-renowned Pilsner, along with many other more obscure styles, is one of the most important countries in the history of brewing.

# Relax in five fantastic old Irish pubs

### 366 The Brazen Head

The self-proclaimed oldest pub in Ireland is full of historical anecdotes and literary drop-ins, including Jonathan Swift, James Joyce, and the poet Brendan Behan.

### 367 Grogan's

Central Dublin's Grogan's has been a hub for literary figures and regulars since its founding in 1899. Opt for a draft pour of Guinness West Indies Porter if you're sick of regular Irish stout.

### 368 Kehoes

A textbook Irish pub with perfect pours of Guinness and Victorian decor, Kehoes dates back to 1803 and has remained virtually unchanged since the end of the nineteenth century.

### 369 Toners

This Baggot Street staple dates back to 1818. Literary greats like Yeats and Kavanagh were regulars and, according to Rory Guinness of the Guinness family, it served the best pint in town.

### 370 Mulligans

This eighteenth-century pub—established in 1782—is famed for being one of Joyce's favorite bars. It has always attracted a writer crowd, and it's rumored that a young John F. Kennedy, working in Ireland for Hearst Newspapers at the time, drank here.

**VARIOUS LOCATIONS THROUGHOUT IRELAND**

## 371 Discover the Emerald Isle's other Irish stouts

Besides Guinness, some of the best stouts you'll
find in all of Ireland come from the small
Porterhouse Brewing chain founded in 1989.
Porterhouse was the brainchild of cofounders
Oliver Hughs and Liam LaHart, who decided to
open a craft beer bar in the town of Bray and
serve German and Belgian imported beer—a
novel, controversial idea at the time, since they
were opting to not carry Guinness or any other
domestic beer. Today, the brewery makes its
own Irish stouts and porters and serves them
at locations all over the world, including in
London and at the legendary Fraunces Tavern
in New York City.

**GALWAY, IRELAND**

## 372 Get giddy with Galway Bay Brewery

Galway Bay Brewery is a modern craft brewery
that originated as a spin-off of the Oslo pub in
the Salthill section of Galway. The core lineup of
beers includes American-style crushers like Full
Sail IPA, Buried at Sea stout, and Althea pale ale.
The owners run a series of pubs throughout the
region, including Against the Grain and The
Black Sheep, so there's no shortage of
opportunities to try their beers.

**CORK, IRELAND**

## 373 Visit Cork's specialty craft beer bars

Start your day in Cork with a visit to one of the
city's two specialty beer bars: The Bierhaus and
The Friary. Both feature dizzying arrays of
hundreds of bottles from all over the world,
including a selection of Trappist beers, American
craft brews, and local Irish ales from breweries
like Dungarvan, Galway Bay, and Porterhouse.

DUBLIN, IRELAND

## 374 Drink Guinness on its home turf

An obvious choice for any beer lover's bucket
list, tasting Guinness—the original Irish dry
stout—in its homeland is an absolute essential
play. If you're visiting Dublin, there are plenty
of options for grabbing a pint or three. You
could begin by visiting the brewery itself, more
specifically the Storehouse at St. James's Gate,
right in the middle of the brewery. It attracts
throngs of visitors—it's said to be Ireland's most
popular tourist attraction—but despite the
crowds, it's a relatively easy visit. Self-guide your
way through seven stories to the top of the
world's largest pint (yes, the building is rather
cheekily shaped like a glass) during which you'll
learn about the history of the beer and company,
and some about the brewing process, too. At
the top, you're rewarded with a fresh pint of
Guinness from the Gravity Bar and a panoramic
360-degree view of Dublin. Finish your pint
and then head back down to explore Dublin's
thriving pub scene, a much better setting to take
in the absolute freshest pints in the city. It's there
that you'll find the truest expression of the
culture that Guinness helped foster within
the city's storied pubs.

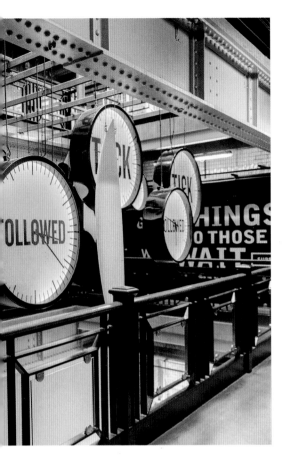

NORTHERN IRELAND

# Learn about brewing at these five Northern Ireland breweries

### 375 Hilden Brewing

Located in Lisburn, Hilden is Northern Ireland's original independent craft brewery. Seek out its flagship Twisted Hop pale ale with aromatic notes of grassy hops.

### 376 Boundary Brewing

This cooperative brewery based in Belfast is owned and run by its members. The focus is American-style craft beers with a bevvy of hazy IPAs and robust stouts. Seek out cans with gorgeous artwork.

### 377 Whitewater Brewery

This upstart brewery near Annsborough is renowned for its Maggies Leap session IPA, which packs a wallop of hops from Australia, New Zealand, and the US. It is a rich and robust beer at 4.7% ABV.

### 378 Knockout Brewing

Founded in 2014 by Joseph McMullan, this small brewery is known for celebrating the rich boxing heritage of its home city of Belfast. Look for Irish Red Ale and Middleweight IPA.

### 379 Farmageddon Brewing

Opened since 2002, this Belfast brewery focuses on classic styles like golden ale, export porter, and English-style IPAs.

THROUGHOUT IRELAND

## 380 Discover Ireland's craft beer scene

With beer deeply entrenched in the Irish psyche, it should come as no surprise that the country would have a thriving, if still emerging, craft beer scene. To find the best that Ireland has to offer, hop in the car and plan a trip across the Emerald Isle. Along the way you'll hit breweries and bars that offer some of the country's best independent beer and ale. In County Kildare, stop into Lock 13 Gastro Pub and Craft Beer House for a pint or two from Carlow Brewing's O'Hara's brand, perhaps the most well-known of the Irish craft breweries. Its Irish Stout gives Guinness a run for its money, with a rich and robust flavor and supremely smooth texture. In County Kilkenny, visit Sullivan's Brewing for its Red Ale, and in County Limerick, Treaty City Brewing is worth a visit for its flagship Harris Pale Ale with big bold aromas of fresh-cut grass, citrus, and melon. There are many other new, up-and-coming breweries throughout Ireland to visit, so check your local listings.

## 381 Taste whiskey barrel-aged ales from Scotland

A storied brewery dating back to the 1980s, Harviestoun creates some of the boldest beers in Scotland, particularly the line of whiskey barrel-aged ales. Old Engine Oil and Ola Dubh are two of the brewery's most revered beers, both known for their rich, robust, and unapologetically viscous textures. Old Engine Oil is a black ale brewed with pitch-black malts and bittering hops that add very little aroma. The overall effect is dark cherries, burnt toast, and crème brûlée. Ola Dubh is conditioned in mature Highland Park 12 Year Old Single Malt Whisky barrels for an elevated ABV (8%) and a smoky, leathery texture. Both are worth seeking out.

## 382 Meet the world's most mischievous brewers

The duo of merry craft beer pranksters known as BrewDog—James Watt and Martin Dickie—are now a worldwide phenomenon, with satellite taprooms, breweries, and bars the world over. It all started in a small Scottish town with its flagship Punk IPA, a take on the aggressively bitter American-style West Coast IPA. Visit the DogTap where you can drink it from the tanks, and while you're at it, try one or more of the always-rotating new and seasonal releases.

## 383 Sample some of Scotland's oldest ales

Founded in 1869 in the Shandon section of Edinburgh, the Caledonian Brewery has been crafting traditional Scottish ale for more than 150 years (albeit with intermittent breaks). The modern era began in 1987, with an updated line of beers, including Deuchars IPA, Flying Scotsman bitter, and Edinburgh Castle brown ale.

EDINBURGH, SCOTLAND

# Grab a pint at five traditional Edinburgh pubs

### 384 The Bow Bar

This no-frills bar focuses on cask ales and single-malt Scotch, with more than 390 whiskies on offer. The beer is dispensed from gleaming, tall brass fountains from the 1920s.

### 385 Joseph Pearce

This living room-style pub (with bookshelves and homey decor) serves a great selection of local beers as well as an array of Swedish ciders and aquavit cocktails.

### 386 The Last Drop

Positioned near an old execution site (hence the name), this atmospheric pub serves a range of real ales and traditional Scottish fare.

### 387 The Caley Sample Room

A true gastropub serving both craft beer and real ale, this spacious bar and restaurant is a great place to catch a game or enjoy a proper breakfast.

### 388 The Sheep Heid Inn

There has reputedly been a bar or public house on the site of the modern-day Sheep Heid Inn since 1360, making it one of the oldest surviving pubs in the country.

BELHAVEN, SCOTLAND

### 389 Sip a textbook Wee Heavy ale

Claiming a history that dates back to 1719, Belhaven is one of Scotland's oldest breweries. The beers range across a variety of styles from the traditional Scottish ales to Twisted Thistle IPA, a golden-hued beer brewed with 100 percent Scottish malts. The 90/- is a classic 7.4% ABV Wee Heavy ale with notes of dark fruit and caramel.

TRAQUAIR, INNERLEITHEN, SCOTLAND

### 390 Learn about brewing in Scotland's oldest inhabited house

Dating back to the early 1700s, Traquair House was originally a domestic brewery serving the Traquair House, the oldest continually inhabited house in Scotland. Abandoned in the 1800s and rediscovered in the early 1960s, today it operates as a commercial brewery producing a variety of real ales. You can visit the mansion to get a glimpse of the brewery and taste the beers on-site.

**390** *Right:* Traquair House is a former domestic brewery that once served Scotland's oldest continuously inhabited house

### ROGERSTONE, NEWPORT, WALES
## 391 Revel in rebellion at Tiny Rebel

Tiny Rebel Brewing was founded in 2012 and quickly won myriad awards and accolades for its modernized craft ales. The flagship Cwtch (which purportedly rhymes with "butch") is a red ale dosed with citrusy American hops for an unconventional flavor and aroma. The brewery operates three bars, including one in Cardiff, where its beer is poured.

### CARDIFF, WALES
## 392 Have a pint at one of Cardiff's oldest pubs

The Rummer Tavern is one of the oldest pubs in Cardiff, with plenty of great beer options, and hearty plates of traditional pub grub. An early 2018 renovation upset some longtime patrons, who complained that the changes made it feel like a sports bar, but the eighteenth-century building still retains much of its charm.

### CAERNARVON, WALES
## 393 Sip real ale among vintage steam-hauled trains

The Welsh Highland Railway Society puts on the annual Real Ale Festival—Cwrw ar y Cledrau/Rail Ale—each spring. You can enjoy a wide range of local ales, including some ciders, along with live music, a selection of local foods, and, of course, vintage steam-hauled trains. It's an entirely fun, niche beer festival event.

### YORK, ENGLAND
## 394 Sample Belgian ales in a Tudor-style hunter's lodge

A hunter's lodge vibe permeates the Tudor-style Trembling Madness Pub, lined with taxidermy heads of all kinds of animals ranging from lions and leopards to wild boar and antelope. Settle in for a pint from one of six drafts or three casks, or choose a bottle from the extensive list, which includes many rare Belgian and Trappist ales.

### MASHAM, ENGLAND
## 395 Get silly with Monty Python-themed beer

Dating back to 1992, Black Sheep Brewery was founded by Paul Theakston of the late Theakston Brewery, a family brewery in Masham. Black Sheep is best known for its line of cask beers (Black Sheep Ale, Best Bitter, Riggwelter) and the Monty Python Trilogy, including Holy Grail golden ale, Flying Circus IPA, and Brian pale ale.

**395** *Right:* Masham's Black Sheep Brewery produces cask ales as well as a range of three Monty Python-themed beers

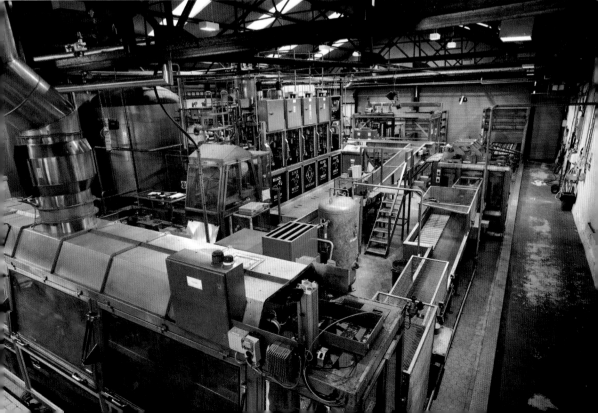

## LEEDS AND MANCHESTER, ENGLAND
### 396 Enjoy modern ales in an old flax store

Northern Monk is a modern UK brewery focused on creating some of the best beer experiences in the world. It has two Refectory taprooms, one in Leeds, the other in Manchester. Northern Monk Refectory LDS is housed in the historic Old Flax Store building on the south side of the River Aire. The session IPA, Eternal, is made with English pale malts and Centennial, Comet, and Mosaic hops for a bright tangerine-like flavor. Try it and fifteen other keg lines at the airy taproom in Leeds.

## OTLEY, ENGLAND
### 397 Drink at one of West Yorkshire's award-winning pubs

Located on a busy corner in Otley, just outside Leeds, The Junction Inn is one of the region's best-known pubs. It has a wide range of real ales from breweries like Timothy Taylor and Black Sheep, and keeps about a dozen on at any given time.

**396** *Above:* Northern Monk Refectory in Leeds sits within the historic Old Flax Store building

## 398 Succumb to the dark side . . .

Northern Monk Refectory hosts Dark City Festival dedicated to dark beers in its rustic-industrial Old Flax Store home every fall. Brewers from the UK (Buxton, Thornbridge, Burning Sky), the US (Finback, Evil Twin), and Europe (Omnipollo, Dry & Bitter) pour their beers shoulder to shoulder. The host brewery creates a special ale for the occasion, typically something dark, rich, robust, and boozy!

HUDDERSFIELD, ENGLAND

## 399 Catch the magic flavors of Magic Rock

Magic Rock Brewing started in 2011 when founder Richard Burhouse and head brewer Stuart Ross opened the doors of their brewery with the goal of enhancing English beer culture with some American-inspired flavors. From the beginning, the aim was to mimic the vibrant US craft beer scene and to re-create flavors that weren't readily available to the UK market. Today, the brewery is considered one of the best in the country, with a core lineup of solid offerings ranging from German-style lagers (Dancing Bier) to the tropically fruity Cannonball IPA.

**399** *Above:* Magic Rock Brewing produces a range of hoppy styles packaged in colorful cans

SHEFFIELD, ENGLAND
## 400 Savor the quirky ales of Saint Mars of the Desert

When Dann Paquette and Martha Holley-Paquette decided to shut down their American contract brewery project Pretty Things in 2015, no one was quite sure where the couple would land next. They were career brewers, and it was rumored they would reopen a brewery *somewhere* in the world. Then, in late 2018, they reemerged in the UK, under the quirky moniker Saint Mars of the Desert (presumably named for Saint-Mars-du-Désert, a small village outside Nantes). Now, they operate the small brewery in the Sheffield neighborhood of Attercliffe, where you can buy beer, tour the brewery, hang out with the Paquettes, and purchase bottles and kegs to go.

MANCHESTER AND LONDON, ENGLAND
## 401 Get your hazy IPA fix at Cloudwater

The UK's undisputed king of hazy IPAs, Cloudwater Brew is considered by many to be one of the best breweries in the UK. Cofounder and managing director Paul Jones is one of the most recognizable faces in modern craft beer. Cloudwater now has three outposts, including a taproom in Manchester and one in London, all pouring New England-inspired hoppy ales.

MANCHESTER, ENGLAND
## 402 Imbibe at Indy Man Beer festival

One of the UK's largest beer festivals, Independent Manchester Beer Convention (aka Indy Man Beer Con) is a world-class showcase for some of the best breweries in the world. It takes place annually in fall on the grounds of the stunning Victoria Baths, making it also one of the most attractive settings for a beer fest. Breweries skew toward the modern and hip, as does the crowd, which is typically a young cadre of hipsters and beer geeks.

### 403 Celebrate friends, family, and beer

Hosted by Cloudwater Brew, the Friends & Family & Beer festival is held annually in the spring in Upper Campfield Market. Four sessions take place over two days, with brewers flying in from all over the world. A range of fringe events, including tap takeovers and panels, accompany the fest.

### 404 Marvel at the selection at Marble Arch Inn

A sloping mosaic floor welcomes you to Marble Arch Inn, the flagship outpost of Marble Brewery, pouring nine cask ales and another eight keg lines. Though the brewery is no longer on-site, this is still the best spot to try the freshest Marble beers. Pair them with a menu of modern British dishes.

**TOP 5**

MANCHESTER, ENGLAND

# Discover Manchester's top five breweries

With more than seventy-five breweries in the Greater Manchester area—including the famed Cloudwater mentioned earlier—these are the top spots to try.

### 405 Marble Brewery

Opened in 1997 as an extension of the Marble Arch Inn, this was one of the first craft breweries in Manchester. Expect beers like Earl Grey IPA and Chocolate Marble ale.

### 406 Manchester Brewing

One of the city's newer breweries is this one established in 2016 under the railway arches. Expect a small, lively atmosphere with games and plenty of American-style brews.

### 407 Runaway Brewery

This small brewery offers tours and tastings at its taproom, which pours a handful of American-influenced pale ales and IPAs as well as a smoked porter and hoppy brown ale.

### 408 Alphabet Brewing

A hop-focused brewery packaging a variety of beers in colorful, design-forward cans, Alphabet is a fun-loving, young brewery peddling beers like Juice Springsteen tropical IPA.

### 409 Beer Nouveau

This nanobrewery was once Britain's smallest commercial operation. Today, it makes classic English-style ales brewed with local ingredients.

RUNAWAY BREWERY

**BURTON UPON TRENT, ENGLAND**

## 410 Learn about the birthplace of IPA

Not as famous as Munich or Pilsen, but Burton upon Trent—a small, unassuming city in the English Midlands—is perhaps the world's most important brewing town. That's because it's the spiritual birthplace of India Pale Ale, first popularized here in the mid-nineteenth century and brewed with water from the local Modwen's Well. The town was home to the first Bass Brewery, and today you can discover its history right on the brewery's original grounds at The National Brewery Centre. Visit the museum and grab a pint at the on-site Tap Bar and Restaurant where the iconic White Shield IPA was once made. There's even an on-site bottle shop stocked with beers from small and independent breweries worldwide.

HOOK NORTON, ENGLAND

## 411 Gain insight into how a gravity-fed brewery works

Founded in 1849, Hook Norton Brewery is a living legend with its tower brewery in which all the stages of the brewing process flow gravitationally from floor to floor (the mash at the top and the fermentation and racking in the bottom). You can see the brewery in action on location and visit the on-site museum. You'll also enjoy a selection of traditional cask ale in the tasting room.

DEVIZES, ENGLAND

## 412 See what a fourth-generation brewery looks like

Founded in 1875, Wadworth Brewery is now in the fourth generation of family ownership. The flagship 6X beer is a malty amber ale with a fruity finish, while a range of other core and seasonal beers, including IPA, is available. You can visit the historic building—a gravity-fed "tower brewery"—which is open for tours and also has a shop and tastings.

LONDON, ENGLAND

## 413 Sip real ale at the GBBF

The Great British Beer Festival (GBBF) is an annual beer festival organized by the Campaign for Real Ale (CAMRA), a UK-based consumer organization that promotes traditional British ales, ciders, and the pubs that serve these beverages. The fest is usually held in London during the first full week of August, from Tuesday to Saturday. In addition to nearly a thousand beers from around the world, the festival is home to the Champion Beer of Britain awards, which give Gold (Supreme Champion), Silver, and Bronze medals to UK-made beers in more than a dozen different style categories. More than sixty thousand festivalgoers attend each year!

**413** *Above:* The Great British Beer Festival is held annually and celebrates real ale and more

## 414 Find the pride of London at Fuller's

Located at the historic Griffin Brewery (which is worth a visit), beer has been made at Fuller's Brewery since at least the seventeenth century. Though the company is now owned by Japan's Asahi, the traditional Fuller's London Pride, Chiswick Bitter, and ESB are still available throughout the world.

LONDON, ENGLAND

## 415 Sip specialty beers in Borough Market

Run by the founders of craft beer shop Utobeer and located
under the same Borough Market roof, The Rake is a specialty
beer bar with an impressive selection of specialty beers from
all over the world (though there's a moderate focus on
American craft beers). Seating is notoriously tight, making
the space feel particularly intimate and warm.

LONDON, ENGLAND

## 416 Partake in a historic pub tour

The City of London is filled with countless renowned pubs.
One of the best ways for tourists to experience them is through
a guided tour like the one offered by Jane Jephcote, CAMRA's
Chair of the London Pubs Group. She offers private pub
crawls for groups of up to six during which you get a half-pint
at each stop while listening to Jephcote delve into the rich
history and culture of each spot.

LONDON, ENGLAND

## 417 Sample a beer brewed for a rare beer club

Founded by Alastair Hook in 2000, and now owned by Asahi,
Meantime was an important microbrewery when there weren't
many opening in the UK. Its coffee porter signaled a shift
toward more updated styles. Other beers include Scotch Ale
brewed primarily for the beer writer Michael Jackson's Rare
Beer Club.

LONDON, ENGLAND

## 418 Discover Shakespeare's local pub

The George Inn was established in the medieval period on
Borough High Street in Southwark. It provides the setting for
beer writer Pete Brown's famous *Shakespeare's Local*, which
explores the history of the pub and surrounding area.

418 *Right:* The seventeenth-century George Inn

SOUTHWARK · BAR

THE GEORGE
Est. 16c.
FAMOUS
ALES, PORTERS & STOUT
IN PERFECT CONDITION
TARIFF

REDUCED PINT

Finest Ale                          4ᵈ
Mulled Ale                          4ᵈ
Special Strong Ale           5ᵈ
Porter + Stout                    3ᵈ
Norfolk Cyder                    3ᵈ

## TOP 10

**LONDON, ENGLAND**

# Wander London's Bermondsey Beer Mile

The current hotspot of London's modern brewing scene is located under a series of railway arches in the southeast neighborhood of Bermondsey. Be sure to check it out when you're in the UK's capital city.

### 419  The Kernel

Founded in 2009 by Evin O'Riordain, a former cheesemonger at nearby Neal's Yard Dairy, The Kernel was the godfather of London's modern DIY beer scene, and the first to settle in the area. Due to its immense popularity, it now only sells beer to go.

### 420  Anspach & Hobday

This Kickstarter-funded brewery was opened in 2014 by Paul Anspach and Jack Hobday. The duo focuses on dark ales like porters, stouts, and smoked beers.

428

### 421  UBREW

As the name implies, this small brewery teaches you how to brew your own beer. If you're not up for a lesson, you can check out the taproom, which features ten different beers brewed by others.

### 422  The Bottle Shop

Another outlier in the Bermondsey Mile is The Bottle Shop, an off-premise store selling bottles from all around the world. It doesn't add to the locally brewed appeal, but it's a nice addition to the neighborhood.

### 423  Fourpure Brewing

Founded in 2013 by brothers Tom and Dan Lower, this brewery references the four "pure" ingredients in brewing: water, malt, hops, and yeast. Specialties include hoppy beers as well as traditional British styles.

## 424 The Barrel Project

A side project from the London Beer Factory (LBF), this taproom features two dozen draft beers, half from LBF and the rest from other breweries.

## 425 Partizan Brewing

Opened in 2012 by chef Andy Smith and brewer Andy Moffat, Partizan focuses on dark ales like Foreign Export Stout, barrel-aged imperial stouts, and black IPAs as well as American-style pale ales and IPAs.

## 426 EeBria

Not technically a brewery, but a distributor pouring a range of craft beer and specialty ales, this bare-bones setup includes empty kegs and pallets, which serve as tables and chairs.

## 427 Southwark Brewing

Bringing a bit of the old school to the hipster Beer Mile set, Southwark focuses on making real ale and serving it from casks.

## 428 Brew by Numbers

Cofounders Tom Hutchings and David Seymour name their beers via a numerical system, which first lists style (01, 02, 03, etc.) and then the iteration of that style; 01/01, for example, is a saison with Citra hops, while 05/03 is an IPA with Amarillo and Mosaic.

HASTINGS, ENGLAND
## 429 Discover a micropub with a history

The historic south-coast town of Hastings (of "1066" fame) has a picturesque old town and bustling seafront. Nestled on the main coast road is a little gem: The Jolly Fisherman. The origins of the pub stretch back to 1769. It was closed down in the late 1950s, but reopened as a family-run micropub in 2016. A range of up to five cask ales and five craft beers are served on tap in a cosy, convivial atmosphere. And be sure to check out the can and bottle menu, which includes a great selection of Belgian beers.

BRIGHTON, ENGLAND
## 430 Be a part of the community

Originally set up in an old dairy building on a farm in 2016 by three friends, Holler Brewery & Taproom opened its Brighton location in 2018 and doubled beer production. The brewery puts the community first, encouraging people to support local breweries, beers, and pubs. You can do a tour or visit its taproom and try the variety of beer styles—all of which are vegan.

## 431 Sip a British barleywine

Barleywine is perhaps the most well-known example of the strong ale category of beers. They are boozy and sweet, with intense flavors of toffee and dark brown sugar. The style originated in mid-nineteenth-century England, with Bass producing the first commercial example. It was marketed in wintertime and meant to mimic the flavors and mouthfeel of fortified wines (hence the term "barleywine"). Barleywines are similar to so-called old ales or stock ales. Barleywines age beautifully, developing sherry-like aromas of toffee, dried fruit, and caramel as they rest in the bottle. Most modern versions are well over 10% ABV, though historically they were closer to 8% or 9%. Two of the best to try are Thomas Hardy's Ale, first brewed in 1968 to commemorate the English writer (and today brewed by Meantime Brewery), and JW Lees Harvest Ale, a vintage ale made intermittently at the Manchester brewery. Try sourcing vintage bottles—these beers can be aged for over twenty-five years with remarkable stability and evolution.

FAVERSHAM, ENGLAND
## 432 Drop into this seventeenth-century brewery

Founded in 1698, Shepherd Neame Brewery is one of the UK's oldest breweries (along with the Three Tuns Brewery in Shropshire). Today, the brewery makes a range of cask ales and other ales for export. You can taste them at the Spanish Galleon Tavern in Greenwich (look for the "Britain's Oldest Brewer" signage on the building).

SELFOSS, ICELAND
## 433 Sample Ölvisholt Brugghús Lava imperial stout

"Lava" is an apt name for this strikingly strong ale from one of Iceland's few craft breweries. An active volcano named Hekla is actually visible from the brewery's front door and occasionally spews lava onto the grounds of the brewery farm. Pitch-black and full of dark chocolate and smoked flavors, this is the perfect beer for watching molten earth breach the ground.

**432** *Right:* Shepherd Neame Brewery produces the strong Bishops Finger

## 434 Celebrate Iceland's repeal of beer prohibition

For nearly seventy-five years, Iceland was under the grip of a sort of prohibition, with full-strength beer sales being banned and no breweries able to operate. On March 1, 1989, however, that ban was lifted and the date has since become known as "Beer Day." The Annual Icelandic Beer Festival, which began in 2012 and has run every year since, celebrates the repeal of prohibition by gathering the world's top young craft beer producers for a three-day party in late February. You'll taste familiar suds from the US, Europe, and the UK, including Fonta Flora Brewery from North Carolina, Iceland's own KEX Brewing, and the UK's Beavertown Brewing. The party begins midweek with tap takeovers around town and other cool events before the official festival kicks off.

**REYKJAVÍK, ICELAND**

# Visit Reykjavík's top three craft beer bars

### 435 Skúli Craft Bar

This cozy bar tucked in the city's nightlife district serves fourteen beers on draft and another hundred-plus in bottles. It has a relaxed, intimate setting, great for dates and conversation.

### 436 Kaffibarinn

If you're looking for a spot to party with craft beer in hand, look no further than Reykjavík's Kaffibarinn, a heady mix of loud music, dancing, and craft brews from around the small country.

### 437 MicroBar

Drop into this laid-back beer bar for flights and tasters of some of Iceland's best brews. Look out for beers from Ölvisholt, Steoji, and Segull 67.

436

## 438 Learn about American-inspired Norwegian beer at Lervig

Founded in 2003, Lervig didn't really come into its own on the international stage until 2010 when the hiring of American Mike Murphy changed the direction of the company. Previously it had focused on German and international style lagers, but Murphy brought an American craft beer sensibility to the job and began putting out hop-forward IPAs, and established a barrel-aging program for big beers and stouts. Today, the brewery is recognized as one of the best and has done numerous collaborations with hipster breweries from around the world. You can tour the mural-adorned building for a behind-the-scenes look at one of Europe's most exciting and nimble breweries.

GRIMSTAD, NORWAY

## 439 Knock back a Nøgne Ø ale

Founder and brewer Kjetil Jikiun was an airline pilot when he began homebrewing recipes based on styles of bold, aggressive ales he would drink during his frequent trips abroad. He became so good at perfecting these recipes that he was encouraged to quit his day job and become a professional brewer. That action became a reality in 2002 when he founded Nøgne Ø brewery on Norway's southeastern shore named for the so-called "naked islands" that Ibsen famously described. The subtitle of the brewery, given by Jikiun and his partners, was *Det Kompromissløse Bryggeri*—"The Uncompromising Brewery"—a plain statement of its mission to make ales of strong personality and individuality, even if they would be challenging to the tastes of the general public. Today, the brewery is Norway's largest craft beer producers with a robust, deep portfolio of aggressively flavored, uncompromising ales and lagers. Still located in Grimstad, the brewery built a new brewing facility right beside the original to expand production and offer a larger range of styles for both domestic consumption and export.

TOP
3   OSLO, NORWAY

# When in Oslo, visit these three bars

### 440 Schouskjelleren Mikrobryggeri

Located in the cavernous, dungeon-like cellar of the Schous brewery, this bar serves a variety of European beers from lambics and Flanders sours to modern Norwegian craft brews.

### 441 Gaasa AS

This airy, light-filled space pours an impeccable list of European and American craft brews alongside Nordic-inspired small plates. In warm weather, grab a seat at the sun-drenched courtyard.

### 442 Crow bar & bryggeri

This bi-level, industrial-chic brewery and tasting room— Oslo's largest craft brewery— serves a variety of house-brewed beers, including Crow's Scream cream ale and Trotskij's Red Ale.

TÓRSHAVN, FAROE ISLANDS, DENMARK

## 443 Discover this craft beer cottage on a remote island

Another country, another Mikkeller bar. Luckily, this one is just as interesting and top-notch as the other outposts around the world. The Mikkeller Tórshavn building (a 500-year-old wooden house) is worth the trip alone, with its thatched roof covered in green grasses and a cute but classic gingerbread house–esque design. Inside, you'll find sixteen drafts (mostly Mikkeller) in a rustic and cozy setting.

COPENHAGEN, DENMARK

## 444 Relax with a pint or two in this cozy space

One big room lit by candlelight and decked with couches and comfy chairs, the small Fermentoren Beer Bar in the Vesterbro neighborhood features a cozy space to sip a variety of suds from around the world. Among the twenty-four drafts are Fermentoren-branded house beers brewed exclusively for the bar by Denmark's own Dry & Bitter Brewing.

COPENHAGEN, DENMARK
### 445 Settle in at this elegant bar
The idea behind the Viktoriagade Mikkeller bar was to buck the trend of manly sports bar-style beer temples and instead create a more stylish, feminine, and artfully decorated space to match the artistic craft beers being served. You'll find plenty of Mikkeller beer on draft surrounded by wooden tables, shiny black tiles, golden lamps and knobs, and daily fresh flowers, all designed by the Danish firm Femmes Regionales.

COPENHAGEN, DENMARK

## **446 Browse this stylish bar's lengthy bottle list**

The stylish, minimalist Himmeriget Bar has an eleven-page bottle list and an additional ten taps of beers from around Europe, and often some rare and specialty ones from the US. If you aren't in the mood for beer, order a cocktail, one of the dozens of American whiskies, or a tipple of Fernet. Many of the cocktails contain craft beer and the vibe is generally sleek, but not uppity. There are often tap takeovers from American brewers passing through town on their way to one of the many annual European festivals.

COPENHAGEN, DENMARK

## **447 Unearth rare lambic at this cool bar**

A celebration of all things tart, spontaneous, and Belgian, Mikkeller and To Ol's Koelschip bar is one of the best places in the world to find rare and obscure bottles of vintage lambic. In stark contrast to Mikkeller's other chic, and design-heavy interiors, Koelschip feels like a traditional Belgian pub, with dark wood floors, dried hop bines adorning the ceiling and banisters, and Pajottenland bric-a-brac plastering the walls. Order from the small bar and dig into a glass of lambic from Brouwerij Boon or Oud Beersel, or a saison from Brasserie Dupont or Blaugies. The ever-changing list often includes rare sour beer drafts from American breweries like Fonta Flora, Jester King, and de Garde. If you're searching for a particular bottle of lambic, you'll likely find it here. Poured from traditional woven wooden baskets, bottles include rare Cantillon and 3 Fontenein lambics and iterations brewed outside the Pajottenland. A word of warning: some of the beers are extremely strong, so order with caution!

**446** *Above:* Himmeriget Bar features an eleven-page list of rare and obscure bottles

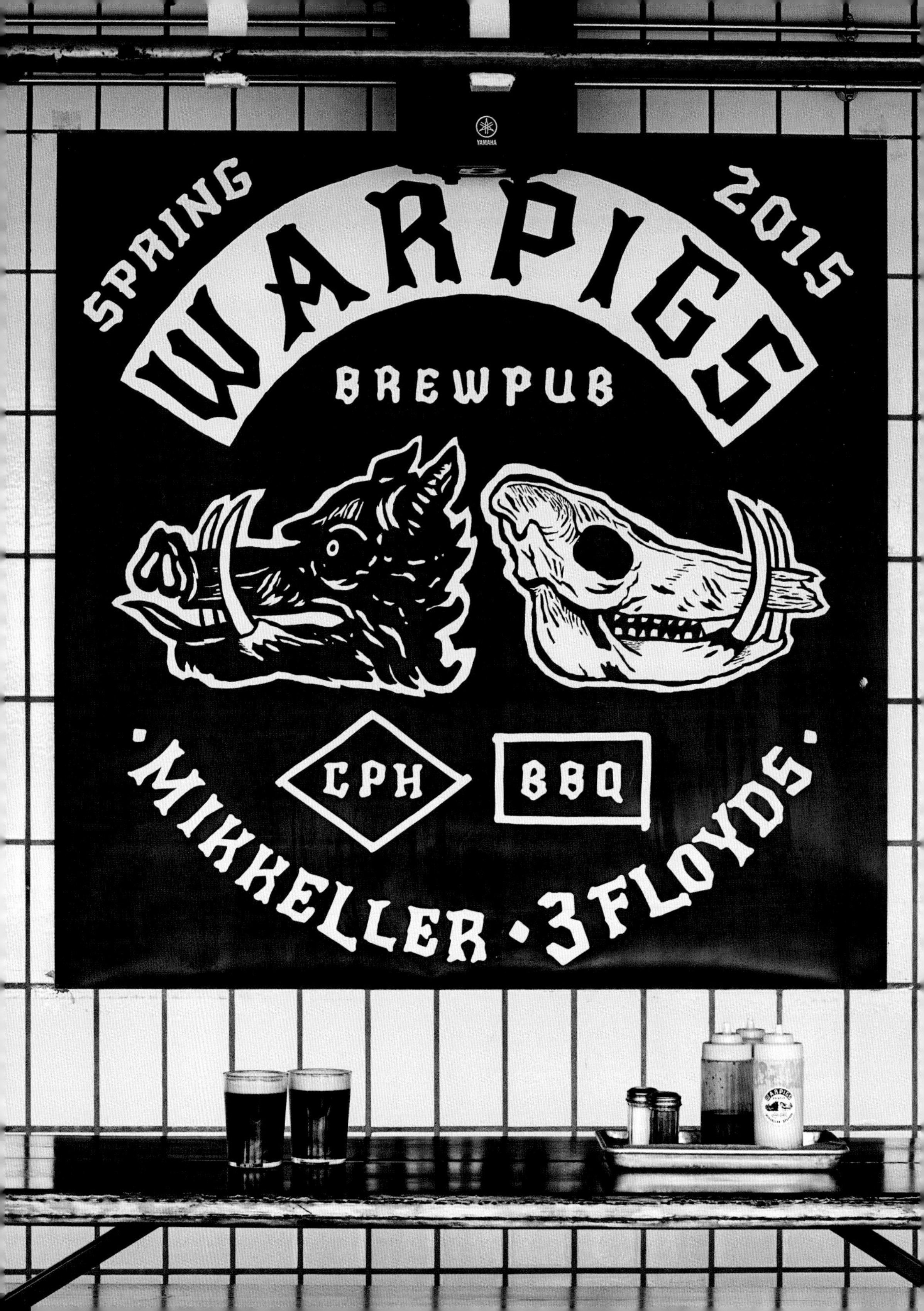
SPRING
WARPIGS
2015
BREWPUB
CPH
BBQ
MIKKELLER · 3FLOYDS

COPENHAGEN, DENMARK
## 448 Make merry with the Mikkeller Beer Celebration

One of the largest collections of hipster-cult modern craft beer anywhere happens annually at the Mikkeller Beer Celebration Copenhagen (MBCC) festival. Held over two days in the spring, thousands of beers are poured to tens of thousands of beer geeks who wait in sometimes seemingly interminable lines for small pours from around the world. It started in 2012 as a much smaller affair held in the Sparta Hallen in Østerbro with almost forty breweries. Today, that number reaches well over a hundred with breweries flying in from all around the world. Various ticket tiers offer weekend-long and early access as well as general admission. Few other festivals offer the opportunity to sample beers from London's The Kernel, Brooklyn's Other Half, and Belgium's Bokkereyder—one of the most revered and esoteric breweries in the world—all under one roof. To round out the festivities, food trucks dish out treats, and live bands and DJs provide auditory entertainment. With its communal vibe and hipster bent, MBCC is truly one of the best beer festival experiences in the world.

COPENHAGEN, DENMARK
## 449 Nosh American-style barbecue alongside Danish beer

A collaboration between Indiana's 3 Floyds Brewing and Denmark's Mikkeller, the small WarPigs Brewpub and barbecue joint slings house-made American-style beers alongside Southern-style barbecue in a decidedly honky-tonk, biker bar-like setting. Pair the smoked brisket and ribs with a house-brewed Big Black Bicycle black IPA.

COPENHAGEN, DENMARK
## 450 Select a beverage from this extensive draft list

With more than sixty drafts listed behind the bar on flatscreen TVs, Taphouse bar is more reminiscent of an American-style craft beer bar than others in Denmark and Europe. The expansive draft list covers everything from local brews like Mikkeller's Monk's Brew Belgian quad to Logsdon Grain Out farmhouse ale from Oregon.

### 451 Embrace your inner hipster at BRUS

BRUS is a brewery, bar, and restaurant with thirty-plus rotating drafts. It is a favorite with the skinny-jean-wearing hipster beer geek set as well as young neighborhood families. Tours are offered some weekends and a small bottle shop provides supplies to go—including food—for a takeaway beer picnic.

### 453 Pair live music with great beer options

The smoky, candlelit Kronborggade 3 bar, adorned with dark wooden booths and dim chandeliers, is a quiet but hip place to sip both local and imported craft beers. A selection of cocktails and ciders rounds out the menu. When indie rock and alternative aren't blasting through the speakers, you'll often find live music, acoustic shows, and DJs filling the air with beats and rhymes.

### 452 Stock up on funky beer, rare cider, and natural wine

Decked out with midcentury Danish furniture, Rødder & Vin is a natural wine, cider, sake, and beer shop that feels more like walking into someone's apartment than a retail store. Proprietor Solfinn creates a welcoming dinner party-like atmosphere that regularly features pop-ups and other industry insider events. He knows nearly everything you would want to know about the beers and wines he sells, and often has a shelf of rare lambic and wild ale bottles for sale. Check out the wildly inventive ciders from Sweden's Fruktstereo and the selection of canned fish and other edible goodies.

452 *Above:* Rødder & Vin sells a small but well-curated selection of beer, cider, and natural wine

## 454 Try traditional Danish cuisine with your beer

A trendy all-day café serving breakfast, lunch, and dinner, the wood-adorned Dyrehaven serves unfussy traditional Danish cuisine paired with a small but interesting list of draft beers. The bottle list features both classics and modern craft beer, including fun stuff from To Øl and Sweden's Omnipollo.

## 455 Check out chic small plates and cult beer

One of the most elegant dining rooms featuring upscale beer service, the small Mikkeller-backed Øl & Brød restaurant and café in the Vesterbro neighborhood features chic small plates (steak tartare with accoutrements) and nine Mikkeller taps ranging from Vesterbro Wit to more complex offerings like Ris a la M'ale brewed with rice, cherries, and almond extract.

COPENHAGEN, DENMARK

## 456 Quaff beer or wine at The Corner at 108

A casual spot that's located on the corner of the upscale Restaurant 108, The Corner at 108 is a café, coffee shop, and wine bar that serves all-day food and drinks, including a small selection of Danish craft beers. The food is refined but unpretentious and pairs well with both the beer and wine on offer.

COPENHAGEN, DENMARK

## 457 Pair *smørrebrød* with local ales

Founded in 2003 by former Carlsberg brewmaster Anders Kissmeyer, the American-style Nørrebro Bryghus brewpub is named for the neighborhood in which it is located. The stylish red tabletop-outfitted brewery dispenses dozens of draft beers most typical of craft beer–style brewers, along with Danish-style *smørrebrød* sandwiches and plates of local products.

**456** *Above:* The Corner at 108 is on the far left, next to North Atlantic House in Copenhagen

## 459 Discover the wide-ranging styles of Amager Bryghus

Amager Bryghus was founded in 2007 by two friends and dedicated home brewers, Jacob Storm and Morten Valentin Lundsbak, both native to the island of Amager. The brewery—situated right next to Copenhagen Airport—exports its unfiltered and unpasteurized beers to thirty countries all over the world. Amager Bryghus has a portfolio of around twenty stable and seasonal beers, but releases a further thirty to forty new beers every year. Although creating mostly hoppy brews, the brewery has gained a reputation for big, dark, intense styles. The unpretentious Amager Boys famously stated: "No matter what you do, don't believe more than maximum 20% of what we write on our beers."

## 458 Drink beer down on the Alefarm

Alefarm Brewing is a family-run craft brewery with a focus on modern hoppy offerings, a wide array of unique, flavorful farmhouse ales, and full-bodied stouts, rich in flavor and character. On a daily basis, the brewery is run by Kasper Tidemann and his wife, Britt van Slyck. Among its hit brews are Citrella, a DIPA at 8% ABV, and Mark My Words, a juicy IPA at 6% ABV. The brewery welcomes visitors and staff are always happy to share a beer with fellow beer drinkers. Its mixed-fermentation saisons are some of the best in the country, and include Celeste (brewed with American and European hops) and Nordic Grape, a pink beer aged on Danish Stevnsbær cherries. Alefarm packages most of its beer in 500 ml cans with artistic design and beautiful, muted-color labels.

## 460 Match great beer with top-notch cuisine

A sleek, modern space located on the ground floor of the North Atlantic House cultural center, Restaurant Barr serves modern Nordic and Scandinavian food along with some twenty beers on draft and an extensive bottle list. Adjacent to the main dining room is a thirty-seat beer bar, a warm, cozy place to stop by for a quick bite or simple weeknight meal.

## 461 Acquire artful ales at To Øl

Meaning "two beers" in Danish, To Øl brewery was started by two homebrewing friends who initially brewed at a school. Classmates Tobias Emil Jensen and Tore Gynther started the project in 2005 and five years later founded the commercial brewery to make floral and hoppy as well as rich and robust modern craft beers. Inspired by the beers they saw—and drank—coming from the US, the duo focused on outlandishly bitter IPAs, mixed-fermentation saisons, and deep, dark stouts. The brewery's labels, typical of many Danish brewers, are art-forward and design-heavy with cheeky names. Find the beers in specialty bars throughout Copenhagen and around the world.

## 462 Gulp brewskis at Brewskival

In the same vein as Mikkeller's Beer Celebration, Cigar City's Hunahpu's Day, and Cloudwater's Friends & Family & Beer fest, Sweden's Brewskival welcomes dozens of international cult breweries to its home turf for this annual summer festival. Set in the southwest corner of Sweden, across a narrow channel from Denmark, Helsingborg's Brewski brewery throws this outdoor beer bash with friends from Alefarm (Denmark), 7venth Sun (Florida), Other Half (Brooklyn), and Jing-A Brewing (China). All told, more than sixty breweries attend with two to three beers per brewery, making Brewskival one of Sweden's largest and most sought-after craft beer festivals.

## 463 Spot Sweden's hippest art and beer duo

Omnipollo is a Swedish beer and art collective founded in 2011 by brewer Henok Fentie and artist/designer Karl Grandin. The mobile brewery follows the contract brewing or so-called "gypsy brewing" model of utilizing existing breweries across the world to make its beer, rather than maintaining its own facility. With Grandin in the mix, Omnipollo has always placed an outsize emphasis on art and design to go along with its creative, American-influenced craft beers. (Think: bold, hoppy IPAs and strong imperial stouts brewed with tons of adjuncts like maple syrup, coconut, and lactose.) The bottles and cans themselves are practically works of art, adorned with all kinds of esoteric and colorful symbols and icons often printed right onto the glass. Some of the most striking are Fatamorgana, an imperial wheat IPA that's frothy and heady; Agamemnon, an imperial stout brewed with maple syrup; and Yellow Belly, a beer wrapped in white paper. In 2015, the duo parlayed their momentum as gypsy brewers into a bricks-and-mortar bar called Omnipollos hatt in their native Stockholm. Partnering with Stockholm's Pizza Hatt—not to be confused with Pizza Hut!—the bar offers an array of Omnipollo taps and inventive, modern pizzas (for example, Parmesan, lardo, lemon, and asparagus) in a trippy, Grandin-designed setting. You can find Omnipollo beers throughout the world.

**463** *Right:* Omnipollo combines cutting-edge beer styles with modern and whimsical art

STOCKHOLM, SWEDEN

# Grab a brew at Stockholm's three best craft beer bars

### 464 Akkurat

Don't be misled by the humdrum digs—this traditional-looking bar offers one of the best beer selections in Sweden with more than twenty drafts and dozens of bottles from local and international cult brewers.

### 465 Oliver Twist

Looking for American craft beers in Sweden? This traditional British-style pub is your place, with a rotating selection of cans and drafts from Oskar Blues, Victory, and Left Hand Brewing, among many others.

### 466 BrewDog Kungsholmen

This bright, colorful bar was the first location abroad for the Scottish brewery. The pub features half BrewDog drafts and half guest taps from Belgian, American, and local Swedish brewers.

LANDVETTER, SWEDEN

## 467 Dig these experimental brews

Inspired by a wave of beer experimentation, Dugges Bryggeri—founded in 2005 just outside Gothenburg—has a penchant for crafting innovative and experimental brews. Founder and brewer Mikael Dugges Engström has a keen eye on quality, and his passion for brewing comes through in the exceptional Idjit! imperial stout, High Five! IPA, and Hiphiphooray! pale ale. With colorful labels and fun, Swedish design, Dugges has doubled its production and now has dozens of new beers available. There is no tasting room or on-site pub, but you can find the beers in specialty bars throughout the country.

ÖREBRO, SWEDEN

## 468 Wise up to one of the world's most obscure and coveted breweries

The obscure Närke brewery's limited-release beers are some of the most coveted in the world, and none more so than the uber-rare Kaggen! Stormaktsporter imperial stout. Brewed with heather honey and matured in oak barrels for an extensive period, the beer has a rounded, mellow character with notes of black tea, tobacco, and blackstrap molasses. The brewery has been in operation since 2003 and has stuck to its small-batch craftsmanship principles, resisting calls to produce more beer on a larger scale. You can schedule a tour and tasting in advance or visit the brewery shop. An exceedingly small number of bars, pubs, and restaurants in both Sweden and abroad distribute the beer.

GOTHENBURG, SWEDEN
### 469 Bang your head at Abyss Bar

Rock out at the famed heavy metal Abyss Bar—located in one of the world's great heavy metal cities—featuring some killer brews from Sweden and abroad. Knock back a Trooper ESB brewed in collaboration with Iron Maiden and the UK's Robinsons Family Brewers, while listening to some live music or a heavy metal DJ. Be sure to check out the rare 1980s concert flyers lining the bathroom walls.

MALMÖ, SWEDEN
### 470 Catch on to Swedish craft

Fifteen house-brewed beers and close to thirty on tap make Malmö Brewing & Taproom a beer lover's paradise. Crack into a Canned Wheat American-style IPA or a smooth and roasty Janky Stout. On the food menu you'll find classic American-style BBQ—brisket, ribs, etc.—served in an industrial-inspired taproom, where you can admire the copper brewhouse on view.

HELSINKI, FINLAND
### 471 Find rare bottles at this tiny bar

Olutravintola Pikkulintu is a tiny bar located in Helsinki's eastern Puotila district and features a huge selection of whiskies and beers. Ignore the Carlsberg signage out front—inside, you'll find one of the best independent beer selections in all of the country, including rarities from Belgium's Cantillon and Sweden's Brekeriet, among many, many others.

UUSIMAA PROVINCE, FINLAND
### 472 Float downriver with buckets of beer

Float down the river with a tether bucket of beer at the roving Kaljakellunta floating beer festival held each summer along Kerava and Vantaa rivers. Thousands participate, bringing various kinds of inflatable dinghies and DIY-constructed rafts to pass down the river while drinking beer. There is no head organizer, exact route, or even an official date, but the festival is typically held the last weekend of July or first weekend of August with varying floating routes and times that are decided last minute via discussions on the festival's social media channels. The beer is BYO, so stock up on your favorite Finnish craft beer.

**FINLAND**

### 473 Seek out Finland's ancient brew

Sahti is one of the oldest traditional beer styles still being brewed, dating back nearly 500 years to the farmhouses of Finland. Turbid, cloudy, and often with an almost viscous body, the beer is traditionally made with a variety of malted and unmalted grains, including barley, rye, and oats, and flavored with both juniper berries and twigs—and only occasionally hops. It can range from dark brown to pale yellow in color and often has a resinous quality. It can also be quite tart due to rustic brewing conditions and exposure to wild yeast and bacteria. Not only are the ingredients unique, but so is the process. Traditionally, Sahti is brewed using a lengthy infusion mash that may last up to eight hours, after which the wort is filtered through a hollowed-out tree trunk called a *kuurna*. Unlike most beers, traditional Sahti wort does not get boiled, but goes straight from the lauter tun to the fermentation vessel (this is where wild yeast and bacteria can be introduced). Commercial examples are typically around 8% ABV and are available in bars and Finnish state-run alcohol stores. Some craft breweries, both in Finland and the US, have re-created the brewing process to make their own novelty Sahtis.

**TALLINN, ESTONIA**

### 474 Drop into a brewery with a private sauna

Estonia's premier craft brewery, Põhjala Brewery crafts modern American-style IPAs and pale ales along with regionally inspired beers like Baltic porter and imperial stouts. The taproom features twenty-four Põhjala and guest beers on tap, Texas-style barbecue, a beer and merch shop, brewery tours, and—one of the coolest taproom amenities—a private sauna, which you and seven friends can rent during normal taproom hours.

**TALLINN, ESTONIA**

### 475 Spend a boozy weekend in Tallinn

Tallinn Craft Beer Weekend (TCBW) is one of the largest international spring craft beer festivals in the Baltic region. It consists of up to fifty of the best breweries from all over the world, as well as the brightest stars of the local brew scene. Festivalgoers can sip unlimited amounts of beers from breweries like Oregon's Boneyard Beer, the UK's Wild Beer, and Estonia's own Pühaste. Throughout the fest, a video monitor keeps track of the day's highest-rated beers as well as the top five beers with most check-ins on Untappd.

**474** *Right:* Põhjala Brewery is widely considered Estonia's best craft brewery

KRAKÓW, POLAND
## 476 Make your way to Kraków's top craft beer bars

Kraków was once a beer wasteland, pouring nearly exclusively national and international pale lagers and insipid ales to crowds of nightlifers out for nothing more than a buzz. Today, it's Poland's craft beer hotspot, the focus of the brew revolution, featuring more breweries and craft beer pubs than any other city in the country. In addition to Pub Omerta (see entry 479), the city features many other bars worthy of bucket-list attention. Start with House of Beer, a spot boasting the biggest range of bottled craft beers in town, plus two bars with dozens of rotating local, domestic, and international beers on tap. Associated with Browar Pinta, a craft brewery, you'll find Viva la Pinta, a pub-style taproom dedicated to pouring the beers of this inventive brewery in a bar located along Kraków's prime tourist district. For hardcore craft beer enthusiasts, check out Strefa Piwa, a temple to beer nerdom with drafts from all over Europe and the US in an engaging setting. Finally, stop into BeerGallery for a fine range of local craft brews.

THROUGHOUT POLAND
## 477 Involve yourself in Baltic Porter Day

Baltic porter is one of the most revered beer styles in the world, though sadly it doesn't get nearly as much attention or general respect as, say, modern imperial stouts. Despite its lineage tracing back to the traditional porters of England, most Polish-born Baltic porters are actually slow, bottom-fermented lagers (rather than ales), which are typically around 8–10% ABV with a smooth, robust flavor and rich mouthfeel similar to many full-bodied red wines. (Some examples are still brewed with ale yeast, however.) There are still many great producers in Poland, including both large breweries and small craft operations. In 2016, Baltic Porter Day was founded by beer enthusiast, former brewer, and bartender Marcin Chmielarz—he hopes to see Poland reclaim the style and make it the national beer of the country.

ŻYWIECZ, POLAND
## 478 Get your hands on a Żywiec beer

Poland's national brewery was founded in 1856 in the south-central town of Żywiec, which was then part of the Austria-Hungary empire. The brand today is majority owned by Heineken and composed of five main breweries: Żywiec, Elbrewery, Leżajsk, Warka, and Cieszyn. Most of the production is still relegated to pale lagers (including the classic flagship Żywiec, which is ubiquitous in Poland and Polish neighborhoods throughout the world), but the brewery also makes some classic styles such as Baltic porter, based on a recipe that purportedly dates back to 1881. The brewery's iconic labels feature a man and woman dressed in traditional Polish garb who are dancing the Krakowiak, a folk dance of the area of Kraków.

KRAKÓW, POLAND
## 479 Drink at one of Kraków's finest pubs

Look for the *Godfather*-themed signage outside the dimly lit Pub Omerta, one of Kraków's finest. Inside you'll find a handful of draft-dispensing craft beer from both local breweries and international ones (for example, O'Hara's Irish Stout, Sweden's Incognito Brewing). The vibe can be a bit craft beer bro-y, but the bartenders and regulars are friendly and inviting.

PRAGUE, CZECH REPUBLIC
## 480 Visit the beer garden at U Fleků

A Prague institution, U Fleků brewery and restaurant, with its dark wood tables, ornate iron chandeliers, and filigreed cathedral-like arches, is one of the best places to drink lager in the Czech Republic. If you're visiting in warm months, the outdoor beer garden is the spot to try the Dark Lager, a 4.5% ABV crusher.

**TOP 5**    CZECH REPUBLIC

# Check out these five Czech lagers

### 481  Koutska 12°
Brewed in the little town of Kout na Šumavě, in the very western part of the Czech Republic, this unfiltered lager is rich with bready notes.

### 482  Pivo Konrad 11°
A golden, full-bodied traditional Czech lager, this beer is only made with water from its own wells, the classic Zatec hops, and local barley.

### 483  Svatý Norbert Velikonoční 13°
This slightly cloudy golden lager has a peppery herbal nose with a touch of citrus on the finish.

### 484  Koutska 18°
This is the brewery's rich, dark specialty lager, which matures for six months to achieve an exquisite rounded, malty character. At 9% ABV, it's one of the biggest lagers you'll find in the country.

### 485  Pilsner Urquell Nefiltrovaný
An unfiltered iteration of the famous Pilsner Urquell, this version is only available on the Plzensky Prazdroj tour and at Na Parkanu in Pilsen. Occasional kegs are exported for special events.

PRAGUE, CZECH REPUBLIC
## 486  *Prost* to polotmavý
Just steps from Prague Castle, the monastic Klášterní Pivovar Strahov specializes in polotmavý, the so-called semi-dark lager unique to the Czech Republic. Dark-red in color, the lagers are rich and nutty with a toasty flavor more similar to Vienna lager than pilsner or Bavarian lagers. The white-walled, copper-adorned brewery was painstakingly restored in 2000 and reopened as a craft brewery with a beer garden and restaurant serving traditional Czech fare. The flagship Norbert polotmavý is a spicy, floral beer with a roasty backbone, while other beers, including Norbert dark lager and even an IPA, are also served.

CHODOVÁ PLANÁ, CZECH REPUBLIC
## 487  Sink into a beer spa
Beside exemplary pilsners, the Czech Republic is known for its pioneering beer spas. And none are more famous or welcoming than the original Chodovar Beer Spa located on the premises of the Chodovar brewery. There is also a hotel and two restaurants, which provide a relaxing, indulgent experience. The beer baths consist of a bath literally in beer, mixed with the local mineral water as well as grains. You soak in the mixture for twenty minutes, followed by a massage and a hot grain pack. If you choose, you'll be treated to a small pour of the brewed-on-premise lager to accompany your bath.

# Explore five Czech craft breweries

### 488 Wild Creatures

Known as the "brewery among the vineyards," this small craft brewery creates spontaneous and wild ales with a decidedly vinous bent. Look for Tears of Saint Laurent, a "Czech grape ale."

### 489 Pivovar Matuška

Pivovar Matuška specializes in traditional Czech lagers as well as American-influenced hoppy ales like Raptor IPA, Apollo Galaxy pale ale, and Černá Raketa Cascadian dark ale.

### 490 Pivovar Nomád

Starting out as a so-called gypsy or nomadic brewery, founder Honza Kočka crafts a range of newfangled beer styles, including the hoppy 7.6% ABV Karel Česká IPA.

### 491 Pivovar Falkon

American-style IPAs, session pale ales, and imperial stouts are the name of the game at this tiny Czech craft brewery, founded in 2012 by an enthusiastic homebrewer.

### 492 Sibeeria

A sister brewery to bottle shop and bar BeerGeek, Sibeeria was founded by couple Olga and Ruslan with the idea of being an experimental brewery in contrast to the traditional lagers of the Czech Republic.

PRAGUE, CZECH REPUBLIC
## 493 Join in Czech's largest beer festival

Czech Beer Festival (Český Pivní Festival) is on par with the Great American Beer Festival and the Great British Beer Festival. Hundreds of breweries, most from the Czech Republic, but also from around the world, gather in Prague's riverfront Letna Park for an entire month (May–June) of workshops, live music, food, and, of course, beer. The festival attracts more than 100,000 attendees over the weeks, who sip pours of ales, lagers, and cask beers from breweries like Pivovar Raven, Permon Craft Brewery, Zichovecký Pivovar, and Pivovar Cobolis. With tents and long, wooden, beer garden–style tables, think of it as a mix between Oktoberfest and a more indie craft beer celebration.

PILSEN, CZECH REPUBLIC

## 494 Call at one of beer's most hallowed spots

One of the most famous—and indeed important—beers in the world, Pilsner Urquell is the original pale golden pilsner, named for its hometown of Pilsen, located 60 miles (95 km) west of Prague. First brewed in 1842, it was crafted to imitate the superior Bavarian lagers coming out of neighboring Germany, which stood in stark contrast to the nasty, unintentionally sour dark ales that were at the time the norm for the Pilsen region. The townspeople banded together to build the brewery on soft sandstone land, into which deep lager caves were dug in order to cold-condition the beer. The new recipe, imported by the Bavarian brewmaster Josef Groll, combined the local soft water of Pilsen with aromatic local hops and pale malts for a crisp, supremely clean, and refreshing beer that's now copied throughout the world. Today, you can walk through the towering gates of the original brewery and tour the facilities, including the lagering caves, and sample the beer fresh from the tanks. Tours are offered in Czech, German, and English, and end with a sample of the unfiltered lager. It's one of the most hallowed beer spots in the world.

AUSTRIA
## 495 Discover an original Vienna lager

Ottakringer Wiener Original is the textbook Vienna lager (a style developed in the city in the mid-nineteenth century). This beer is brewed with Viennese malts—an amber-hued malt that's darker than typical pilsner varieties—for a nutty finish, plus Saaz hops for a spicy, grassy aroma. The recipe dates back to the early twentieth century and is still produced in its namesake sixteenth district of Vienna.

VIENNA, AUSTRIA
## 496 Party at Austria's version of Oktoberfest

A celebration of Austrian heritage and culture, the annual Wiener Wiesn-Fest (September–October) is essentially Austria's version of Oktoberfest, complete with folk music and dancing, huge plates of traditional food, and copious amounts of local beer poured from servers in lederhosen and dirndl. The festival's largest tent is sponsored by the brewery Gösser.

VIENNA, AUSTRIA
## 497 Drink beside Belvedere Palace

Setting up in 1924, Salm Bräu Brewery serves traditional Austrian-, Czech-, and German-style beers, including Pils, Helles, and Böhmisch G'mischt (an obscure, dark Czech-style lager). Located next to Vienna's historic Belvedere Palace, the digs are rustic with aged wooden chairs and tables, and copper lamps fashioned after the brewery's copper brewhouse.

ENGELHARTSZELL, AUSTRIA
## 498 Try Trappist beer from this Austrian monastery

In 2012, the Austrian monastery of Stift Engelszell was recognized as the eighth Trappist brewery in the world, and the first Trappist beer producer in Austria. Gregorius Trappistenbier, named for the first abbot from the congregation of the Trappist fathers of the monastery, is a high-gravity, quad-style ale with sweet cherry notes and a rich, robust mouthfeel.

BAD RADKERSBURG, AUSTRIA
## 499 Sip modern beers in the birthplace of Styrian Golding hops

Located in a quaint spa town in the southeast Austrian state of Styria—the ancestral birthplace of the famed Styrian Golding hop—the modern Bevog Brauhaus-Brewery makes American-inspired hoppy ales like Zo Session IPA, Tak Pale Ale, and Rudeen Black IPA. Tours are offered with advanced bookings and feature a gratis tasting afterward.

**499** *Right:* Bevog Brauhaus-Brewery produces American-inspired hoppy ales

SAIGNELÉGIER, SWITZERLAND
## 500 Become an acolyte of BFM

Founded in 1997 by Jérôme Rebetez, a trained oenologist (wine scientist), Brasserie des Franches-Montagnes (BFM) is one of the world's great breweries and the most revered Swiss craft brewery period. It is known for pushing the boundaries of beer, taking influence from Rebetez's wine background and its setting in the Jura region, to craft exciting and crossover styles that nod to traditions of Belgium, but result in beers that are entirely unique. After winning 50,000 Swiss francs in 1997 on the TV show *Le rêve de vos 20 ans* ("Your Dream at 20"), Rebetez started the brewery to fulfill his dream of creating wild, complex, and anti-mainstream beers. Since its beginnings, BFM has evolved, but stayed true to its roots. Its most famous beer is Abbaye de Saint Bon-Chien, an 11% ABV dark strong ale with vinous notes from a prolonged aging in wooden barrels with wild yeast and bacteria. The primary batch of Bon-Chien each year is blended from different barrels, but "Grand Cru" versions of single-barrel beers are also released occasionally. Other beers include √225, a saison aged in used Bon-Chien barrels, and Cuvée Alex Le Rouge, a "Jurassian" imperial stout.

# Taste exciting brews in Switzerland's top five beer bars

### 501  The International

Zurich's premier beer destination, The International boasts dozens of styles from breweries around the world. Eight drafts feature mostly European cult breweries (Lervig, Birrificio Italiano), while many others are served in bottles.

### 502  Biercafé Au Trappiste

This Bern bar is a compact, traditional European pub with stone walls, dark wood tables, and a varied selection of top-notch beers. Sip on a famed Fantôme Saison or an Old Numbskull barleywine from California's AleSmith.

### 503  The Alehouse

A Zurich gastropub with twenty drafts and traditional French-style brasserie fare, this bar pours a mix of traditional ales and lagers (Augustiner-Bräu) and newfangled, hipster craft offerings (Beavertown, Storm & Anchor).

### 504  Le PiBar

This cozy Lausanne beer temple offers a dizzying selection of bottles (Cantillon, Amager Bryghus) and fourteen drafts from a mix of international and Swiss breweries (Hoppy People, Brasserie de l'Atelier).

### 505  Hüsi Bierhaus

Set in a traditional Swiss house in Interlaken, this photogenic bar offers many specialty beer options alongside a menu of traditional German-influenced Swiss food. The nighttime vibe from the outside is exceedingly charming.

SAINTE-CROIX, SWITZERLAND

## 506  Visit this brewery inspired by three women

Raphaël Mettler is the founder and brewer of Brasserie Trois Dames, which has been producing Belgian-inspired brews since 2003. Named for the "three ladies" in Mettler's life—his wife and two daughters—this Swiss brasserie is a farmhouse-inspired operation set within a small building in the village of Sainte-Croix. In 2008, the brewery released the Flanders-style Grande Dame Oud Bruin ale, which gets a fruity kick from fermented apricots from the Valais region of Switzerland. Other classics include Saison Framboise, brewed with raspberries and aged in red wine barrels, and Forêt Noire, a chocolate torte-inspired dark ale blended with cherry wine and fermented cherries.

# Europe—South & West

An entire book could focus on the bucket-list breweries of Germany and Belgium alone. The two countries, though disparate style-wise, are arguably the two most influential traditional beer centers of the world. In Germany, in addition to fabulously clean and classic lagers, seek out the smoky rauchbiers of Bamberg and the crisp kölsches of Cologne. In Belgium, visit the monastic Trappist breweries as well as the saison and farmhouse ale producers of Wallonia.

France, Italy, Spain, and Portugal might be more renowned for their cuisines than their beer, but these days each has something wonderfully creative to offer. From Italy's culinary-influenced brews to Spain and Portugal's fledgling beer markets, you're sure to find innovative and inventive beers wherever you go.

BERLIN, GERMANY
## 507 Discover Berliner weisse, the original "Champagne of the north"

Berliner weisse is the specialty beer style synonymous with the city of Berlin. One of the best places to try it is at the admittedly touristy Alt-Berliner Weissbierstube, a cozy café specializing in the city's nearly forgotten style. Berliner weisse is a light, refreshingly tart wheat ale soured with lactobacillus. It was once ubiquitous throughout Berlin and northern Germany, but like so many regional specialties, it succumbed to the rise of international lagers and pilsners amid the advent of industrial brewing. At Alt-Berliner, servers still dispense the beer *"mit Schuss"* (with syrup) into customary widemouthed goblets with shots of sweet raspberry or woodruff syrup. Order it *sans Schuss* for a true Berliner weisse experience. Most of the Berliner weisse served at Alt-Berliner comes from the Kindl brewery, an industrial, large-scale producer. For a taste of old-school Berliner weisse made in small batches from authentic recipes, head to the Arminiusmarkthalle, a sprawling food hall that features lunch counters and a beer bar affiliated with BrewBaker, the maker of a lemony tart Berliner weisse. Unlike Kindl, BrewBaker's Berliner is fermented with brettanomyces, a traditional Berliner weisse method used to give the beer a complex, funky character.

# Discover Berlin's five best craft breweries

### 508 Hops & Barley

This small brewery and bar opened in Berlin's Friedrichshain district in 2008. The specialty is traditional German styles with a diversity of hops that are typically not found in most German beers.

### 509 Heidenpeters

This small but hip brewery located in the Markthalle 9 in Kreuzberg offers a high-quality selection of modern craft beers.

### 510 BRLO

Named for the Slavic word for Berlin, this craft brewery creates superb examples of helles, pale ales, and porter beers served in an outdoor *biergarten* called the BRWHOUSE.

509

510

### 511 Vagabund Brauerei

Drop into this tiny nanobrewery for American-style specialties, including hoppy wheat ales, pale ales, and IPAs, plus more experimental brews like tingly Szechuan Saison brewed with Szechuan peppercorns.

### 512 BrewBaker

This small brewery is best known for reviving the traditional Berliner weisse–style beer. Its version is triple-fermented with saccharomyces, brettanomyces, and lactobacillus, and is bottle-conditioned.

### WÜRGAU, GERMANY

## 513 Visit a very old Franconian brewery

Licensed since 1550, Brauerei Gasthof Hartmann is one of the oldest in Franconia. The specialty is Felsentrunk, a gently smoked amber beer; also try Edelpils, a hoppy pilsner, and Erbschänk 1550 schwarzbier. Positioned in the center of a small village, the premises also include an on-site hotel, inn, and restaurant, though the decor feels somewhat dated.

### BAYREUTH, GERMANY

## 514 Sample lagers with the brewhouse on view

At more than 230 years old, Becher Bräu is the oldest brewery in this part of Bavaria. Visit the brewery's old-fashioned restaurant and tasting room where you can sample traditional lagers with customary dishes. Be sure to check out the glass-enclosed brewhouse, which is visible from the back of the building.

### BAYREUTH, GERMANY

## 515 Discover a pillowy weisse beer

Wheat beer is the specialty at Maisel Brewery, whose history dates back to 1887. Maisel's Weisse Original has a fruity, clove-spiked aroma with a pillowy body and crisp, easy-drinking finish. A spin-off brand, Maisel & Friends, features American-style craft beers as well as a company museum located in the original brewery building.

### BAYREUTH, GERMANY

## 516 Drink dunkel in kitschy surroundings

Though Schinner Braustuben is now a full-fledged contract brewery—producing its beers in another brewery's facility—its original location still welcomes visitors for a traditional Bavarian meal and large pours of its textbook dunkel in somewhat dated, kitschy surroundings. The flagship Schinner 1860 Urstoff is a frothy helles lager with a grassy aroma and delicate, bitter finish.

### BAMBERG, GERMANY

## 517 Savor the gently smoked beers of Spezial

Brauerei Spezial is Bamberg's second rauchbier producer after Schlenkerla, but it crafts the smoked beers with a deft, gentle touch that doesn't overwhelm your palate the way Schlenkerla might. In fact, the beers taste downright tame comparatively. Founded in 1536, the name "Spezial" came into use around 1630 and has been synonymous with the brewery ever since. Spezial's range of rauchbiers includes traditional lagers, Märzen, and wheat beer as well as so-called "Ungespundet" beer, an unfiltered, full-bodied lager that literally translates as "unbunged." The brewery also houses an inn and restaurant—a one-stop shop for traveling beer nerds.

## 518 Sip smoky rauchbiers at Schlenkerla

In stark contrast to the clean flavors typically associated with German beer are Bamberg's historic smoke-laced rauchbiers. The finest examples are found in the middle of the city center at a brewery called Schlenkerla. Brewed with smoked malt, the beers are imparted with an intense medley of barbecued meat, Islay scotch, and caramel malt flavors. The Schlenkerla tavern features a Gothic ceiling known as the Dominikanerklause, and legend has it that a brewery has been located on this site since 1405, when it was a pub known as Zum Blauen Löwen ("At the Blue Lion"). Today, the brewery taproom offers a variety of smoked malt beers, from the flagship Aecht Schlenkerla Rauchbier (brewed from a Märzen-like base beer) to smoked wheat beers and seasonals. Depending on what time of year you're visiting, you may find specialties like Fastenbier (a smoked bock-style beer brewed for Lent), Kräusen (a blend of traditional and young smoked lager), or a Christmas ale called Schlenkerla Oak Smoke (a doppelbock brewed with oak-smoked, rather than beechwood-smoked, malt). A selection of Bavarian dishes is served to accompany the beers. Think: crispy pork knuckle with smoked beer sauce, sauerkraut, and potato dumplings, and coarse sausage studded with grains of smoked malt.

**BAMBERG, GERMANY**

## 519 Try Bamberg's newest brews

Located literally next door to Schlenkerla, Ambräusianum is the newest and smallest brewery in the city of Bamberg. The centerpiece is a beautiful copper brewery located in the middle of the pub, making it a picturesque setting for visitors. Try the Hell and Dunkel lagers, as well as the Weizen and seasonal bock beers.

**519** *Above:* Ambräusianum is the relative upstart of Bamberg's historic brewing culture

BAMBERG, GERMANY
### 520 Swig unfiltered lagers at Mahrs Bräu

The region of Franconia in northern Bavaria is perhaps the most interesting part of Germany when it comes to brewing. It supposedly boasts the most breweries per square mile in the world, and contains the widest array of original beer styles in Germany. Within the city of Bamberg alone, with just 75,000 inhabitants, there are around ten breweries—and Mahrs Bräu is one of the city's finest. This family-run establishment, with roots in the region dating back to 1895, boasts an old-world brewpub with traditional fare and a beer garden. Mahrs eschews the region's smoked beers in favor of traditional lagers and pale ales, all brewed in a traditional German copper brewhouse. Its flagship is a 5.2% ABV Ungespundet Lager (simply referred to as "A U" or "*ahhh oooo*") with a yeasty aroma. It's pleasantly smooth and only lightly carbonated. Also check out Mahrs Pilsner (a robust take on the style), Hell (an extremely light pale ale), and Bock (a strong, velvety beer). The beers are slightly more expensive than you'll find in the rest of Germany, but their extremely high quality is worth every last cent.

BAMBERG, GERMANY
### 521 Learn about the history of Franconian brewing

Founded in 1979, the Franconian Brewery Museum Bamberg (Fränkisches Brauereimuseum in der Bierstadt Bamberg) is a fascinating place to learn about the history of brewing in this world-class brewing city. With nearly 2,000 artifacts to take in, the museum highlights the process of brewing—from brewhouse, malting, fermentation, and storage cellars to lagering vessels, filtration mechanisms, and bottling devices—as well as the cultural importance of beer in the Franconia region. A lecture hall and educational facility offer year-round courses and beer seminars that cover a wide range of topics specific to Franconian brewing. There are also demonstrations of brewing, malting, and cooperage techniques.

**COLOGNE, GERMANY**

# Try the best Kölsch in these Cologne venues

Kölsch is the namesake beer of Cologne. It's often thought of as a lager-ale hybrid, but strictly speaking, it is a pale ale, a holdover from the prelager days of German brewing.

### 522 Brauerei Päffgen

This boisterous, wood-adorned tavern serves traditional unfiltered Kölsch dispensed from wooden barrels. Päffgen's beer has a remarkably fresh hop character and pairs perfectly with the tavern's plates of traditional German fare.

### 523 Braustelle Helios

Cologne's first craft brewpub is a friendly, laid-back space, a fixture of the Ehrenfeld neighborhood, attracting both locals and craft beer tourists. The premier brew is Helios, Braustelle's take on its hometown beer.

### 524 Gaffel Kölsch

Gaffel Am Dom is located adjacent to Cologne's massive Gothic cathedral. Gaffel, along with Reissdorf Kölsch, is perhaps the best-known Kölsch in all of Cologne, with a sprightly bitterness and a pronounced hop character.

**OBERPFALZ, GERMANY**

## 525 Seek out the zoigl communal brews

Named for the zoigl star, zoiglbier is a communal-style brewing native to the Oberpfalz region located between Franconia and the Czech border. Zoigl is the word for "sign," which in this context means a six-pointed star similar to the Star of David consisting of two interlocking triangles. The first triangle represents the three elements—water, fire, and earth—while the second denotes the traditional brewing ingredients—malted barley, hops, and water. Traditional zoigl breweries are communal and owned by either the local municipality or a consortium of homebrewers. The brewers come together to create a base wort (often brewed on a wood-fired kettle), which is then distributed among the private cellars. Once the beer is ready, the zoigl star sign is put up outside the house, which essentially becomes a pub.

FREISING, GERMANY

## 526 Visit the world's oldest continuously operating brewery

The oldest continuously operating brewery in the world is Bavaria's Weihenstephan Brewery. It is most famous for its hefeweizen beers with notes of banana and clove, and a refreshing full-bodied flavor. The grounds were established as a Benedictine abbey in the year 725 and brewing officially began in 1040—it has been in operation in one form or another ever since. Tours give you an in-depth look at the brewing process, and the museum's "To the Origin of Beer" exhibition documents the brewery's history. A tasting room and restaurant offer beers and traditional, unfussy Bavarian cuisine.

HALLERNDORF, GERMANY

## 527 Absorb traditional Franconian culture

Traditional Franconian culture exudes from Brauerei Rittmayer brewery and restaurant in Upper Franconia, whose specialty is an amber-hued kellerbier. Seasonal releases include bock beer and a winter wheat beer. Order a beverage and plate of Franconian charcuterie to enjoy in the fenced-in beer garden with the nearby church steeple towering overhead.

MUNICH, GERMANY
## 528 Drink Märzen from wooden barrels

Augustiner Bräu is Munich's oldest independently owned brewery, founded in 1328 within an Augustinian monastery. Today, the brewery crafts some of the best beers in Germany, including its Augustiner Helles, a pale lager with a smooth, rounded flavor. One of the best places to try the beers is at Oktoberfest. Its traditional Oktoberfest Märzen is one of only two still served straight from the original wooden barrels.

MUNICH, GERMANY
## 529 Discover a famed Munich brewery

One of the most important brands in terms of advancing lager production, Spatenbräu can trace its roots back to fourteenth-century Munich when it ran a small brewpub. Today, the company is owned by Anheuser-Busch InBev, but it still produces some exemplary beers, including Münchner Hell and Doppelbock Optimator.

MUNICH, GERMANY
## 530 Get thee to the Oktoberfest museum

Formally known as the Beer and Oktoberfest Museum (Bier- und Oktoberfestmuseum), this beer and cultural museum is housed in the oldest historic townhouse in Bavaria, dating back to 1340. It was restored and reopened in 2005 and today features exhibitions about the history of brewing and how Bavaria became the center of the world of beer production. Stop in at the on-site bar and restaurant serving traditional Bavarian food and, of course, plenty of beer.

MUNICH, GERMANY
## 531 Sip strong beers at starkbier festivals

The Strong Beer festival (Starkbierzeit) is the spring alternative to Munich's fall Oktoberfest. Many of the breweries in Munich, including the big four— Paulaner, Augustiner, Unions, and Löwenbräu—hold their own small starkbier fests, which celebrate with special strong beers at 7.5–8% ABV. This is a more low-key event than Oktoberfest.

MUNICH, GERMANY
## 532 Consume history in a glass

Formed in 1972 from the merger of Hack and Pschorr breweries, the traditional Hacker-Pschorr Bräu crafts a line of historical lagers, including an unfiltered kellerbier, a weissbier brewed with Hallertau Herkules hops, and its classic Münchner Gold featuring three varieties of locally grown malts. The Hacker-Pschorr Oktoberfest Märzen is one of the few traditional Märzens still served at the festival.

### 534 Check out the original Paulaner

Though now an international brand with small breweries in far-flung regions like Shanghai and Moscow, the original Paulaner brewery in Munich is still worth a visit. Established here in 1634 by the Minim friars of the Neudeck ob der Au cloister, the brewery's specialty is weissbier, including the textbook hefeweizen.

FORCHHEIM, GERMANY

### 535 Witness the crowning of the Forchheimer "beer queen"

In what is a truly engaging and magical beer festival, the annual Annafest Franconian folk festival celebrates the dozens of small, family-run *bierkellers* ("beer cellars") that turn out to showcase their beer and traditional Franconian foods. The festival dates back to 1840 and is held on Saint Anna's Day in late July at the Forchheim beer gardens. The setting is the shady oak forest, known locally as the *kellerwald* ("cellar forest"), with seating and accommodation for nearly 30,000 daily revelers. Estimates suggest that nearly 500,000 people pass through the festival grounds each year. There are carnival-like amusements, but the main attractions are the twenty-plus *bierkellers*. Positioned throughout the forest along a wandering path, each *bierkeller* has its own shelter-like structure where beer and food are served. Many offer outdoor *biergarten*-like seating. Breweries include Mahrs Bräu, Brauerei Griffin, Neder Bier, and Brauerei Eichhorn, and many others from around the region. Every two years, a new Forchheimer Bierkönigin ("beer queen") is selected, whose role includes numerous public appearances throughout the reign.

MUNICH, GERMANY

### 533 Book at tour at the Hofbräuhaus brewery

Book a tour in this sprawling, modern facility to see how a historic brewery has modernized into the twenty-first century. Dating back to 1589, Staatliches Hofbräuhaus München is now a global enterprise. Visit the brewery in Munich for the best experience of sampling the original beers. Tours feature pours right from the tanks and end with a Bavarian snack in the Bierstüberl brewpub.

MUNICH, GERMANY

## 536 Join the massive party at the original Oktoberfest

The most famous beer festival in the world is this annual two-week blowout that starts in mid-September in Munich's Theresienwiese— an open-air fairground south of the city center. Every year, millions of revelers from all over the world gather under giant tents erected by one of the six participating breweries. The festival strictly regulates what beer can be served here with the most general rule being that it must be from one of the large breweries that brews inside the city of Munich. These include Augustiner Bräu, Hacker-Pschorr Bräu, Löwenbräu, Paulaner, Spatenbräu, and Staatliches Hofbräuhaus München. The primary beer served is an amberish-colored lager called Märzen, a style closely related to Vienna lager. The mild, moderately bitter brew is around 5% ABV with aromas of toffee and bready flavors. Within Germany, only the aforementioned breweries can market their Märzens under the Oktoberfest moniker, but many international breweries use the name to denote a special brew released during the fall. Oktoberfest is the largest folk festival in the world, featuring many events, games, and rides besides beer drinking. It has spawned countless copycat festivals around the world, though none are nearly as grandiose, authentic, or well attended as the original Munich one.

ANDECHS, GERMANY

### 537 Discover the complex beers of Andechs

There are just a handful of operational monastic breweries in Germany today, and Klosterbrauerei Andechs, located in the Upper Franconia region, is by far the best and most well regarded. Brewing has taken place at the monastery for centuries, but it wasn't until the mid-twentieth century that a separate facility was built for the monks dedicated to their beer production. Now set at the foot of the Heiliger Berg ("Holy Mountain"), the brewery is the monastery's largest business enterprise. It makes a range of traditional German-style beers, but its most well-known are Doppelbock Dunkel, Weissbier Hell, and Weissbier Dunkel. Rich, complex, and smooth, each beer is like a symphony of holy flavors distilled into a single glass. Perhaps the brewery's best beer, however, is its festbier (also known as Andechser Spezial Hell), which is a lighter alternative of the traditional Märzen lager. In fact, it's not a Märzen at all, but a fairly straightforward helles beer with killer grassy and floral hop aromas, and a light, biscuity malt sweetness. You can embark on a brewery tour, but no tastings are included. A brewpub or Bräustüberl is located at the main monastery with outdoor seating and magnificent views of the Bavarian Alps.

### 538 Get attuned to altbier

Uerige Hausbrauerei is renowned for its altbier, a native
German top-fermenting brown ale that's indigenous to
the Westphalia region surrounding Düsseldorf. Uerige's
recipe dates back to 1862 and combines three types of
malt with Umbel hops and a proprietary yeast strain for
a full-bodied, bitter, and highly aromatic beer. Perhaps
its best-known beers, however, are Sticke and
DoppelSticke, two boozier beers that are brewed in
limited quantity. In fact, Sticke is released just twice
a year at the brewery—always on the third Tuesdays
of January and October. The large brewery and public
house feature many rooms for different occasions,
including some with pristinely restored stained glass
windows and carpentry work.

THROUGHOUT GERMANY

### 539 Sip a schwarzbier

Schwarzbiers look bold and bitter, but these
black (*schwarz*) lagers are deceptively refreshing
and crisp. They're often toasty with a mild but
pleasing burnt aftertaste and a lighter body and
drier finish than most dunkels and bocks. The
dark malts used impart a mild bitterness and an
acidic, chocolate flavor that mellows with the
long lagering process. The style was popularized
by the Köstritzer Brewery in the central German state of Thuringia,
which has been making schwarzbier since the sixteenth century.
One of the most well-known examples is Köstritzer Schwarzbier.
The style has become popular abroad, too. Remember, just because
a beer is dark doesn't mean that it is strong! Most schwarzbiers
clock in at less than 5% ABV.

KAUFBEUREN, GERMANY

### 540 Say "hello" to Hallertau hops beer

Aktienbrauerei Kaufbeuren in
Bavaria can trace its brewing
heritage back to 1308. Today,
it makes high-quality beers
using only Hallertau hops
and local grain from the
surrounding area. Try its
Hell ("light"), a refreshing,
easy-drinking pale lager,
and Edel, a more robust,
bready lager.

DORTMUND, GERMANY

### 541 Peruse the artifacts at this brewery museum

Brewery-Museum Dortmund is chock-full of artifacts—beer-delivery trucks, ceramic mugs—and brewery memorabilia. You will get a behind-the-scenes guide to the city's fascinating history of industrially brewed beer.

GRAFENHAUSEN, GERMANY

### 542 Taste the world's best pilsners

Located in the Black Forest region, the state-owned Badische Staatsbrauerei Rothaus crafts two of the best pilsners in the world: Rothaus Pils and Tannenzäpfle Pils. The iconic labels feature "Biergit Kraft," a blonde woman dressed in traditional garb holding two steins of beer.

ALKMAAR, THE NETHERLANDS

### 543 Visit this Dutch national beer museum

National Beer Museum De Boom—the Netherlands' national museum dedicated to beer—is housed in a former brewery. Here, you'll learn the history of brewing culture in this country through exhibitions and artifacts.

HAARLEM, THE NETHERLANDS

### 544 Sample modern beers based on traditional recipes

Founded in 1994 and named for the 112-liter barrels once used to ship beer from its hometown of Haarlem to locales all over the world, Jopen Bier Brewery's aim was to recover Haarlem's brewing traditions and show them on a global stage. The brewery is housed in a former church

called Jopenkerk in the heart of the city and includes a sparkling copper brewhouse behind the bar. Lagering tanks are set behind the kettle, and within the brewery is a café and restaurant serving a variety of Dutch food and Jopen beer. A second facility and tasting room are set on the outskirts of Haarlem, in an industrial park called Waarderpolder, where you'll find tours and tastings offered in English on Saturdays.

AMSTERDAM, THE NETHERLANDS

### 545 Pair traditional Dutch dishes with beer at Café Foeders

Named for the tall, upright wooden tanks used to age Flemish beer, Café Foeders bar is a craft beer lovers' dream with around thirty drafts of both traditional Belgian beers and modern imported craft ales. Located near the Amstel River, the space is decorated in a traditional Dutch style with dark woods. On draft are Belgian classics like Rodenbach and La Chouffe in addition to many other regional specialties. Food-wise, order the *grijze garnaaltjes* (gray shrimp), which come ready to peel and are served alongside Flemish red ales and oud bruins, or try the *pottekeis* (a cheese spread on bread), which are served with lambic and other styles.

AMSTERDAM, THE NETHERLANDS

### 546 Spot this brewery beside a windmill

Look for the adjacent windmill and you'll know you've found Brouwerij 't IJ located in a former bathhouse. Open since 1985, the brewery is named for the IJ body of water, which was once a bay (it is now a river inlet). Check out the Belgian-style IPA—called simply I.P.A.— and the Belgian-style tripel Zatte, a golden ale with notes of fresh fruit and bubblegum.

AMSTERDAM, THE NETHERLANDS

### 547 Bend an elbow at the quirky, esoteric In de Wildeman

In de Wildeman is a quirky bar with loads of charm and character—check out the vintage ceramic mugs and tin beer signage adorning the walls. There are literally hundreds of beers available both on draft and in bottles. Lambic enthusiasts in particular will love the selection of vintage bottles served traditionally from wooden wicker baskets.

BODEGRAVEN, THE NETHERLANDS
## 548 Find some of the Netherlands' best craft beer at de Molen

Founded in 2004 at the historical De Arkduif windmill along the Oude Rijn river, Brouwerij de Molen is a relatively young but instantly classic brewery making some of the best beers in the Netherlands. Visit the windmill and you'll find a brewery café, tours, and a bottle shop selling not only beers brewed on-site, but other rare and interesting bottles and an assortment of merchandise. Flavor-wise, the brewery is all about experimentation and delivering big, aggressive flavors. One of its top-rated beers is Hel & Verdoemenis (Hell & Damnation), an exceedingly expressive imperial stout brewed with aged malts. The brewery has made more than 700 different beers, many of which have been one-off offerings available only in the brewery café and tasting room.

AMSTERDAM, THE NETHERLANDS

# Enjoy a brew at Amsterdam's best three "brown cafés"

Amsterdam's so-called "brown cafés" are similar to the pubs of Dublin—public gathering spots that attract a mix of artists, literary notables, and ordinary folks out for a beer. Here are three of the best.

### 549 Café De Dokter

Founded in 1798 by a surgeon, this medical-themed bar was a favorite of doctors and medical students from the nearby University of Amsterdam. Today, it's dimly lit with stained glass windows and a variety of beers on draft and in bottles.

### 550 Café Chris

Dating back to 1624, Café Chris is routinely acknowledged as Amsterdam's oldest brown café. The interior is all dark woods and vintage mugs (check out the ones lining the ceiling) and the beer is a local if somewhat uninspired selection.

### 551 Café Hoppe

Since 1670, this bar has been dispensing beers and pouring small glasses of gin for patrons.

551

### 552 Delve into Dutch-only pours at this bar

Positioned in the heart of Amsterdam, the copper-adorned Proeflokaal Arendsnest serves exclusively Dutch-only beer from the country's 400-plus breweries. With more than fifty beers on draft and another hundred-plus in bottles, you're sure to find something unique and pleasing. Be sure to check out the canal-side terrace.

### 554 Get a historical perspective on brewing

Located at the historic Château de l'Avouerie d'Anthisnes, Musée de la Bière et du Péket offers a historical perspective on brewing—how it started and why Belgium became the heart of brewing culture. The tour ends in the castle's vaulted cellars with a tasting and also explores the depths of the castle's dungeon rooms.

### 555 Go back in time at Europe's largest brewery museum

Bocholter Brouwerijmuseum was founded in 1979 and takes you through the history of brewing in the region from 1758 to the present. It includes technological artifacts like a traditional malting facility, a grand brewing hall, a barrel and bottle workshop, and even a re-creation of a raucous barroom.

### 553 Try this Trappist ale from the Netherlands

One of just two Trappist breweries in the Netherlands, De Kievit Trappist Brewery produces one of the best (if totally obscure) Trappist ales in the world. Zundert 8 Trappist is a chestnut-colored ale that is bottle-conditioned with live yeast. According to the brewery, it is a "slightly unruly" beer, meaning it can be somewhat unpredictable and may take some time to fully appreciate. The only other beer produced here is Zundert 10, a 10% ABV Belgian quad-style ale. The abbey does welcome visitors, but not those looking for a beer-fueled experience. The guesthouse is open only to those who seek a quiet, respectful place for a retreat, who must adhere to the rules and guidelines. It caters to individuals looking for a rest and even silence rather than beer tourism. Luckily, the abbey is a quick drive or train journey from Antwerp and Rotterdam. You can buy bottles at the abbey shop, but the brewery is not open to visitors. Distributors can be found throughout the Netherlands and Europe, and cafés and bars in the surrounding region may also stock the beers.

### 556 Quench your thirst in a castle garden

The Ter Dolen Castle Brewery tour focuses more on the history of the castle and grounds than the brewing process, but a beer in the garden awaits at the end. Armand is the Belgian strong ale and Kriek is a 4.5% cherry-infused abbey ale.

SOY, BELGIUM
## 557 Meet Brasserie Fantôme's whimsical brewer

Be sure to call at least a few days ahead to visit the eclectic Brasserie Fantôme. You will be kindly rewarded with the jovial presence of Dany Prignon, the sole proprietor. Prignon is a whimsical brewer who uses an ever-evolving variety of spices, herbs, and flowers in his special saisons. In fact, his enigmatic approach to brewing leads many to seek out his beer throughout the world, particularly in the US, the UK, and Scandinavia. Fantôme saisons vary from fruity and evanescent to robust, dark, and funky. One interesting rumor is that Prignon doesn't even like his own beers; he instead prefers stronger Trappist ales and soft drinks.

MECHELEN, BELGIUM
## 558 Spend the night in a brewery

Located halfway between Antwerp and Brussels, in the town of Mechelen, is Brouwerij Het Anker, maker of the famed Gouden Carolus ales. A brewery has existed on this site since the middle fifteenth century (at one time it served the on-site hospital), but in 1990 Charles Leclef, fifth generation of the Van Breedam family, took over the brewery and installed modern brewing equipment. The renovation also included an on-location three-star hotel where guests can sleep overnight and watch the brewery come alive over breakfast. As of 2010, a distillery and restaurant are also part of the compound.

VILLERS-DEVANT-ORVAL, BELGIUM
## 559 Don't miss Belgium's most mysterious beer

Ask nearly any brewer or beer geek what the best beer in the world is and you'll likely get a range of answers. One of the most common, however, will undoubtedly be Orval, one of Belgium's most famous Trappist beers. The beer is revered for its complex, beguiling aromas and flavors, and its chameleonlike ability to evolve and change on a dime. Visit Brasserie d'Orval/Abbaye d'Orval where the legendary beer is made and roam the monastery grounds dating back to 1132. The present-day brewery was built in 1931, and is open to the public just two days a year, on so-called "open door days." Orval produces only two beers: regular Orval, an amber-hued saison-like beer with brettanomyces; and Petite Orval, a smaller, less boozy version of the same beer available only at the café next door called À l'Ange Gardien. If you're not around on open door days, grab a goblet of the beer and plate of local cheese (also produced at the abbey) at the café.

**559**  *Right:* Belgium's Orval is one of the country's most famous Trappist beers

**BREENDONK, BELGIUM**

## 560 Dive into a Duvel

Founded in 1871, Brouwerij Duvel Moortgat is one of the largest family-owned breweries in Belgium. Its flagship beer, called simply Duvel, is a textbook strong golden Belgian ale with fruity, yeasty notes and a dry finish. Recent variations have included dry-hop additions with specific hops like Citra, Sorachi Ace, and Mosaic. Today, the company owns a variety of other breweries in Belgium (Brasserie d'Achouffe, De Koninck Brewery) and in the US (Ommegang, Boulevard, Firestone Walker). You can tour the brewery, drink in the tasting room, and even sign up for a guided degustation and tasting with a certified beer sommelier. Be sure to book in advance.

BRUSSELS, BELGIUM

## 561 **Visit the authentic, tavern-like Brewers' House Museum**

Located in the basement of Het Brouwershuis—the headquarters of the trade association of brewers in Belgium—the small, dark, tavern-like Maison des Brasseurs or Brewers' House Museum features artifacts of brewing history in Belgium. The price of entry includes a beer at the bar.

BRUSSELS, BELGIUM

## 562 **Flip out at this famed lambic and gueuze bar**

Moeder Lambic Original is a famed lambic and gueuze spot that is widely considered one of the best beer bars in the world. The menu is heavy on rare and vintage gueuze and kriek served from bottles and on draft, but it also features an assortment of Trappist ales and saisons. There are now two locations in Brussels, but the original offers a superior experience. (The second location, known as "Fontainas," sits near the famous Manneken Pis statue.) Come thirsty, but don't expect a full dinner—the short food menu features just a few snacks, like local cheeses, bread, and charcuterie.

BRUSSELS, BELGIUM

### 563 Taste some of the most revered beer in the world at Cantillon

Brasserie-Brouwerij Cantillon was founded around 1900 by Paul Cantillon and is currently run by his great-grandson Jean Van Roy, who brews every ounce of beer the brewery produces. On-site are a tasting room and shop where you can taste rare vintages of lambic and purchase merchandise.

BRUSSELS, BELGIUM

### 564 Gaze at the treasures in this museum

Next door to Cantillon is Brussels Gueuze Museum, which is dedicated to lambic production. Established in 1978, a visit features a tour of the Cantillon brewery where you can see vintage brewing equipment, examine historical brewing documents, and see where and how Cantillon's lambic beers are aged.

### 565 Savor Oud Beersel's Oude Geuze Vieille and Oude Kriek Vieille

Originally founded as a lambic producer in 1882, Oud Beersel now brews traditional gueuze and kriek as well as a line of nonlambic beers. The highlights are the Oude Geuze Vieille—a blend of one-, two-, and three-year aged lambic—and Oude Kriek Vieille, a lambic infused with cherries.

**TOP 3**

BRUSSELS, BELGIUM

# Dine at Brussels' three best beer restaurants

### 566 Bia Mara

Uberfresh fish and chips paired with an esoteric array of craft and traditional beers make this one of the best places for casual dining in Brussels. Try the Bia Mara special edition of Zinnebir from Brasserie De La Senne.

### 567 Nüetnigenough

A cozy, warm, living room–like space decked out with art nouveau and art deco artifacts. The food is hearty Belgian pub fare, while the beer list is full of obscure new Belgian craft beers.

### 568 Café Mort Subite

Opened since 1928, this classic Brussels café and brasserie serves traditional bistro fare with house-branded lambics (faro, kriek, framboise).

568

## 569 Find the famous 3 Fonteinen lambics

Besides Cantillon, Brouwerij 3 Fonteinen (3 Fountains or water source) is one of the most famous and revered lambic and gueuze producers in Belgium. Initially founded in the late-nineteenth century as a *geuzestekerij*—a gueuze blendery where lambic wort is purchased from other breweries and then blended— today it brews most of its own lambic, but still purchases a certain quantity from neighboring producers like Lindemans and De Troch. Armand Debelder is the current proprietor who learned his gueuze blending skill, knowledge, and passion from his father, Gaston Debelder. You can tour the blendery with advanced reservations or eat at the connected bustling Restaurant 3 Fonteinen.

LENNIK, BELGIUM

## 570 Seek out vintage lambic on Sunday mornings

In de Verzekering tegen de Grote Dorst is the famed lambic café in Belgium's Pajottenland region, whose name translates as "In the Insurance against Great Thirst." It's only open on Sunday mornings, on official Church holidays, and whenever a funeral is being held at the adjacent St. Ursula Church. The café and bar features one of the largest selections of rare and sought-after lambic, gueuze, and kriek bottles in the world. The pub was built in 1842, though it's gone through some changes in the intervening centuries, and is one of the main attractions of Eizeringen. For fifty-one years, a local woman named Marguerite ran the pub, but decided to close it on Christmas Eve 1999. However, two brothers—the Panneels—took over and spent five years restoring the venue. Today, it's rightly regarded as one of the best beer bars in the world for its outlandish selection of vintage lambic. Every other year (on the even years), the pub holds a lambic festival called The Night of Great Thirst, which invites both Belgian and international lambic-style beer producers.

LEMBEEK, BELGIUM

## 571 Guzzle some of the famed Boon gueuzes

Located in the town that likely gave lambic its name, Brouwerij Boon is housed in a former iron foundry near the river Senne. Boon (pronounced "Bone") crafts traditional long-aged lambics that are big in body and flavor, but well-rounded enough to convert even the most sour-averse drinker. The beers are wood-aged and blended to create balanced and approachable gueuzes. Book a tour and sample Oude Gueuze Boon, which has a mandarin-like fruitiness with a rich, firm body, and Gueuze Mariage Parfait, a blend of old and young lambic; it is stronger and has a minty aroma and a vanilla character from the oak.

**571** *Left:* Founder Frank Boon with one of Brouwerij Boon's creations

BOUILLON, BELGIUM

## 572 Quaff a Cuvée de Bouillon

Founded in 1996, Brasserie de Bouillon is a relative upstart among Belgium's historical breweries. The small, family-owned brewery makes four beers, including Cuvée de Bouillon, a 6.5% ABV bottle-conditioned blonde ale, as well as La Medieval amber ale and La Bouillonnaise brown ale. Book a tour and tasting.

THROUGHOUT BELGIUM

## 574 Sample Saison d'Erpe Mere

The first beer made by Brouwerij de Glazen Toren in Erpe-Mere, Saison d'Erpe Mere is a classic saison, blonde in color and hopped with Hallertauer hops for a spicy, hoppy, and fruity aroma. Like most de Glazen Toren beers, the bottle is wrapped in thin paper adorned with the brewery's logo.

LE ROEULX, BELGIUM

## 575 Sup a St-Feuillien beer

Established in 1873, Brasserie St-Feuillien produces abbey-style ales, including Triple and Brune Reserve as well as farmhouse-style saisons and more modern styles like IPA. The brand was dormant for a few years toward the end of the twentieth century, but is open today to visitors on the weekends and hosts monthly beer and cheese pairings on certain evenings.

**574**  *Right:* Saison d'Erpe Mere is a textbook Belgian saison with floral and fruity notes

ELLEZELLES, BELGIUM

## 573 Visit this brewery in Belgium's beautiful hill country

Located in Belgium's "hill country," Ellezelloise Brewery was purchased by the Brasserie des Géants in 2006, another local beer producer, to become Legende Brewery. Specialties include Quintine beers, a blonde ale and a pale ale, both of which are quite strong (>8% ABV), and a robust 9% ABV stout called Hercule. The surrounding hillsides are lush and idyllic. Book a tour in advance.

**GOOIK, BELGIUM**

## 576 Explore the age-old art of lambic blending

Tours of De Cam Cultureel Centrum gueuze blendery are offered every Sunday and give you a rare behind-the-scenes peek at the art of lambic blending. Formally called Oude Geuzestekerij De Cam Gooik, the blendery is located inside a 500-year-old building known as "des Heeres Landcamme." You can see the hundred-year-old barrels used for aging the lambic, which is purchased from other Pajottenland brewers.

**MONTIGNIES-SUR-ROC, BELGIUM**

## 577 Enjoy Abbaye des Rocs brews

Abbaye des Rocs is a family-run brewery that was founded in 1979, and was one of the first new "microbreweries" in Belgium. Now run by the founders' daughter Nathalie Eloir and her partner Georges Levecq, the microbrewery specializes in Belgian-style ales. Its flagship blonde ale is perfectly balanced with lively citrus notes and hop bitterness. You can visit Abbaye des Rocs and its off-site Watermill facility.

**TOURPES, BELGIUM**

## 578 Pin down this quintessential saison

The prototypical saison by which all others are judged, Saison Dupont is one of those classic beers that should be on every beer lover's bucket list. Highly carbonated and overly effervescent, the cork pops with a piercing burst and the liquid flows forth in all its orange-hued glory. In the glass, a billowing, fluffy white head forms, dispensing big aromas of white pepper, lemon peel, orange zest, and an earthy funk. The beer itself is thirst quenching and beguiling, an ale to ponder sip after sip as it unfurls its delicate, complex flavors. Lucky for us, bottles are exported throughout the world, under the label "Vieille Provision."

**BLAUGIES, BELGIUM**

## 579 Imbibe in beer from a true family-run farmhouse brewery

A true family farmhouse operation, Brasserie de Blaugies is a small brewery built into the garage of the family estate. Owners Marie-Noëlle Pourtois and husband Pierre-Alex Carlier first began brewing saisons and other farmhouse-style ales in their garage in 1988. When mashing is finished, Pourtois backs the tractor into the garage and unloads the spent grain for the livestock. Throughout Belgium, the beers, such as the textbook Saison d'Epeautre, are revered as some of the best examples of a bygone era of brewing—that of small, family farm breweries. Group visits are available by appointment (minimum fifteen people), and the beers are distributed throughout Belgium to in-the-know beer spots.

PIPAIX, BELGIUM

## 580 Observe a brew day at a Belgian saison brewery

Brasserie à Vapeur is a Wallonian saison-focused brewery that opens the last Saturday of every month and welcomes visitors to observe the brew day (a rare treat!). While you're observing the brewing activities, knock back a Saison de Pipaix, the brewery's traditional take on the iconic Wallonian saison. Reservations must be confirmed in advance.

PIPAIX, BELGIUM

## 581 Tour the hop fields of Belgium

Owned by the Dubuisson family since 1769, the traditional Brasserie Dubuisson produces Belgium's very own Bush beers (though no relation style-, quality-, or otherwise to the US's Busch beers). Tours include a walk through the hop field next to the brewery, the old and new brewing halls, fermentation areas, and the bottling line. A tasting follows.

BRUGES, BELGIUM

### 582 **Feed your senses at an interactive museum**

Bruges Beer Experience is an interactive beer museum that features exhibits like a virtual hop field and an impressive bottle wall, as well as a bar and café where you can sample sixteen different draft beers from all over the country. A gift shop sells T-shirts and other memorabilia in addition to bottles of beer to go.

# Drink at Bruges' best three bars

### 583 't Brugs Beertje

This cozy but bustling bar near the city center boasts a menu of more than 300 beers organized by region. The specialty is West Flanders beers, including rare bottles and half a dozen taps.

### 584 Café Rose Red

This bar, located on the ground floor of the Hotel Cordoeanier, features an extensive list of obscure and rare Trappist ales and other Belgian beers, many from Flanders.

### 585 Le Trappiste

Located in a thirteenth-century cellar that's been meticulously restored with original arched ceilings and columns, this bar features more than a hundred bottles and fifteen taps from which you can order flights.

584

ROESELARE, BELGIUM
## 586 Pucker up with a Flemish sour ale
Flanders is home to a variety of beer styles,
but the most iconic is Flanders red. The style is
synonymous with Brewery Rodenbach, which today is part
of the Palm Breweries group. However, the brewery dates
back to 1821 when Pedro Rodenbach emigrated from the
German Rhineland region. Soon after arriving in Flanders,
Rodenbach's grandson Eugène visited England and learned
about brewing dark ales, aging in wooden vats, and
blending. He returned and formulated what we know as
Rodenbach. Palm has spent a lot of money preserving the
original brewery and showcasing the vintage Rodenbach
cellar, which is filled with foeders—huge upright wooden
tanks. Try the medium-tart red ales like Rodenbach Classic
and Grand Cru (both blends of aged and new beer) or opt
for the rare Alexander—by appointment only. First brewed
in 1986, Alexander is a blend of two-thirds old ale and a
third younger ale, aged in wood on macerated cherries.
It's tart and sour with red wine–like tannins and funk.

MOUSCRON, BELGIUM

## 587 Discover Belgium's best hoppy ales

Founded in 1996, Brouwerij Brasserie
De Ranke—the name is a reference to the vines
on which hops grow—is a modern brewery
producing hop-forward Belgian pale ales, saisons,
and other mixed-fermentation ales. Originally
operating out of an existing brewery (Deca),
in 2005 the owners decided to start their own
brewery in Dottenijs, located in the province of
Henegouwen. You can visit a small but handsome
taproom where a range of beers is served on draft
and in bottles, and book a tour for a fee at the
adjacent brewery. XX Bitter is for all intents and
purposes the flagship beer—a bitter, hoppy pale ale
made with Brewers Gold and Hallertau Mittelfrüh.

ESEN, BELGIUM

## 588 Order an Oerbier

Oerbier from De Dolle Brouwers is one of the
most complex, intriguing beers in the world.
Brewed with a combination of six malts, whole
cone Poperinge Golding hops, and a
combination of special yeasts and bacteria, the
9% ABV amber-hued ale is stunningly delicious
with notes of caramel and toffee, but has a tart
finish that gives it a vinous character. It's one of
the world's best beers to age, evolving and
morphing into many different aromas and
flavors. In fact, the brewery encourages keen
drinkers to seek out different vintages to
compare side by side. A Special Reserva edition,
aged in Calvados barrels with a boosted ABV of
13%, is also available.

ESEN, BELGIUM

## 589 Take a gulp of the beer made by these mad brewers

De Dolle Brouwers ("The Mad Brewers") is a small, artisanal brewery that was
founded in 1980 in a historic building whose brewing history dates back to the 1800s.
The brewery makes some of the most aggressively flavored but balanced beer in West
Flanders. Of note are the Arabier, an 8% ABV hoppy beer made with whole leaf from
nearby Poperinge—the center of Belgium's hop-growing region—and Oerbier Special
Reserva (see previous page), the brewery's take on the local oud bruin–style ale. If
you visit around Christmastime, do not leave without a bottle of Stille Nacht
Christmas ale, a strong beer with fruity, figgy notes.

WESTVLETEREN, BELGIUM

## 590 Imbibe like a monk

Brouwerij Westvleteren/Saint Sixtus Abbey is perhaps the most exclusive of all the Trappist breweries in
Belgium, with sales available only at the brewery itself—by appointment only. The abbey produces just
three beers (Blond, 8, and 12) and distributes them directly to consumers via a regimented reservation
system. Its most famous beer, colloquially known as "Westy 12," is a high-gravity, quad-style ale with
robust notes of dried dark fruit and spices that was first brewed at the beginning of World War II. You
have to call ahead or reserve purchases online during specific times, and unfortunately you are not able
to tour the brewery.

# Sample five leading lambics

The current variety of lambics available can be overwhelming. Here are five of the absolute best that are sure to not disappoint.

592

### 591 De Cam Lambiek Special

A young, smooth, and fruity lambic imbued with three fruits, including yellow gooseberries, blackberries, and sour cherries.

### 592 Tilquin Oude Quetsche Tilquin à L'Ancienne

A blend of one- and two-year-aged lambic refermented on fresh purple plums (Quetsche véritable d'Alsace) for four months. Tart and fruity, it's an approachable beer even for those who don't love lambics.

### 595 Boon Mariage Parfait

This blend is the perfect marriage of three-year-aged lambic with a small percentage of young lambic for a balanced, approachable beer with notes of lime zest, tangerine, and a palate-refreshing acidity.

### 593 3 Fonteinen Hommage

An unfiltered, unpasteurized blended lambic brewed with whole fresh raspberries from the Pajottenland region as well as sour cherries.

### 594 Cantillon Fou'Foune

This blend of lambics aged 18–20 months is imparted with the fragrant aromas of French Bergeron apricots.

## 597 Get yourself a grisette or bière du pays

Two lesser-known traditional farmhouse-style ales (closely related to saison) are grisettes and bière du pays. Grisettes are usually lower in alcohol and lighter in body than saisons. Historically they were aggressively hopped and usually brewed with a significant percentage of malted wheat. Though there is some debate over the name, grisette's primary consumers were Hainaut miners who would return from the mines covered in gray dust (*gris* is "gray" in French). Bière du pays simply means "country beer," but it's sometimes called a "table beer" (especially versions made in the US). Bières du pays are low-alcohol, light, and crisp beers meant for everyday sustenance, much like a French vin de pays ("country wine").

## 596 Combine Trappist cheese with Trappist beer

In de Vrede is a bright, modern café located next door to Brouwerij Westvleteren/Saint Sixtus Abbey and pours all three beers offered by the brewery along with a selection of sandwiches, Trappist cheese, pâté plates, and desserts. You can purchase other monk-made memorabilia and occasionally bottles to go.

## 598 Relish a witbier in its home village

Witbier—meaning "white beer" in Flemish—is another example of a beer style that was once nearly extinct, but is now widely popular following an unlikely rebirth. Called *bière blanche* in French, witbier was developed as a regional specialty in the area east of Brussels, including the village of Hoegaarden, in the farmlands of Brabant. The region was rich in barley, wheat, and oats, and all were utilized in traditional witbiers. The practice of adding spices to beer was traditional here, and witbiers commonly used coriander and orange peel. All but extinct, the style was revived by Pierre Celis in 1966 when he created the famed Hoegaarden beer (now owned by Anheuser-Busch InBev) modeled on the traditional white ales of the namesake region.

# Meet the top brews from Belgium's six Trappist breweries

There are twelve Trappist breweries in the world, a full half of which are in Belgium. Here are the best beers from each of the Belgian Trappists.

### 599 Chimay Bleue

A 9% ABV dark ale, Chimay Blue is the textbook classic Chimay ale with fruity, peppery notes.

599

### 600 Westvleteren 12

Also known as the "yellow cap" beer, Westy 12 is a bottle-conditioned 10.2% ABV strong beer introduced in 1940.

### 601 Trappist Achel 8 Bruin

This amber-hued dark ale is smooth and silky with notes of figs and toffee. Even at 8% ABV, it goes down easily.

### 602 Rochefort 10

Aka "blue cap," this strong, dark ale clocks in at 11.3% ABV with a robust dried dark fruit character.

### 603 Westmalle Tripel

One of three beers produced by this brewery, Tripel is a 9.5% ABV beer first brewed in 1934.

### 604 Orval

This classic saison-like ale fermented with brettanomyces is widely considered one of the best beers in the world.

602

603

FLANDERS, BELGIUM
## 605 Taste a tart "old brown" ale

Also called Flanders Brown, oud bruin ("old brown") is a style of beer that originated from the Flanders region of Belgium. The "old" in the name refers to the aging process, which typically takes up to a year in barrels after the beer is brewed and then a secondary fermentation—another several weeks to a month—followed by bottle-conditioning for several more months. All told, the process is nearly two years in the making. The result is a tart, funky, and somewhat malty vinous brown ale. The most well-known Belgian makers are Ichtegems, Liefmans, and Petrus, while many US and new European breweries make their own takes on the style.

GUSSIGNIES, FRANCE
## 606 Hunt down this rare bière de garde

Cuvée des Jonquilles—a bière de garde from Brasserie Au Baron—is a small-release French farmhouse ale named for the brewery's surrounding daffodils. Extremely limited in production, the beer is difficult to find. But if you do come across it, expect a beautifully complex aroma mixing notes of yeast and floral hops with touches of caramel and mint.

LUCINGES, FRANCE
## 607 Cherish beer brewed with water from the French Alps

Located outside Geneva in the Haute-Savoie region of France, Brasserie des Voirons is a small brewery founded in 2013 by partners Christophe and Barbara, who were experienced in the restaurant industry, wine importing, and even ballet. They use organic hops, barley, and wheat from Germany and Belgium with water sourced from the French Alps to create their exemplary beers. Blanche is made from a base of barley and wheat for a crisp and refreshing brew. Blonde is a softer, rounder, and creamier style, while Rousse is firm and high-toned with a malty cherry sweetness and a touch of minerality. Be sure to make an appointment to visit the brewery.

ESQUELBECQ, FRANCE
## 608 Visit a family brewery in France

Proprietor Daniel Thiriez oversees the rustic Brasserie Thiriez in the middle of rolling farm country of French Flanders near the Belgium border. Thiriez trained in brewing at a Belgian university and his beers are inescapably Belgian-influenced farmhouse ales, which originated in a time when borders between France and this part of Belgium did not exist. The typical Thiriez ale boasts an earthy, slightly wild character with a pronounced hop bitterness. The beers haven't changed much since the brewery's founding in 1996, immune to trends that ebb and flow through the industry. You can stop in at the brewery for a tour and tasting, which might be led by Daniel himself, his wife, or one of their grown children. The flagship beer is the deep golden yellow La Blonde d'Esquelbecq with a creamy mouthfeel and a hint of orange peel on the finish. It's quite bitter from the local hops. Another favorite is Thiriez Extra, a Belgian pale ale that's hopped like an American IPA.

**608** *Right:* Brasserie Thiriez is a family-run brewery in rolling farm country

FRANCE

# Find the five best French bières de garde

**609 Brasserie de Saint Sylvestre 3 Monts**

From the Nord-Pas de Calais region of northeast France, this golden-colored ale is brewed with hearty Flemish hops and aged in barrels.

**610 Brasserie Theillier La Bavaisienne**

This beer from a small family brewery in Bavay is a classic French bière de garde with a slight acidity on the finish and pleasant tartness that keeps you coming back for more.

**611 Page 24 Bière de Printemps**

This springtime beer is bright and floral with a deep blonde color and complex but delicate bitterness.

**612 Brasserie La Choulette Les Sans Culottes**

With its Champagne-like carbonation, this bière de garde is luxuriously earthy with notes of honeycomb, white grape, and lemon zest.

**613 Brasserie Castelain Blonde**

Aromas of spice and fruit dominate this textbook dry bière de garde with a floral, bitter finish.

AIX-NOULETTE, FRANCE

**614 Delight in the floral qualities of these ales**

The region of French Flanders where Brasserie Saint Germain is located was once home to nearly 2,000 breweries. Today just twenty or so survive, and this brewery, which produces beers under the better-known Page 24 label, is one of the best. Specializing in traditional farmhouse ales of yore, it reveres hops and brews with a local variety, which give its beers a bright floral bitterness.

# Visit these five craft beer bars in Paris

### 615  La Fine Mousse

Twenty craft beer taps and an extensive bottle list await you at this cozy 11th arrondissement bar and restaurant with seating along an often-crowded counter or on more relaxed couches.

### 616  La Cave à Bulles

A gathering place for craft beer enthusiasts, this laid-back bottle shop offers some of the best beers from all over the world in a relaxed setting.

### 617  Le Supercoin

Bend an elbow at this garage rock-themed craft beer bar in the 18th arrondissement, which features a wide range of French craft brews.

618

### 618  Les Trois 8

High-quality artisanal beer and natural wine are served at this boisterous but chic spot. A blackboard lists draft beers, and bottle pours of both wine and beer are available.

### 619  Express de Lyon

Don't let appearances fool you. This seemingly typical French brasserie boasts an exquisite list of craft beers on draft and in bottles.

**CÉRÉ-LA-RONDE, FRANCE**

## 620 Drop in on this farmhouse brewery in the Loire Valley

A small family brewery founded by the brothers Hardouin, Brasserie de la Pigeonnelle makes some of the most classic Belgian-inspired farmhouse ales in France. The brothers started off working in the beer-distribution industry in Paris, and after years of working with imported brands like Cantillon and Dupont, they decided to start making their own beers based on these styles. Once they decided to go at it full steam ahead, they moved the operation into a family property in Touraine in the Loire Valley. Maintaining a deep love for the beers of Belgium—ranging from aggressively tart styles to lighter farmhouse ales— they started looking around for local ingredients to use. Being in the Loire meant they discovered a number of good, honest certified organic growers doing everything they needed to make completely organic beer. The first beer was called Loirette, a farmhouse-style ale made as simply as possible with malted barley, organic hops, water, and yeast. The next beers were Salamandre, a pale blonde ale, and Biere du Chameau, a wheat beer. Located on a rural farm, you can visit the brewery tasting room, but are unable to tour the facilities.

PORTO, PORTUGAL
## 621 Revel in beer flights in Porto

Catraio Craft Beer Shop is a narrow, sliver of a space. It offers bottled and canned beers, including from the UK's Beavertown and Portugal's own Gíria Craft Beer. You can get flights of draft beers in taster sizes and outdoor tables are set up in front of the shop.

PORTO, PORTUGAL
## 622 Relax in a tree-shaded beer garden

A rustic but sleek decor fills the indoor-outdoor Letraria—Craft Beer Garden Porto in the city's Fontaínhas section. Inside, order from a lengthy drafts list or do a flight of six. Outside, tuck into one of several tree-shaded nooks and crannies that make up the comfy but rustic beer garden.

LISBON, PORTUGAL
## 624 Pair tapas with local draft pours

Set in a quiet neighborhood near Lisbon's Botanical Garden, Cerveteca Lisboa offers dozens of bottled beers to stay or to go in addition to fourteen drafts from Portuguese and other European brewers. The owners and bartenders are friendly and eager to help you find something you'll love, and the bar offers a daily selection of small tapas, including local cured meats and cheeses.

LISBON, PORTUGAL
## 623 Enjoy a fun rock 'n' roll spirited craft beer experience

Founders Bruno Carrilho and Nuno Melo were on a road trip when they decided to open the colorful Cerveja Musa Brewery. Today they operate the brewery and an on-site taproom—decked out with exposed brick walls, polished concrete floors, and other minimalist decor—which serves a dozen of the brewery's American-style inspirations, including the 6.5% ABV Born in the IPA, Red Zepplin hoppy red session ale, and Ale is Love cocoa milk porter. Bottles are also available in brightly colored labels and names referencing famous rock musicians—Mick Lager Vienna lager, Frank APA (pronounced "appah," like Zappa) pale ale, and Baltic Sabbath Baltic porter.

### BARCELONA, SPAIN
## 625 Devour beers made in a brewery that used to be a garage

Located in a former garage, Barcelona's Garage Beer (not to be confused with Garage Project from New Zealand) makes modern American-style beers for the city's burgeoning independent beer scene. Drop into the taproom for a view of the fermentation vessels and brewhouse behind a glass window in the back and order a pint of Soup IPA, brewed with Citra and Mosaic hops, or Apricots, a New England–style double IPA brewed with stone fruits to enhance the fruity hop character. The vibe is casual and a little hipster with low-slung seating and a mix of stools and high-top tables.

### PAMPLONA AND BARCELONA, SPAIN
## 626 Investigate the seasonals at this brewery

Founded in 2009 in Pamplona—a one-time Hemingway outpost—Naparbier gets its name from a combination of the Basque word for its home province Navarra (*Napar*), and the German word for beer (*bier*). While the brewery was founded on just two beer styles (pilsner and dunkel), it now produces more than fourteen seasonals, including five year-round offerings. The focus is on fresh, local beers made for the community, but a creative streak also runs through head brewer Juan Rodriguez, who can craft innovative recipes, too. Check out Pumpkin Tzar Russian imperial stout brewed with habanero chiles and squash.

Photo credit: Dan Wilkinson AKA @craftbeerlovin' on Instagram hotndelicious.com

### BARCELONA, SPAIN
## 627 Discover new, rare, and unusual beverages at Kælderkold

A low-ceilinged, black-and-white tile bar serving beer and cocktails, Kælderkold is one of Barcelona's best spots for discovering new, rare, and unusual beer from Europe and North America. Check out the *Twin Peaks*–esque red room in the back with black-and-white floor tiles and red leather furniture.

**628**    *Above:* MASH, held annually in Barcelona, is a collaborative beer festival created by a number of Spanish breweries

## 628 Get smashed at MASH Craft Beer Fest

MASH Craft Beer Fest is a collaboration between Barcelona's Garage Beer, Edge Brewing, and the American importer Shelton Brothers. This annual festival brings together some of the world's youngest and hippest brewers for a two-day event celebrated under the October Barcelona sun. You'll find beers from Sweden's Stigbergets, Maine's Oxbow Brewing, the UK's Northern Monk Brewing, and Poland's Browar Stu Mostów, among many others. In addition to Garage and Edge, local representation has included Agullons (Mediona), Soma Beer (Girona), and Cyclic Beer Farm (Barcelona). Beer is dispensed on a token system for €2–3 per pour. Local restaurants provide myriad food options (Malte, Fogg Bar, Chivuo's), while all-day music comes from some of the city's hottest young DJs. An on-site bottle shop, sponsored and run by BierCaB, sells cans and bottles from local and participating breweries. All told, the festival is one of the coolest in the world with plenty of local vibes and flavor.

### BARCELONA, SPAIN

**629 Find local brews at BierCaB**

Ten of BierCaB Bar & Brewery's thirty drafts typically feature local brews, while the others come from the rest of the world and offer a range of pilsners, IPAs, sours, and stouts. The sleek, modern room is a great place to dive into the deep bottle list—featuring some real stunners and vintage offerings—while a menu of fresh fish, meat, and snacks rounds out the always-stellar experience.

### PADUA, ITALY

**630 Sip suds in the White Pony Beer Pub**

Drop into the White Pony Beer Pub & Beershop to sample wares from Padova's White Pony Microbrewery as well as imported selections like Alvinne Wild West sour ale. The house-brewed beers skew mostly to the strong beer categories, like Black Sheep imperial stout and Strongest Than Ever barleywine.

### CAMPODARSEGO, ITALY

**631 Try Italy's take on the hazy IPA**

One of the leaders of Italy's modern craft beer movement is Crak Brewery in the Veneto region near the city of Padua. It is fleshed out with a lively taproom pouring plenty of double dry-hopped (DDH) hazy IPAs and robust, cocoa-infused imperial stouts. One of the latter is Dark Chili Pond, a chile- and chocolate-infused collaboration with Florida's Cigar City Brewing, whom the brewers met in Estonia at the legendary Tallin Craft Beer Weekend. Other collaborators include Brooklyn's Other Half (which helped the brewery make a vanilla, cocoa, hazelnut, and dark cherry stout called Croccante). In Italy, the brewery's beers are available to order online, and for the rest of the world, check them out at the hippest local beer fest you can find—they typically make the rounds.

### 632 Sample experimental beers made inside a penitentiary

Pausa Café is most famously known as the "prison brewery," an actual brewery located inside a penitentiary in northern Italy. It is part of a program that helps bring inmates back into the job market (the Pausa Café brand also roasts coffee and makes bread and baked goods, among other things). Though the brewery isn't open to the public for obvious security reasons, the beers are available throughout Italy, Europe, and the US, and include some stunning examples of Italian craft beer creativity. Taquamari, for instance, is brewed with a blend of tapioca, quinoa, amaranth, and basmati rice (hence the name) for a smooth, saison-style beer. Tosta, meanwhile, is a 12.5% ABV barleywine-style ale infused with cocoa.

### 633 Fall in love with these ales at Loverbeer

Combining a love for Belgian-style sour ales with the regional fruit and *Vitis vinifera* grape varieties surrounding the Piedmont-based brewery, Birrificio Loverbeer, owned by brewer Valter Loverier, crafts some unique and exciting wine-inspired fruited ales. Take BeerBrugna, for example, a wild sour ale aged with local Piedmontese Damaschine plums, which lend the beer a distinctive nutty fig and banana bread flavor. Or BeerBera, a play on the local wine Barbera, which incorporates barbera grapes with a lambic-inspired-based beer fermented with wild yeast and aged in oak barriques. You can taste these and many other beers at the brewery itself, open only by appointment with Loverier.

### 634 Learn about the beginnings of craft beer in Italy

If the founding of Italy's craft beer movement can be credited to one individual, that person would be Birra Baladin's Teo Musso. He began Baladin as a beer-centric bar, but in 1996 installed a brewing system and began experimenting with indigenous ingredients and rare and unusual spices, grains, and culinary ingredients. Thus set the hallmark of Italian craft beer—Belgian-inspired, innovative, creative, and wine-influenced—for the decade-plus to come. Though the era of American craft beer influence has now fully permeated, with hazy IPAs and sweet adjunct stouts, Italy is still synonymous with the foundations built on Musso and Baladin's legacy.

VENICE, ITALY

## 635 Unwind with a brew along the Venetian canals

A canal-front spot to sip beers from all over the world, Ormesini da Aldo is Venice's premier beer spot. Grab a seat at one of just a handful of outdoor tables and soak in views of gondolas passing by. A fridge inside offers bottled beers from Italy's Birrificio del Ducato and Birrificio Pontino, among many others.

ITALY

## 637 Taste the magic of Tipopils

Though technically in the same beer family as Italy's best-known beer, Tipopils pilsner from northern Italy's Birrificio Italiano has nothing to do with Peroni. Tipopils, a hoppy American-influenced Italian pilsner, may be the best-loved beer among beer geeks everywhere. At first sip, there's nothing particularly impressionistic about the beer—in fact, the brewery admits, "It might seem the most normal of our own beers, yet it is the one that leaves its mark the most, the one that makes you fall in love." However, after several pints, you'll likely be singing this beer's praises. Its key is the embodiment of the ideal light beer that has been impressed upon most of the world over the past century. It is a perfect example of that craft, a paramount balance of crispness, malts, hops, and elegance that comes together. It is distributed globally.

TORRECHIARA, ITALY

## 636 Ensconce yourself at a brewery in a castle on a hill

Located in a castle positioned atop a hillside of vineyards in Italy's Emilia-Romagna region (near the town of Parma), the quirky Birrificio Torrechiara aka Panil Brewery makes a variety of Belgian-influenced beers. The most well-known outside of Italy is the famed Panil Barriquée, a Flemish-inspired sour brown ale. The ale is complex, nuanced, and balanced, and undergoes a triple fermentation—in stainless steel, oak barrels, and finally in the bottle itself—and is unpasteurized for that authentic wild yeast flavor. Other beers include Divina, a spontaneous ale, and Raphael, a vinous red ale aged in oak. On-site there's a café offering bottles to drink or to go.

BOLOGNA, ITALY
### 638 Drink fresh beer in the heart of Italy's culinary region

Birra Cerqua is a handsome brewpub that pours some of the freshest beer in this culinary-obsessed town. Four house-brewed beers are always available, including Four Hops American IPA and PorQUA porter, and you'll find a small selection of edibles on offer.

BOLOGNA, ITALY
### 639 Pair pizza with beer

Gourmet wood-fired pizza and specialty craft beer sing in perfect harmony at Ranzani 13. The restaurant's menu features more than forty items to choose from—check out the burrata, cured duck breast, and orange pizza—while the beer selection features specialty drafts and an extensive bottle list from across Europe.

SORAGNA, ITALY
### 640 Sip a spicy Verdi stout

Along with Baladin and Del Borgo, Birrificio del Ducato—was one of the forerunners of Italy's initial craft beer boom. It still creates some of the best beers in the country with perennial favorites like Verdi Imperial Stout—brewed with chile peppers for a subtle but noticeable heat—and the signature Viæmilia, a pretty, highly refined lager with floral notes. The beers pair particularly well with the food of nearby Parma, a region known for long-aged hams (Prosciutto di Parma) and cheese (Parmigiano Reggiano). Catch them at beer bars throughout Italy, Europe, and the US.

FLORENCE, ITALY
### 641 Grab a pint near Florence's Santa Maria Novella terminal

Located near Florence's main train station, Birrificio Mostodolce brewpub features a tidy collection of brews made in-house, including Martellina Belgian strong ale (brewed with a local honey variety) and Pepita, a crisp and light pilsner. Food-wise, dig into generous plates of pastas, pizzas, and sandwiches.

MONTEPULCIANO, ITALY
### 642 Enjoy a tipple in Tuscany

Birrificio L'Olmaia is a small brewery in Tuscany's Val d'Orcia region—surrounded by picturesque vineyards and rolling golden hills. It produces English-, Belgian-, and American-inspired beers. Try La "9," an English strong ale with notes of candied bitter orange and caramel. Visit the small shop and tasting room for beer to go and merchandise.

**BORGOROSE, ITALY**

## 643 Try an Italian imperial pilsner

Founded in 2005 a couple of hours' drive northeast of Rome in a small village along the A24 highway, Birra del Borgo crafts a range of American- and Belgian-inspired ales with that textbook Italian twist. The flagship beer, ReAle, is a traditional British IPA with intense aromas from the addition of American-grown hops, while Duchessa is a spelt saison with notes of banana, pineapple, and tropical fruit, and a pleasantly dry finish. One of the brewery's highest-profile beers is My Antonia, an "imperial pilsner" that began as a collaboration with the US's Dogfish Head Brewery. (The collaboration has since dissolved due to Del Borgo's acquisition by Anheuser-Busch InBev in 2016.) Newly flush with capital, the brewery now has multiple locations in Rome.

**ROME, ITALY**

## 644 Sail the seas of beer

Un Mare di Birra (the "sea of beer") festival is an annual event held in Rome in the spring. Publicans from the city's best-known beer bars gather to pour their most exclusive and special beers. In 2011 and 2016, the festival literally took to the seas for beer-fueled overnight excursions to Barcelona aboard a cruise ship.

**NAPLES, ITALY**

## 645 Check out this hip, young bar

Throngs of young craft beer enthusiasts flock to the small, brightly lit Hoppy Ending bar and bottle shop in the Vomero neighborhood. Four always-rotating drafts dispense beers from across Italy and Europe, including modernized hoppy IPAs from Crak Brewery. Be sure to check out the skateboard decks adorning the walls.

**VALLETTA, MALTA**

## 646 Consume esoteric brews in Malta

67 Kapitali is a small café and craft beer bar serving Maltese foods and a range of esoteric beers. It offers a fun, convivial experience. The Guinness sign out front (which has been lettered over with "CRAFT BEERS") sets the tone for an irreverent, fun-loving spot where nine craft beers are offered on draft along with Maltese snacks.

# Drop into Rome's ten best craft beer bars

### 647  Stavio

Housed in three exposed brick-arched rooms in a former grain storage space, this gastropub offers a variety of sour beers and natural wines.

### 648  Birra Più

The staff at this small bottle shop and bar are big fans of American-style craft beer, so expect plenty of imported IPAs and pale ales in addition to locally brewed varieties.

### 649  Bir & Fud

Located practically across the narrow cobblestone street from Ma Che is the newer Bir & Fud, featuring regional Italian craft beers.

### 650  Hey Hop

This bar in the southern Garbatella section of Rome offers rare and unusual beers from Italy, Europe, and the US. Knock back a tart Fantôme Saison or an AleSmith Wee Heavy.

### 651  My-Ale

Specializing in Birra Artigianali (artisanal beer), My-Ale features craft beers from all over Italy, including Milan's BrewFist and Rurale. The decor creates a cozy spot for a quick drink and bite.

### 652  Pizzarium

Gabriele Bonci, Rome's undisputed pizza master, serves his fare at this tiny shop with a small, interesting selection of craft beer. With nowhere to sit, enjoy your pizza and beer streetside.

### 653  Brasserie 4:20

With more than forty beers on draft in the main beer hall, this brewpub offers one of the largest selections of draft beer in Rome. An extensive list of vintage Belgian beers rounds out the stellar experience.

### 654  Open Baladin

One of Rome's original craft beer destinations, Open Baladin is an outpost of northern Italy's Birra Baladin. Dozens of taps feature Teo Musso's unique creations like Nora, a spiced ale brewed with the ancient grain Kamut.

### 655  Be.Re.

Located steps from the Vatican, this Ma Che–affiliated spot serves esoteric craft beer (some in ceramic mugs) alongside *trapizzini*, triangular sandwiches filled with savory stuffings like chicken cacciatore.

### 656  Ma Che Siete Venuti A Fà

Known locally simply as Ma Che (pronounced "mah kay"), this spot in the Trastevere area is easily Rome's best-known craft beer bar. Rare and exotic drafts are on offer as well as a rotating Cantillon tap.

GREECE

# Step inside these three top Greek craft breweries

### 657 Solo

If you're seeking high-quality craft beer on the island of Crete, this is your place. Based in the Kallithea region near Heraklion's industrial zone, Solo brews American-inspired hoppy ales, including IPAs and imperial IPAs.

### 658 Santorini Brewing

Santorini's small eponymous brewery offers a range of styles and flavors, including Crazy Donkey IPA and Slow Donkey barleywine. A small tasting room offers samples and bottles to go.

### 659 Septem Microbrewery

Located on Evia, Greece's second-largest island, Septem brews seven different ales and lagers, each named after a day of the week. Try Thursday's Red Ale or Saturday's Porter.

ST. PETERSBURG, RUSSIA

## 660 Live it up in St. Petersburg's top beer bar

Located near the city center, Top Hops is a hip craft beer pub that offers spectacular views of the Fontanka River. The bar's name is self-evident, boasting an extensive but well-curated collection of local and imported craft beer. On tap are twenty rotating drafts and in bottles nearly 200 additional lagers and ales from breweries in Russia, Belgium, the UK, the Netherlands, the US, and Scandinavia. You'll also find a nice selection of hard ciders from France and Spain. Food-wise, dig into a selection of Tex-Mex dishes—burritos, chips and guacamole, quesadillas, tacos, and nachos—while you listen to an eclectic mix of reggae, jazz, and soul piping through the sound system.

### 661 Drink beer from all over the world at RULE

Close to thirty drafts dispense beers from all over the world at RULE Taproom, a dimly lit, hipster beer temple. Settle in with a short pour of Buddy Bear, an 11% ABV barleywine from the Netherlands, or Thribble Currant American wild ale from California's Anderson Valley Brewing. Don't miss the cheeky handcraft tap handles designed from quirky artifacts.

### 662 Take your friends to this bar for craft beer

All Your Friends is a no-nonsense bar that offers a good variety of Russian and imported craft beers to a bearded and tattooed clientele. TVs show sports and games, so it isn't the best spot for deep conversation, but the bar's commitment to offering interesting and obscure craft beer is as deep as any spot in the capital city.

### 663 Spend time in one of the best beer bars in the world

Perennially ranked by websites like RateBeer and Untappd as the best beer bar in Russia, the long-standing Craft rePUBlic offers one of the best selections of Russian craft beer anywhere in the world. With nearly two dozen beers on draft, a full half are typically from the motherland, while the rest are sourced from the US, Belgium, Denmark, and even more obscure locales like Hungary. Meanwhile, the bar's whitewashed interior, with its low ceilings, blonde woods, and arched roof, is reminiscent of the moloko bars featured in the movie *A Clockwork Orange*. The clientele is typically young and hip, most with knowledge of craft beer, but not snobby about it.

# Middle East & Africa

Given the region's modern propensity toward widespread alcohol prohibition, it may seem odd today that the Middle East is the birthplace of brewing. But indeed it was ancient Sumerians living in the Fertile Crescent who provided the first written accounts of intentional beer brewing, with a recipe for a nutritious, grain-based fermented beverage that was essentially liquid bread. Today, brewing isn't exactly widespread in the region, but there are a few strongholds where you'll find contemporary breweries and brewpubs. Lebanon and Israel in particular feature several well-established craft brewers, while Jordan is finally seeing its first breweries come online.

   Meanwhile, Africa offers its own traditional brewing traditions that are ripe for exploring. In South Africa, there's the Zulu beer tradition, and in Ethiopia and Eritrea, tella beer made from pulverized *gesho* and malted barley. Throughout the continent, you'll find a special variety of high-alcohol Guinness brewed specifically for certain markets. The urban centers of South Africa also feature modern craft breweries, many of which utilize native South African hop varieties.

### YEREVAN, ARMENIA
## 664 Grab yourself an Armenian brew

If you ever find yourself in Armenia's capital city, be sure to drop in on Dargett Craft Beer, an open, airy brewery with about half a dozen different Americanized craft brews on draft. These include the citrusy, piney Milestones black IPA and Armenia Invicta, an imperial IPA brewed with Italian friends at Canediguerra brewery.

### FUHEIS, JORDAN
## 665 Drink Jordanian beer with a view

Founding a brewery in Jordan—a country where the population is more than 90% Muslim—is no small feat. So when Yazan Karadsheh opened his Carakale Brewing in 2013, it was a major stepping stone in establishing a craft beer scene. The move was two long years in the making, with Karadsheh petitioning the government to give him a brewery license and then convincing local officials to approve a manufacturing facility for the brewery. Located just miles north of the Dead Sea, Karadsheh produces gateway craft beers that appeal to the country's small drinking population, a group who are familiar with European exports like Heineken and Amstel. His first beer was called simply Blonde Ale, which is a light, crisp, and refreshing sessionable beer with gentle toasty flavors. Next was an English-style Pale Ale, which aimed to introduce Jordanians to the idea of hoppy beers. Since then, Karadsheh has expanded his portfolio to include experimental beers like Dead Sea-rious gose, brewed with salt from the

Dead Sea and pink grapefruit from Jordan Valley, and Black Camel Spider imperial porter infused with Jordanian dates and Bedouin coffee roasted with cardamom. You can visit the brewery, which has magnificent views of Jordan's Blue Canyon, and enjoy a tour and tasting.

**BATROUN, LEBANON**

## 666 Sip beside the seaside

If you find yourself feeling thirsty in Lebanon, take a trip to the Colonel Brewery. Founded in 2014, it is Lebanon's most modern craft brewery. The chic seaside brewpub offers American and European-style fare (burgers, nachos) to pair with its small but tasty selection of beers. Try Black Irish stout, a robust and bitter sipper, or Colonel Lager Beer, a properly bitter Czech-inspired pilsner.

**MAZRAAT YACHOUA, LEBANON**

## 667 Enjoy some of the Middle East's finest beer

Founded in 2006 by Mazen Hajjar, 961 Beer was for years one of the Middle East's only craft breweries. Today, it has grown to produce more than 300,000 cases annually, including its regular series of Witbier, Porter, and Red Ale, as well as specialty brews like Lebanese Pale Ale, an English-style IPA spiced with Lebanese za'atar, sumac, anise, and mint. The brewery is located in the foothills of Mazraat Yachoua, overlooking Beirut and the Mediterranean Sea. You can sample the beer at the Route 961 bar and restaurant in Beirut.

**BEQAA VALLEY, LEBANON**

## 668 Try a fresh, locally brewed lager

The idea behind Beirut Beer was to create a simple, refreshing beer similar to the great international lagers of the world (Heineken, Coors, etc.) that was 100% Lebanese owned and made. The beer itself—made by brewery Kassatly Chtaura—is pale, slightly bitter, and completely unassuming. You could say that it is nothing to write home about, but the idea of drinking a fresh, locally brewed lager should appeal to any beer lover.

**TAYBEH, RAMALLAH, PALESTINIAN TERRITORIES**

## 669 Drink at one of the Middle East's first modern breweries

Often cited as the Middle East's first microbrewery, Taybeh Brewery was founded in 1994 by brothers Nadim and David Khoury. Legend has it that, despite most Palestinians' religious aversion to alcohol, President Yasser Arafat was an early supporter of the brewery because it meant less reliance on alcohol from Israel. Today the brewery produces six different beers: Golden, Light, Dark, Amber, Non-alcoholic, and White.

**BIRZEIT, RAMALLAH, PALESTINIAN TERRITORIES**

## 670 Sip a shepherd's brew

Located in a predominantly Christian town north of Ramallah, Birzeit Brewery—or "shepherds brewery"—is one of the Middle East's most exciting new breweries, focusing on modern craft beer styles. Its core lineup includes Shepherds Blonde (actually a pilsner), Shepherds Amber ale, and Shepherds Stout, a classic American-style stout with notes of espresso and dark chocolate. Seasonals include Summer Ale, Wheat, and even a Christmas beer infused with cinnamon and clove for the holidays. In 2016, the brewery founded Shepherds Beer Festival, a two-day beer, music, and comedy festival that was one of the first of its kind in the region. You can make an appointment to tour the facility—a quaint block building on the outskirts of town.

**669** *Right:* Taybeh Brewery in the Palestinian Territories

TEL AVIV, ISRAEL
## 671 Drink at the Dancing Camel

Founded in 2005 in a circa-1930s grain storage facility, The Dancing Camel Brewery was Israel's first craft beer producer and is now one of the most well-regarded outfits in the Middle East. Operating as a brewpub with Western-inspired dishes—sausages, fries, pretzels—the brews range from the classic Blond Ale to a Leche del Diablo wheat ale infused with *shaata*, a locally grown chile variety.

TEL AVIV AND JERUSALEM, ISRAEL
## 672 Sit curbside at the BeerBazaar

With locations in both Jerusalem and Tel Aviv, BeerBazaar is Israel's mini-chain of scrappy craft beer spots. The digs aren't much to look at—folding chairs and tables, rough-hewn street-side bars—but the beer is attractively presented and includes some of the best breweries of the region.

JERUSALEM, ISRAEL
## 673 Get thee to the Jerusalem Beer Festival

Held annually since 2004 in summer (usually August), this open-air craft beer festival is one of the most important events of the year for Israel's burgeoning craft beer industry. It now comprises more than 120 different Israeli craft brews, ranging from the country's largest producers to its smallest indie boutique breweries. Live music from rock bands, rap acts, and DJs fills the air—this lends the festival a concert- or rave-like feel—and an array of restaurants serve beer-friendly snacks and plates. There's even an on-site market for shoe, clothing, and souvenir shopping.

የአ/ገብርኤልና
የወ/ገብርኤል
ምግብና ጠጅ ቤት

## ETHIOPIA AND ERITREA
### 674 Track down tella in Ethiopia and Eritrea

Known as tella, talla, farsoo, or suwa, the traditional Ethiopian and Eritrean brew is made with a hodgepodge of grains, adjuncts, herbs, roots, and spices for a truly unique beer. The primary base is typically sorghum and *teff* (a type of annual bunch grass), but may also include raw wheat, barley, and corn. Instead of hops, a combination of dried spices, herbs, and roots are added as bittering agents, including *gesho* (a type of buckthorn). Honey may be added for fermentable sugars and to dry out the finish. The typical ABV range is around 3–6% and the brew often has a smoky, somewhat sour flavor from wild bacteria and yeast. Most tella is homebrewed, so you won't likely find it at a bar or restaurant. Instead, you'll have to find a tella house (often just someone's private home), which are popular gathering spaces.

## HARAR, ETHIOPIA

### 675 Sample this sweet stout

Chocolaty Harar Hakim Stout is designed after the export stouts that were once so popular in Ethiopia. Brewed by the Harar Brewery, it features rich notes of raisins, plums, and figs with a toasty aroma and dry finish. You'll find the beer is surprisingly refreshing and easy drinking, despite its rich character.

## CASABLANCA, MOROCCO

### 676 Sample European exports in Casablanca

Craft beer isn't really a thing in this part of the world, but Casablanca's La Bodega, a small Spanish-style restaurant, bar, and nightclub, offers a small but solid selection of imported European beers. Try a refreshing Hoegaarden witbier paired with a plate of chorizo and jamon made from Pata Negra pigs.

**TOP 9**

## SOUTH AFRICA

# Set your foot inside one (or more) of South Africa's top nine breweries

South Africa has a young, burgeoning craft beer scene. Here are nine of the best places to sample it.

### 677 Drifter Brewing

Located in Cape Town's seaside Woodstock neighborhood, this young craft brewery is best known for its Ocean Aged beer series in which bottles of beer are literally aged under the sea for a year.

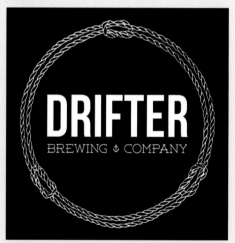

### 678 Mad Giant

Founded in 2014, this Johannesburg-based brewery and pub crafts up-to-the-minute beverages like Jozi Carjacker New England-style IPA, and Whisky Barrel Porter, a whiskey barrel-aged porter.

### 679 Jack Black's Brewing

Specializing in routine European-style ales and lagers, Cape Town's Jack Black's features a spacious taproom with dark wood communal tables, growler fills, and several drafts.

### 681 Anvil Ale House

This Dullstroom-based brewery produces an array of European and American-inspired beers. Try Mjölnir, a West Coast-style IPA, or Biere d'Saison, a warm, fermented Belgian-inspired farmhouse ale with fruity aromas.

### 683 Sedgefield Craft Brewery

This tiny family-run brewery handcrafts each batch of beer on-site—Blonde Ale, Irish Red Ale, and India Pale Ale—and offers tall pours to sip in the small but comfy outdoor *biergarten*.

### 684 Urban Brewing

Cape Town's Urban Brewing is an industrial-chic oasis serving well-crafted ales, lagers, and ciders in the Hout Bay suburb.

### 685 Berg River Brewery

Located on the banks of the Berg River in Paarl, this brewery features a wooden-walled tasting room and event space with around four German-inspired beers available on draft and in bottles.

### 680 Craft Wheat & Hops

A bistro and restaurant specializing in craft beer and tapas, Stellenbosch's Craft Wheat & Hops features fifteen local beers on draft as well as another twenty in bottles. The wood-fired bakery and kitchen make it a comfy place to drink.

### 682 Beer House

Two locations of this craft beer bar and restaurant—Cape Town and Johannesburg—offer what are likely South Africa's largest selection of craft brews. It has a color-coded system, which helps you to pick between light and refreshing beers (yellow) or fruity and funky flavors (purple).

682

MULTIPLE AFRICAN COUNTRIES

## 686 Discover "African Guinness"

Despite the fact that most Africans don't celebrate
St. Patrick's Day, they still love drinking Guinness—
its sales make up more than 40% of the beer sold
throughout the continent. However, the Guinness
found here isn't the frothy Guinness Draught or extra
stout you'll find in bars and stores from Dublin to
New York, but is instead a gussied-up version called
Foreign Extra Stout. The "African Guinness" is based
on a high-strength recipe that was exported here
during colonial times (the eighteenth and nineteenth
centuries), and persists to this day. How is it different?
Instead of 100% malted barley, a significant portion
of corn and/or sorghum is added to the malt bill,
which can produce a more bitter flavor, but mellower
mouthfeel and texture. Since the 1960s, it's been dosed
with a flavor extract brewed in Ireland called a
"concentrated essence," which lends it that house flavor
that is unmistakably Guinness. It's also considerably
higher in alcohol (around 7.5% ABV) compared to the
4.5% of regular Guinness. A similar version is also quite
popular in Caribbean and Central American countries.

SOUTHERN AFRICA

## 687 Take part in a Zulu beer tradition

Umqombothi, a traditional beverage native to the Zulu
culture of southern Africa, is made using a combination
of maize, sorghum, and malted barley. It is typically
brewed over a wood-fired kettle called a *potjie* and
left to steep overnight. Slightly sour and funky, it's
purportedly full of vitamin B and is an integral part
of several Zulu culture ceremonies and rituals.

**686** *Left:* "African Guinness" is a stronger version of the Irish
drink and has a more bitter flavor

# Australia &
# New Zealand

Without a doubt, Australia and New Zealand are two of the most exciting places for modern beer making. Both feature robust industries chock-full of boundary-pushing, experimental, and unquestionably impressive breweries. It doesn't hurt that both Australia and New Zealand grow some of the most coveted hops in the world.

In Australia, look for beers made with Galaxy and Vic Secret hops for big notes of passion fruit, citrus, and peach. In New Zealand, check out brews made with the inimitable Nelson Sauvin variety, with a distinct gooseberry and white wine-like character.

### CAIRNS, AUSTRALIA
### 688 Help save wildlife while drinking beer

Tropically based Barrier Reef Brewing rates its passion for wildlife first before brewing, and actively donates a portion of its profits to charities that support welfare and maintenance of its local fauna. You can visit its Two Turtles (some of the animals it donates funds to) Taproom, and try the brewery's core range, which features beer with 5% ABV or below.

### BRISBANE, AUSTRALIA
### 689 Sip suds in a converted bus depot

Starting in a 1940s steel bus depot, whose features Newstead Brewing retains, the second venue is more sleek and contemporary. The brewery has thirty-two taps offering a core range, seasonals, and differing small-batch brews—a fantastic excuse to check out both spots.

### BRISBANE, AUSTRALIA
### 690 Pair local seafood with local beer

Green Beacon Brewing has a nautically themed core range and the team is passionate about local seafood matched with its beer. Visit earlier in the week to enjoy wider choices with food trucks present. Try the summer-quenching 7 Bells passion fruit gose. Growth has seen the brewery receive accolades at the Australian International Beer Awards.

### BRISBANE, AUSTRALIA
### 691 Check out this boozy bi-level bar

With beer on tap both upstairs and downstairs at the Bloodhound Bar, as well as a great selection of bottled brews, expect to find the occasional gem on tap (for example, Canadian Les Trois Mousquetaires' Porter Baltique) with great bar snacks and pub meals. It holds a range of events upstairs, from open-mic nights to zine fairs and local book launches.

## 692 Toss back a brewski or two

The North American slang for "beer" name suggests the atmosphere encouraged at the Brewski Bar. With more than 150 beers, local regulars include Newstead and Green Beacon; nationals Boatrocker, Hop Nation, and 3 Ravens; and international examples from Belgium, Germany, New Zealand, Scandinavia, the UK, and the US. There are six rooms to enjoy beer and noms, with an American-inspired menu—vegetarian and vegan options are also available.

## 693 Perfect your pinball game at this "barcade"

Netherworld is a "barcade" that offers arcade games from the 1970s to the present day. Along with twenty-four beers on tap and delicious burgers, you can find board games, pinball machines, and retro consoles. You can also attend regular gaming nights (*D&D*, anyone?), live music, movie screenings, and trivia.

## 694 Soak in the history at this historic hotel

For a tipple in an essential part of Brisbane's colonial history, visit any of the rooms (two bars, one dining room) in the heritage-listed Port Office Hotel, which first opened in 1864, and has survived floods. The food menu online is extensive, but it's best to use your preferred beer app to see what's offered on tap.

BRISBANE, AUSTRALIA

### 695 Order in at a local watering hole

The cozy Scratch Bar lists its bottled and canned beer according to ingredients and drinking preference: mid, session, hops, malt, and yeast. What's pouring on its nine taps is listed on its website and you'll find that this is updated frequently. There's not much available foodwise—there are cheeseboards—instead, you're encouraged to have food delivered or brought in.

BRISBANE, AUSTRALIA

### 696 Get your game on at this bar

Featuring a mix of national and a smattering of international beers on tap, Saccharomyces Beer Café also offers bottled and canned beer. Visit in person to discover what is in stock, or peruse its Untappd and Now Tapped venue links. You'll find enticing food and drink specials, trivia evenings, and happy hours. The café frequently hosts brewery tap takeovers, beer launches, comedy, or pinball nights, and the occasional movie screening thrown in. You can also book functions, and they're conveniently close to South Brisbane train station.

**696**   *Above:* Saccharomyces Beer Café offers an array of local drafts plus nightly events

## 697 Take a break from brewery hopping at this hip restaurant

Take a break from the brewery tours, visits, and tastings, and focus on the culinary offerings at the stylish, intimate Catbird Seat Bistro restaurant. Ask the staff what's available on tap, and peruse the modest bottled beer list for a great intro to local craft beer staples with a couple of internationals, including Anchor Steam Ale.

## 698 Drink better-than-average beer at this local franchise

Although Ze Pickle is a franchise with its four locations in popular vacation destinations, don't judge it as average. Its twelve taps feature Australian staple beers and breweries, with a few reserved for internationals from Denmark, Italy, and New Zealand. While there, you can munch on Mexican snacks and American comfort food.

## 699 Taste the rainbow of dessert-influenced beers

Every brew Bacchus Brewing makes has some weird, wonderful flavor spin on many standard styles. Expect flavor combinations like Peanut Brittle Gose, After Dinner Stout (think choc mint without the sweetness), or the subtly flavored White Chocolate Pilsner. When you visit, you'll find twenty-plus taps and scores of bottles to choose from (on average it makes three beers a week, but can make as many as twelve different ones a day). To satisfy your appetite, there are also rotating food trucks that cater alongside the brewery kitchen. Over the years, the brewery has picked up a slew of national awards, and although it's been in operation since 2005, it was from 2010 onward that saw it adopt its unique approach.

## 700 Go bar- and brewery-hopping in a helicopter

Got money to burn while Down Under? Consider watching the world go by from above, while following an unusual and extremely scenic route using a unique transportation mode: the helicopter. Pterodactyl Helicopters offers a couple of beery excursions: for the Pub Lunch Tour option, you'll visit eight pubs and one brewery (The Scenic Rim Brewery) in southeast Queensland. For the Country Pub Crawl, for two to six people (two-person minimum applies), you can take a whirlwind all-day tour of five country pubs for a quick beer in locations west of Brisbane.

**TOP 7**

VARIOUS WINE REGIONS THROUGHOUT AUSTRALIA

# Visit the seven best breweries in Australian wine country

### 701 Cheeky Monkey Brewery

The beer at this Margaret River brewery is made with fresh rainwater. It has a small core range and also produces cider.

### 702 Colonial Brewing

Colonial Brewing has two facilities: the "western" Margaret River brewery opened in 2004, and expanded to create an "eastern"' brewery in Port Melbourne in 2015. Both welcome customers.

### 703 Lobethal Bierhaus

Forty-five minutes from the city in Adelaide Hills, this brewery has twelve taps and four handpumps. It uses locally sourced produce, and once brewed its standard Pale Ale with quinces for a BrewBoys collaboration. The result? Quince Ale.

### 704 Murray's Craft Brewing

Considering itself "brewers first, and winemakers second," Murray's boasts seven grape varieties grown on premises. Try the Port Stephens' brewery's Whale Ale and Angry Man, plus limited Anniversary Ales or Heart of Darkness, and rare collaborations like Sutton Hoo with New Zealand's Townshend Brewery.

### 705 Burleigh Brewing

Located at Burleigh Heads on the Gold Coast, this husband-and-wife-run brewery is strictly just outside of wine country. Try Black Giraffe Black Coffee Lager, which deserves the five medals it has won at the World Beer Championships.

704

### 706 Red Hill Brewery

Having rebranded in 2018, this Mornington Peninsula brewery is famous for its annual hop harvest of organically grown Hallertauer, Tettnanger, Golding, and Willamette, which attract people from all over the state.

### 707 Granite Belt Brewery

If you want luxurious accommodation neighboring national parks, this brewery near Stanthorpe is worthy of consideration. Don't forget to try the brewers' platter: four dishes matched to Granite's beers.

**BYRON BAY AND MURWILLUMBAH, AUSTRALIA**

## 708 Become a more adventurous drinker at this brewery

Stone & Wood Brewing started off in Byron Bay in 2008 before expanding enough to need a second facility in Murbah in 2014. It's the Byron Bay one that welcomes tourists and visitors, so drop in and enjoy its range alongside an ever-changing menu of bar snacks. The sessionable Pacific Ale is one of those beers that everyone seeks once more timid drinkers commit to being more adventurous—it has tropical fruit notes and a refreshing, crisp finish, and is a staple in the national beer landscape. Try the brewery's occasional seasonals, such as Jasper Ale, a hoppy red that has a contrasting flavor profile to its flagship beer. Notably, the newer Melbourne-based Fixation Brewing started out brewing on its premises before its southern relocation.

CURRUMBIN, AUSTRALIA

### 709 Taste the "X" factor in this award-winning XPA

With its sleek, minimalist cans and beers with catchy names for one-offs like Black Metal Disco (stout), All Day Breakfast (porter), or Captain Sensible (Australian pale ale), Queensland microbrewery Balter Brewing has been attracting the attention of craft beer lovers, particularly with its flavorsome but incredibly sessionable award-winning XPA. Book a brewery tour, which includes a tasting paddle of four beers, and a branded "stubby" holder (foam receptacle to hold your cold can or bottle while drinking), with a maximum of ten participants. Balter has collaborated with breweries such as Brewmanity and Bavarian Brewing Competition.

SYDNEY, AUSTRALIA

### 710 Drink from generously sized cans

Established in 2012 in Sydney's Northern Beaches, Modus Operandi Brewing has won over drinkers with its trademark big, labeled cans (be sure to try Sonic Prayer and Former Tenant from its core range). The seasonal beers also come in the same generously sized cans. The brewery has collaborated with Bridge Road Brewing, Fixation Brewing, and Wheaty Brewing Corps—the latter for whom it has a permanent guest tap on-site (the second reserved for Little Bang). With twelve beers on tap, there's bound to always be something interesting to enjoy, and its "method of operation" means that, while you can experience food and live music at the brewery, the beer is always the first priority.

SYDNEY, AUSTRALIA

### 711 Sip ales infused with rare Australian ingredients

Based along Sydney's Northern Beaches, NOMAD Brewing makes thought-provoking bottle- and keg-conditioned brews that come in eye-catching cans or bottles—whose availability has only increased since the brewery started canning. When it first set up in 2013, NOMAD had three core beers, and its Jet Lag IPA—with the trademark addition of native finger lime—remains as popular as ever today. The team loves using rare native Australian ingredients or barrels in the limited releases. The Freshie Moka gose, using local coffee, is inspired by a Napoli tradition of sprinkling salt into your morning espresso. The brewery has attracted attention from international colleagues such as Birra del Borgo, Jester King, Stone, and Dogfish Head's Sam Calagione—he asked the brewery to create a special beer (Cross Pallet Nation, an American amber/red ale) for the launch of his magazine, *Pallet*, in 2015. The Transit Lounge is the brewery's bar, which has eleven taps, a guest tap, and an excellent bottle selection. Families and their four-legged friends are welcome to hang out in the beer garden, and enjoy live music and food truck fare on weekends.

## 712 Choose among hundreds of beers

With several spaces to drink come rain or shine, more than a hundred beers to choose from at its bottle shop (corkage applies to drinks on-premises), and ample usual suspects on tap, The Oaks Hotel is a must-visit establishment. Pop in for a drink or a meal (pub classics, pizza, steaks, and bar snacks) in any one of its beautifully decorated rooms (1940s decor and features), or the beer garden.

**712** *Above:* Hundreds of different beers await drinks enthusiasts at The Oaks Hotel

## 713 Discover breakfast cereal-inspired beers

Sydney-based 4 Pines Brewing started in 2008 before being acquired in 2017 by Anheuser-Busch InBev. It has a solid core range of nine beers, and a special seasonal series called Keller Door, located downstairs in the same building as its Manly (upstairs) brewpub. The Brookvale Truck Bar is where the brewing magic happens, and there are two other venues that do food and beer. Some notable seasonals include Big Brekky Porter, available in bottles for a limited time. Out of its core range, the ESB is a reliable, satisfying drop, as it isn't a style often focused on nationally.

SYDNEY, AUSTRALIA

### 714 Visit the site of the Australian Beer Festival

Boasting a beer selection listed according to state, The Australian Heritage Hotel is also home to the annual Australian Beer Festival, the first of which was held in 2005. The hotel has also collaborated with Akasha to produce Red Kelly Red IPA, a smooth, easy-drinking experience.

SYDNEY, AUSTRALIA

### 715 Explore exclusive brews at Sydney's oldest pub

Established in 1841, Lord Nelson Brewery Hotel is Sydney's oldest continually licensed pub, and Australia's first brewpub in 1986. While its Three Sheets and Old Admiral beers are widely available, it's worth visiting to drink the exclusive brews on tap and look at the building's colonial features.

**715** *Above:* Traditional beers and heritage flow at Sydney's oldest pub, Lord Nelson Brewery Hotel

## 716 Quaff American-influenced beer from a can

Making outstanding hoppy beers that are widely available nationally in cans, try Akasha Brewing's US West Coast-style IPA Hopsmith—triple dry-hopped with a citrus, pine, fruity, bitter profile featuring all-American hops. The child- and pet-friendly brewery has various food trucks present on weekends, and also offers growler fills.

### 717 Learn how beer is cellar-aged

If Redoak Brewery's award-winning tap brews aren't reason enough to visit, then drop in for its cellar-aged rarities, or the extremely popular beer classes. Here, you will learn about the frothy beverage and enjoy a four-course "beer degustation™." Established in 2004, this Sydney brewery works closely with local producers and is fully solar-powered.

### 718 Taste international rarities alongside pizza

Local laws mean booze and decent live music are not as plentiful as in other Australian cities, but expect some internationally rare drops at Frankie's Pizza. Be sure to try Rogue Marionberry Braggot/ Mead or Mikkeller Mikropolis bourbon lambic with a dazzling array of Australian "tinnies" and bottles listed by style. Chomp with pizza available by the slice, or order one to share.

### 719 Drink local beer on a rooftop

Formerly the Palace Hotel, The Local Taphouse is a double-story 1920s building that hosts twenty regularly updated taps and rooftop music. Stop in for a few drinks and enjoy events such as trivia, board games, homebrew, and beer-appreciation sessions, plus a Sunday "host a roast" for small groups. Enjoy burgers, steaks, and parmas, or dine more formally at its restaurant.

## 720 Cool down with a piña colada-inspired IPA

The story goes that, bonding over their mutual love of fishing and boating, two homebrewers set up Willie the Boatman in 2014, and the year after, the brewery was open to the public and supplied to other bars, pubs, and bottle shops around inner-west Sydney. You can visit the tasting room and enjoy food from a rotating food truck roster booked in advance. The Australian brewery has collaboratively brewed with bottle shop owner mates Bucket Boys on the If You Like Piña Colada NEIPA, and has a core range and several limited-release brews.

SYDNEY, AUSTRALIA
## 721 Admire art while sipping local boutique beers
Bitter Phew has twelve taps rotating and a mission statement of wanting to "make craft beer accessible to Sydneysiders and welcome all beer enthusiasts" by also offering local and international boutique beers. Sit at the bar or table, order in food from nearby Mr Crackles (American-style rolls, dogs, and sides) or BL Burgers, and admire the art displayed from pals Badger & Fox Gallery.

BEECHWORTH, AUSTRALIA
## 722 Indulge in ale brewed with local oranges
One of the first craft beer breweries that helped to influence the popularity of drinking better rather than more, head brewer Ben Kraus started Bridge Road Brewers in 2005 after a European beer tour. The brewery is a three-hour drive from Melbourne, but a trip worth making, given the local produce available. Join a tour, which includes a four-beer tasting paddle (bookings recommended). Be sure to sample Little Bling, a session IPA, Chestnut Pilsner, and Robust Porter from its core range. From its Mayday Hills range, the Marmalade release is memorable (using regional oranges), and Chevalier Saison (with occasional variants, such as the addition of elderflower) is just as fancy as a decent bottle of plonk, best enjoyed alongside an equally special meal.

## 723 Track down an award-winning Thai red curry pale ale

The majority of Bright's tourist traffic occurs during winter as the town is just outside the Victorian Alpine region; it is a similar distance to Beechworth from Melbourne. Embracing sustainable practice and carbon neutrality where possible, Bright Brewery is also solar-powered and uses fresh mountain water to brew. Beers to try include its annual Stubborn Russian Russian imperial stout, the seasonal Black Diamond black/Cascadian dark ale, and other seasonal highlights, which in the past have included Pumpkin Harvest Ale and the 2017 GABS festival brew Yippee Thai Yay, a Thai red curry pale ale. You can expect a family-friendly experience with loads of special brews on tap, and damn good food.

## 725 Unearth the secret of Vic Secret hops

Developed in Australian state Victoria in 2000, Vic Secret hops have been commercially available since 2013, and share ancestry with the older variety Topaz, though Vic Secret possesses more flavor and aroma possibilities than its relative, and is similar in that respect to Ella and Galaxy hops. When added late to the kettle, brews become earthier, and depending on how much is used, can intensify pine and resin. If dry hopped, pineapple notes may also be more evident.

## 724 Discover Galaxy hops

Galaxy hops are a mid-1990s German Perle descendant that took nine years to make. The hop often adds clean citrus, distinct passion fruit aromas when dry hopped, and musky tropical fruit, apricot, Key lime, earthy blackcurrant, with peach and mellow bitterness. Favored in American pale and IPA, wheat beer, saison, ESB, and brettanomyces-fermented beers, it's a stalwart in Stone & Wood's Pacific Ale, and Mountain Goat's Fancy Pants and Hightail ales. Stone & Wood runs an annual "Tour of the Galaxy" at the Bushy Park Hop Harvest (in Tasmania), which is well worth considering if you have the time and plan to head that way. Citra, Amarillo, and Centennial hops are common substitutes.

## 726 Pair chocolate porter with Aussie meat pies

Located outside Melbourne in the Mount Macedon ranges, Holgate Brewhouse is the perfect out-of-town getaway destination, and has its own accommodation. Established in 1999, it's one of the older craft breweries around. Its choc porter Temptress is a must-have, and recommended with desserts or the quintessential Aussie meat pie—it has won a slew of awards nationally and abroad.

MELBOURNE, AUSTRALIA

## 727 Ride the flavor rollercoaster at this experimental brewery

Cliché-sounding as it may be, every first sip or gulp of a unique Moon Dog Craft Brewery beer is never something you can fully prepare yourself for. While some find the taste combinations apposite to the chosen beer style, many continue to be intrigued by the flavor rollercoasters of beers like Marmajuke IPA (with definite marmalade notes), Ogden Nash's Pash Rash imperial stout (flavored with Redskins— a red, raspberry-flavored chewable candy), ice cream spider-inspired IPAs (lime- or raspberry-flavored), or quintessential Australian black and tan combos (part dark beer, part much lighter beer)—one was called Coughlin's Diet and came in a two-bottle pack. It's the annual variations or treatments of its Black Lung stout that you should hunt down, and if you do try the offerings on tap locally or at the brewery, the core beers are readily available alongside brew alchemies new and old. Be prepared for what's on tap to sometimes taste markedly different to bottled versions, even if newly released (Jaffawocky choc-orange NE DIPA was remarkable in this respect). The brewery has a ten-tap bar, which serves pizza and assorted non-beer options, and also runs tours.

## 728 Dig up Australia's funkiest offerings

In 2011, when La Sirène Brewing came onto the Melbourne microbrewery scene to focus on *bière artisanale*, drinkers paid attention because Australian French/Belgian-inspired farmhouse ales with their funk, yeast, and focus on wild fermentation tend to be associated with continental Europe. Before setting up Urban Farmhouse Brewery in outer northeast Melbourne, the team worked in the state's Highlands region, better associated with winemaking. The brewery's dark beer Praline has something of a following, so keep your eyes peeled for variants (barrel-aged, one-off kegs, or the Imperial Praline), or the collaboration with Seven Seeds coffee roasters, Seven Sirens. Demand saw La Sirène can Urban Pale and Citray Sour, which are session-type, table beers. The brewery isn't open to the public, but you'll find its products in several beer venues or bottle shops in Melbourne. In addition to the aforementioned beers, try Harvest Ale and Petit Sour on tap, and the popular (bottled) Farmhouse Red. Limited-release bottle range Avant Garde, Fleur Folie (honey beer), and Bière de Cerise are ones to buy and cellar. The brewery has collaborated twice with Jester King (a rare, expensive treat nationally) to produce Song of Binding (saison) and Song of Blending (American wild ale).

ORBOST, AUSTRALIA

### 729 Catch a beer brewed in a circa-nineteenth-century butter creamery

"Beers from the deep sou'east" is the tag line for Sailors Grave Brewing, situated near the coast of Victoria state. Since 2016, husband-and-wife team Chris and Gab Moore have used the town's abandoned butter and produce factory—which is said to date from 1893—for brewing beer. The brewery's trademark is using locally grown and sourced ingredients, which inspire wonderfully odd twists on seasonal farmhouse ales and collaboration brews (for example, Australian Gothic, a sour farmhouse IPA with wormwood grown in the brewery's garden). It supplies statewide regularly, and frequently dreams up new weird drops for drinkers to excitedly hunt down, honoring Aussie desserts (Peach Melba Pavlova Cream Sour ale), or making use of the coast's offerings in oyster stouts, or seaweed and salt in goses.

MELBOURNE, AUSTRALIA

### 730 Play video games with a side of beer at this bar

Initially Perth-based, independent game designer Louis Roots' Melbourne Bar SK venue offers a constantly rotating game selection with bespoke controllers, while managing to keep a fridge stocked with tasty cans. Expect occasional collaborations on its four taps, and the staff are always happy to give recommendations.

MELBOURNE, AUSTRALIA

### 731 Find a European-style beer hall in Melbourne

GABS cofounders Guy Greenstone and Steve Jeffares set up the thirty-tap Stomping Ground Brewing featuring a Euro-style beer hall, and support Melbourne's arts culture (for example, Midsumma). In summer, Melbourne Airport features its Terminal 3½ and a pop-up tent in the city's art precinct, La Boca. Try the seasonal Pridelweiss and Gipps St. pale ale.

MELBOURNE, AUSTRALIA

### 732 Discover the dogs of this beer bar's Instagram

With around twenty taps and no exclusive brewery to supply contracts, the Great Northern Hotel is often home to the American Pint of Origin during Melbourne's Good Beer Week. The pub meals and weekly specials are fantastic, and the hotel features a beer garden, a bistro, and a private function room. Bring your dog and get snapped on the canine-devoted Instagram (@dogs_of_gnh).

## 733 Rock the boat at this brewery and distillery

Boatrocker Brewers & Distillers has come a long way since its head brewer started selling its first beers from his car in 2009. Matt Houghton brewed at others' facilities to make a pale ale and a pilsner. People he knew enjoyed them, and so did judges at international beer awards, as evidenced by the medals awarded. It was late 2012 when the brewery's own facility became feasible. First, Houghton purchased sixty wine barrels, with equipment to follow. Once completed, Australia's first barrel room and cellar door was real, and it now possesses more than 300 ex-wine, whiskey, and bourbon barrels. It continues to be one of the country's largest barrel-aging spaces, and has its own distillery arm, Hippocampus Spirits. The on-site family-friendly Barrel Room has eight taps, with beer also bottled or canned. Food-wise, expect pizza, cheese, charcuterie plates, and snacks. Tailored beer flights or spirits tastings are available on request, or choose your own and enjoy in the beer garden or amid barrels. Excellent introductions to Boatrocker's range are the raspberry-based Berliner weisse Miss Pinky, or any of the Ramjet yearly imperial stout variations, like those infused with Starward Whisky one year, or coffee for another. In early February, the brewery holds the annual Boatrocker Barrel Fest. Bookings are recommended for groups of eight or more.

## 734 Crush a tropical pale ale

KAIJU! Beer only started making beer in 2013, and has since attracted many loyal drinkers. KAIJU! Krush Tropical Pale in cans is its most available, accessible classic, and Cthulhu on the Moon Black IPA and Hopped Out Red return every so often and are must-tries. For Collingwood's Bar SK, KAIJU! whipped up a special version of its Krush (Skrush Tropical IPA) to celebrate the bar's first birthday. Limited releases Betelgeuse Double Red Ale (brewed for GABS 2015) and Where Strides The Behemoth double India black ale (Australian International Beer Awards gold medalist) are phenomenal drops that pop up periodically.

## 735 Find out why beer belongs with food

One of the first Melbourne venues to emphasize the relationship between beer and dining when the city's craft beer boom began, The Royston gastropub helped to pave the way by focusing on stocking microbreweries' products and avoiding contracts with macros. You can book online to dine more formally or nibble on snacks and share plates amid national and trans-Tasman beer from thirteen taps, one a handpump, and all updated regularly. Bottled and canned beer selections are available, but it's best to visit the venue to find out what's stocked. It's especially convenient as it's close to Mountain Goat Beer, and often participates in Good Beer Week events.

# Drink at Melbourne's top eleven bars

### 736  The Catfish

This friendly bar crams local brews and Philly-style cheesesteaks (with vegetarian/vegan options available) with live comedy and music in the upstairs room. Its mascot (catfish) has an old TV as a tank.

### 737  Boilermaker House

This upmarket venue has twelve taps featuring local, national, and international beer releases, plus extensive charcuterie and cheese selections. The bar specializes in beer and whiskey matches.

### 738  Carwyn Cellars

A storefront with an encyclopedic range of alcohol, the twenty-tap backroom highlights local and international breweries' core and limited brews. Food can be delivered from nearby Kustom Burgers or The Moor's Head.

### 739  The Alehouse Project

Serving a great mix of staples and rare local releases, this bar features brewery showcases and is conveniently close to local transport.

### 740  The Terminus

A stalwart Good Beer Week venue, you can expect family-friendly dining, bar snacks, a beer garden, and an amazing list of tap beer and bottled beers listed according to style and country.

### 741  Foresters Hall

This hall and its counter have more than thirty taps. There is also the upstairs Golden Clamshell, and a menu like its sister venue The Terminus.

### 742  Beermash

Beermash holds its own by offering eclectic international releases not usually on tap elsewhere. Admire the staff-drawn tap "tiles" if you head in for a late-night tipple.

### 743  Mountain Goat Beer

A flagship brewery since 1997 (despite Asahi acquiring it in 2015), this bar boasts a Randall infuser, dietary-requirement-friendly pizzas, Rare Breed limited releases, and a free drink if you cycle down.

### 744  Slowbeer

Try a fresh drop from five regularly changing taps, or pore over its extensive range.

### 745 Tallboy & Moose

A brewpub located in a northern suburb, this family-friendly space offers "canimals" to go, and boasts an Indian-Scottish menu with flavorsome delicacies like haggis or black pudding pakora.

745

### 746 The Local Taphouse

With twenty taps, a massive list of bottled beers, and British-style pub food, this friendly watering hole attracts newcomers and regulars, and is home to the monthly beer-appreciation club Ale Stars.

MELBOURNE, AUSTRALIA

**747 Snag a pun-filled pint at Two Birds Brewing**

The "two birds" are Jayne Lewis, head brewer, a Little Creatures and (pre-Asahi buyout) Mountain Goat alumnus, and Danielle Allen on marketing, setting up Melbourne's first female-run brewery in 2011. Taco and Sunset are great intro beers, but watch out for punny-bottled limited releases like Jucius Caesar NEIPA and Et Tu, Brut? IPA.

GEELONG AND FREMANTLE, AUSTRALIA

**748 Get lit with Little Creatures**

Bought out by Lion in 2012, Little Creatures Brewing was a Western Australian brewery opened in 2000, when a bunch of mates decided they wanted to brew really hoppy beers. In 2016, its inner Melbourne-based beer hall shut down to concentrate efforts on establishing a second brewing location on the East Coast. Craft beer drinkers may recall the increasing availability of its Pale Ale and the brewery's trademark angel logo Pipsqueak apple cider, and later its mid-strength, bright red-labeled Rogers' American Amber Ale. The blue-labeled Geelong-brewed Furphy Kölsch ("furphy" also being slang for "tall tales") has risen in popularity, thanks to an aggressive marketing campaign.

TASMANIA, AUSTRALIA

**749 Pack a picnic and bring your dog when visiting this farm brewery**

The Derwent Valley-based Two Metre Tall Farmhouse Ale & Cider is especially known for its barrel-aged and spontaneously fermented ales and ciders, with fruit in the ales. On the premises you'll find a beer garden, a cellar, and the Farm Bar serving its range on handpump. There is no food on-site, so bring a picnic, or use the barbecue facilities. Don't leave without trying Cleansing Ale, the brewery's signature brew—it's crisp, not too sour, with well-balanced acidity. If purchased outside the brewery, pay attention to brew and bottling date. Best enjoyed with soft cheese like Tasmanian Camembert or Brie after three to four months of bottling time.

**749** *Below:* Two Metre Tall is a bona fide farm brewery

# Five things to get involved with during Melbourne's Good Beer Week

### 750 Opening Night Party

Beer DeLuxe at Federation Square, located opposite the iconic Flinders Street Station, acts as the ten-day festival's "hub." Entry is free and you'll find good tunes, industry folks, and beer devotees celebrating till late.

### 751 Beer education events

"Beer School" events often sell out. Past incarnations have seen blind tastings with The Crafty Pint, beer-style identification, and brewing know-how through "Beer Geek" experiences, such as Brewniversity with Stomping Ground.

### 752 Beer and food pairing

Southern grill-loving restaurant Le Bon Ton regularly holds a three-course feast matched with flown-in Brooklyn Brewery brews. Northern Git matches Brit grub with Samuel Smith and Buxton Brewery beers. Honorable mention: beer and cheese anything.

### 753 Specialty tap takeovers

A crash course in learning what beers are available locally, nationally, and internationally, the week-long Pint of Origin occurs throughout the city. Entry is free, and many of the venues have regular punters.

### 754 Fun and games

Think: lawn bowls, pétanque, video-game contests, mini golf, "dunk the brewer," a scavenger hunt, and movie/music/board game/karaoke nights. There's also a family-friendly day with the classic egg-and-spoon and sack races.

PERTH, AUSTRALIA
### 755 Sip suds in Swan Valley

Being a Coca-Cola Amatil subsidiary, Feral Brewing made Hop Hog and Karma Citra household names. Opening in 2002, its "experimental brewpub" is located in the Swan Valley (the state's oldest wine region), has a barrel-aging shed, market garden, restaurant, and beer garden. With sixteen taps, it offers brewery-exclusive beers that are worth sampling.

PERTH, AUSTRALIA
### 756 Sup a specialty keg in inner-city Perth

Located in inner-city Perth, Nail Brewing has been integral to the state's craft beer scene even while being a "roving" operation. Its Clout Stout initially celebrated the brewery's tenth anniversary, and a new batch has been released every year since 2010. The brewery offers keg-only releases via its Brew Log collection on tap (sample Flaming Lamington if it's available).

METRICUP, AUSTRALIA
### 757 Discover both edible and drinkable delights at the BeerFarm

Since 2015, the dog-friendly BeerFarm has housed a brewery. A hay shed repurposed as a tavern, and the roundhouse-cum-brewery on former dairy land harks back to its farming history. You can expect excellent food with these brews due to its black Angus beef being raised and fed on local pasture, honey that comes from its own bees, cheese from its Jersey cows, and vegetables grown on-site.

ADELAIDE HILLS, AUSTRALIA
### 758 Drink pure, unfiltered beer at this award-winning brewery

Using traditional recipes and only four ingredients (malt, hops, yeast, and water), and leaving its beer naturally unfiltered might sound restrictive, but Prancing Pony Brewery has attracted international awards. The brewery's Hunt for the Red Velvet Russian imperial stout DIPA cross (made for GABS 2017) and Magic Carpet Midnight Ride have proven extremely popular with drinkers nationwide. Next to the brewery, the Brewshed sports sixteen taps with one-off specialty beers, small-batch brews available only at the Brewshed Beer Awards. Book a brewery tour and find that it's worth investigating the claim that beer goes best with pizza, parmas, chips, burgers, salads, schnitzels, and chicken wings.

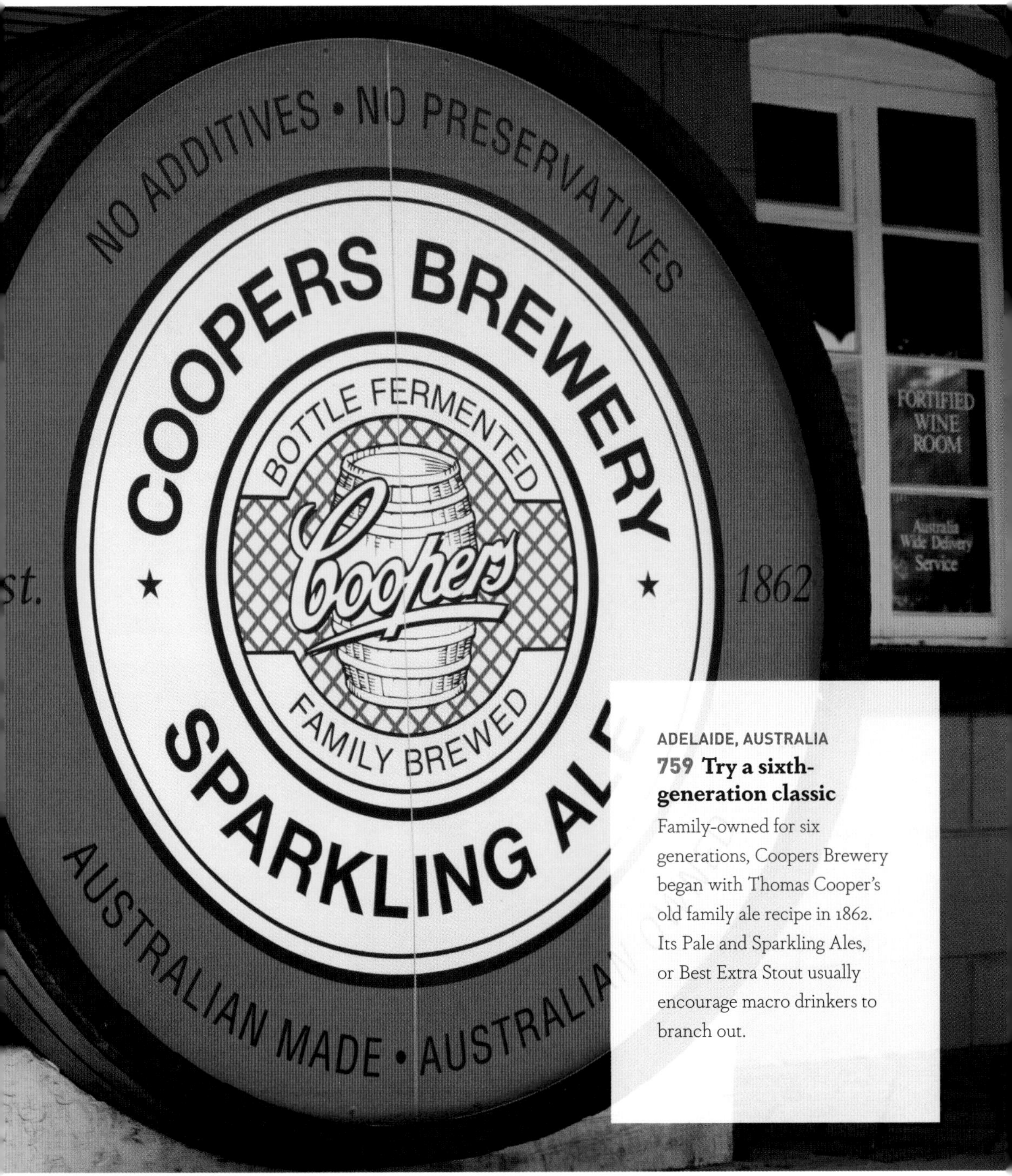

NO ADDITIVES • NO PRESERVATIVES

COOPERS BREWERY

BOTTLE FERMENTED

*Coopers*

FAMILY BREWED

SPARKLING ALE

est.

AUSTRALIAN MADE • AUSTRALIAN

1862

FORTIFIED
WINE
ROOM

Australia
Wide Delivery
Service

ADELAIDE, AUSTRALIA
**759 Try a sixth-generation classic**

Family-owned for six
generations, Coopers Brewery
began with Thomas Cooper's
old family ale recipe in 1862.
Its Pale and Sparkling Ales,
or Best Extra Stout usually
encourage macro drinkers to
branch out.

### ADELAIDE, AUSTRALIA
## 760 Explore beer brewed in Barossa Valley wine country

The name Big Shed Brewing Concern recalls origins of brewing out of a shed in 2002 in a rented property located in the state's wine country (Barossa Valley). The brewery pays tribute to Australian chocolates or ice creams of "Golden Gaytime" with the core Golden Stout Time dessert stout, and the brewed 2016 GABS rarity Beery Ripe cherry porter with coconut, glacé cherries, cacao, and lactose.

### ADELAIDE, AUSTRALIA
## 761 Say "arrr!" with Pirate-themed beers

Pirate Life Brewing blew away consumers with its trademark hoppy beers when it started out in 2014, and it wasn't long before Anheuser-Busch InBev bought it out in 2017. It has done some collaboration beers with big names such as the Trans-Pacific Partnership 2, an American strong ale with Ballast Point Brewing, the Captain Nameless Rum Barrel Aged Baltic porter with Stone Brewing, and Citrus US East Coast-style IPA with a bunch of AIBA 2017 champions (Stone & Wood, Two Birds, and the now-defunct BrewCult) for GABS 2017.

**761** *Right:* Discover the hoppy creations of Pirate Life Brewing

## 762 Forgo gaming and cocktails in favor of great beer

It might be easier to start with what The Wheatsheaf Hotel doesn't offer: no gaming machines, no cans, and no cocktails. This is beer-venue pilgrimage material: an international-heavy bottled beer list (first by style, then by brewery), live music, art from up-and-coming visual artists, and its own brewing arm Wheaty Brewing Corps. The pub's handpump taps feature six of its own beers, and six other nationals through a custom-installed Glasshopper (a glass and stainless steel infuser filled with hop flowers, coffee beans, and various spices, herbs, or fruit). This "retro-infuses" beers, three of which are national guest taps. The hotel is extremely social media and tech-savvy (with downloadable smartphone apps).

## 763 Check out some custom-built taps

Passionate about the national beer scene, specialist beer bar Tahi Cafe & Bar attracts a lot of recommendations for tourists, having been around since 2008. It boasts eight custom-made taps built from recycled car manifolds. Check its regularly updated website to find out what's on.

## 764 Get wired with these hoppy ales

Head brewer Søren Eriksen started 8 Wired Brewing out of Renaissance Brewing in 2009 with whom he'd worked the year before. He then moved with his family to Warkworth in 2013, where two years later, they set up their own brewery. Its name is a nod to the Kiwi tradition of typically using a "number 8" gauge of wire in electric fencing, and is shorthand for an ingenious, DIY attitude, which also hints at Eriksen's beginnings as a homebrewer in Perth, Australia. The brewery's beers are available

on six continents (excluding Africa), and RateBeer lists Eriksen as the sole Southern Hemisphere brewer in its top 100. Try to get your hands on Big Smoke, Hopwired IPA, Hippy Berliner, iStout, Super Conductor, and Tall Poppy to get an idea of the execution across broad beer styles. On its premises, you will find barrel-aged (10% of its output) and limited-release kegs, some of which make it abroad, and regularly across the Tasman to Australia. Here, collaborations have occurred with Bridge Road, Newstead, and Wheaty Brewing Corps (with Spanish Naparbier).

**765 Taste the best of Antipodean ales at this roving festival**

The Great Australasian Beer SpecTAPular (GABS) festival was born when Guy Greenstone (of Stomping Ground Brewery fame) and Steve Jeffares both worked at The Local Taphouse in Melbourne, and in 2011 decided to start an Australian beer festival. What started as a beer extravaganza in Melbourne's Royal Exhibition Building (mid-May) and The Local Taphouse in Sydney (early June, now held at Sydney Olympic Park) quickly grew into one of the world's top twenty beer festivals, and grew to be held in Brisbane (late April at the Brisbane Convention & Exhibition Centre) and across the Tasman in Auckland (mid-June at the ASB Showgrounds). Every year, brewers make keg beer and cider especially for the festival, and punters face a myriad of excruciating choices as to what to sample, buy paddles of, or commit to in a half-pint serve. These brewy concoctions aren't always entirely successful from a consumer standpoint, but it's become an essential part of every Australian-based beer obsessive to attend and be resignedly defeated by palate fatigue, because there's just no way to predict what new brews will appear. In December, everyone is encouraged to nominate beers for the Hottest 100 Craft Beers poll, and results are announced early the following year.

### COROMANDEL PENINSULA, NEW ZEALAND
## 766 Turn up the heat at Hot Water Brewing

Hot Water Brewing aims to make beer that everyone will enjoy drinking, so expect anything from classic styles to more adventurous ones, using internationally sourced malts and national hops. Its beers often feature at local food and music events. The brewery also has accommodation available.

### WAIHEKE ISLAND, NEW ZEALAND
## 767 Get your beer boogie on

Since 2016, with a self-confessed amalgamation of influences like heavy music, custom van culture, and US West Coast and Kiwi roots, Boogie Van Brewing makes beer its staff loves to drink. Book a guided tour with six mates minimum, or buy fills to go from what's on the six taps.

### WAIHEKE ISLAND, NEW ZEALAND
## 768 Sip beer inside a speakeasy

Alibi Brewing opened in late 2017 under the Tantalus Estate restaurant, and has a Prohibition-era speakeasy lounge where you can sample beer brewed on-site. Expect small-batch releases, amped-up classic styles (Tony Stoutano), and fruit and hops nationally accessible to feature alongside hazy NEIPAs.

### WAIPU, NEW ZEALAND
## 769 Sip New Zealand's prized pale ale

McLeod's Brewery opened in 2014, and since its head brewer Jason Bathgate joined in 2016, the brewery has attracted a lot of national attention. It won accolades at the 2018 Brewers Guild of New Zealand Awards and its Paradise Pale Ale was voted Beer of the Year in 2017. The brewery is located behind McLeod's Pizza Barn, one of several places where its wares are served on tap.

**WAIHEKE ISLAND, NEW ZEALAND**

### 770 Get wild on Waiheke

Established in 1998, Wild on Waiheke has four core beers and a popular non-alcoholic ginger beer on tap, all available to go. Tap 7 is reserved for unusual, experimental beers, and everything is brewed in unpasteurized small batches, so must be kept chilled.

**AUCKLAND AND KUMEU, NEW ZEALAND**

### 771 Grab a beer and a bite from a food truck

With two locations that have slightly varying opening hours, and a mouthwatering food truck lineup listed well in advance on its website, The Beer Spot offers you forty beers to choose from to drink in-house or to go. There is also ample on-site parking.

**770** *Below:* Waiheke Island Brewery is part of the Wild on Waiheke compound

NEW ZEALAND

# Try these five Kiwi pilsners

772

### 772 Emerson's NZ Pilsner

Using Nelson-grown Riwaka hops, expect a dry finish reminiscent of Marlborough's Sauvignon Blanc, citrus, and passion fruit flavor and scent from this beer affectionately known as a "Kiwi classic."

### 773 Harrington's The Rogue Hop Organic Pilsner

A subsidiary of Lion, this beer shares much of the taste profile of Emerson's NZ Pilsner, with the addition of Rogue kettle hops, pronounced gooseberry flavors, and a cleaner, fresher finish.

### 774 Townshend's Black Arrow NZ Pilsner

Established in the hop-growing region and using ancient water drawn from the Motueka aquifer, this brewery and pilsner commands apt industry recognition.

### 775 Mac's Hop Rocker Pilsener

Brewed using Cascade for bitter grapefruit florals, and Nelson Sauvin for a Sauvignon Blanc flavor profile, this is a pilsner for drinkers who enjoy complexity and non-aggressive bitterness.

### 776 Tuatara's Mot Eureka

Previously known as Bohemian Pilsner, Mot Eureka is widely available. It is the most bitter example listed at 44 IBU, and boasts an authentic Czech yeast in its recipe.

AUCKLAND, NEW ZEALAND
## 777 Drink beer from a hand-crafted bottle

Hallertau Brewery & Biergarten organizes its brewing
schedule around festivals that occur near or at the
brewery—such as the Chilli & Hop Beer Festival and the
Glorious Society of Bangers & Beer (where the sausages
incorporate a Hallertau beer). The core range is quite
simply numbered, while the Heroic range showcases
hop-driven brews. The brewery also dabbles in a couple of
sour beers. The seasonal range's labels are illustrated and its
bottles (each being unique) made by a local potter. Try
Little Beast barleywine, a drop that hobbits would no doubt
down multiple tankards of, if given a choice.

AUCKLAND, NEW ZEALAND
## 778 Get a taste of Yakima in the Southern Hemisphere

Thanks to Liberty Brewing's love
affair with Yakima hop varieties,
you can be assured of West
Coast-style and hop-forward beers.
C!tra, its double IPA, Yakima
Monster, an American pale ale,
and Knife Party IPA are worth
prioritizing. Other national brews
are also available in-house.

AUCKLAND, NEW ZEALAND
### 779 Hoist a pint of cask ale

Opened in 1995, the English-style Galbraith's Alehouse is a brewpub and restaurant housed in a heritage-listed building (formerly a library in the early twentieth century). It features in-house brews focusing on cask ales and pilsners. There are five rotating guest taps devoted to other national breweries like Urbanaut, Liberty, and McLeod's, a range of more than a hundred bottled beers, a nitro tap, and growler fills. The bottled range has won awards from the Australian International Beer Awards, the International Brewing Awards, the Brewers Guild of New Zealand, and the New World Beer and Cider Awards.

AUCKLAND, NEW ZEALAND
### 780 Swill beer with the vultures

At Vultures' Lane, you'll find twenty-two regular rotating taps (including nitro and cask beers), and more than seventy-five bottles in the fridge—the meticulous care used to catalog them is stunning. The separate bottle and tap beer lists are updated frequently (the Untappd venue's listing being most accurate) and are classified according to style, with additions for sessionables, alcoholic ginger beer, and cider. You can get growler fills and beer to go, plus the family-friendly pub offers daily food specials, with the option to sit outside. Not bad for a place that takes its name from the nicknames of the various undesirables ("vultures") frequenting and inhabiting in the 1920s.

AUCKLAND, NEW ZEALAND
### 781 Knock back brews from a nomadic brewer

Self-described "beer giraffe" Andrew Childs' quirky, roving Behemoth Brewing has no fixed location, despite the wide availability of its products nationwide. You can also find them in Australia—under the name Chur Brewing, where it has produced beers for festivals such as Beervana, GABS, and the Australian International Beer Awards. It has collaborated with Emerson's and Funk Estate (Threeway international IPA) and Gigantic Brewing (Too Big to Fail triple IPA), and has infused stouts with single-origin coffee from Thailand (Drink Tomorrow No. 1 double/imperial stout). With gorgeous label art and playful, pun-riddled names, this is still a brewery to take very seriously, as its brews are also extremely adventurous. The Trial By Jury NEIPA stands out particularly, as it uses an experimental New Zealand hop variety known only as Hort 4337.

AUCKLAND, NEW ZEALAND

## 782 Design your own beer recipe at this pub

"I would give all my fame for a pot of ale . . . " (*Henry V*, William Shakespeare) inspires the name of The Shakespeare Hotel & Brewery, the nation's first micro-brewpub. Established by publican Thomas Foley in 1898, imported Melbourne red bricks were used in the building's construction, and in 1986, the then owner introduced microbrewing on the premises. The resulting beer is not flash-pasteurized or filtered, and comes on tap or in 500 ml bottles. Classic beers are offered (pilsner, pale ales, and IPAs) with the odd seasonal (an Irish stout or a Munich lager). Heritage listing means its accommodation has accessibility issues, despite dedicated dining, bar, and function spaces. If you plan to stay in the area for more than five weeks, why not consider having the team help you design your own beer recipe, which can then be kegged and tapped?

AUCKLAND, NEW ZEALAND

## 783 Embrace the uptown funk

With around twelve local tap beers and thirty-plus stocking the fridge, Uptown Freehouse has daily food specials to take advantage of. Check out the menu, which has sections listing special dishes "By land" or "By sea," and most of the culinary offerings are standard pub fare, including humble but irresistible toasties.

782 *Below:* The Shakespeare Hotel & Brewery was New Zealand's first micro-pub

AUCKLAND, NEW ZEALAND

### 784 Nerd out with more than 100 bottles

Sadly, a freehouse does not necessarily entail free beer, but freedom from macrobrewery contracts and having full control over what is on tap. The Lumsden Freehouse is kid- and dog-friendly, has fifteen taps, and an encyclopedic range of more than 120 bottled beers and ciders—it's an essential venue for any beer nerd to check out.

PALMERSTON NORTH, NEW ZEALAND

### 786 Pair beer with local and sustainable foods

With around twenty taps, two handpulls, and a fridge dedicated to rare, special tipples, expect Brew Union Brewing's entire range on tap alongside national brews. You can feast on a seasonal menu incorporating fresh local and sustainable ingredients in a Portland-inspired family-friendly venue. You can also get fills to go.

AUCKLAND, NEW ZEALAND

### 785 Drink "epic" and extreme beers

Before 2007, Epic Beer brewed at Steam Brewing with the mission to "make epic beers that will provide epic experiences for people who love beers." Inspired by a California beer research trip, once Luke Nicholas took over Epic several styles became more hop-driven. Its American Pale Ale, with twenty-five hop flowers, has won Champion Beer at the New Zealand International Beer Awards, for example, and was a guest at the inaugural GABS 2011 in Melbourne. Most hop nerds are familiar with the brewery's work, and know to enjoy Hop Zombie and Lupulingus IPAs, or the Armageddon IPA (with its cleverly engineered 6.66% ABV and 66 IBU). Extreme, but in a left-field way, is the glorious Epicurean Coffee & Fig imperial oatmeal stout, which has a yearly vintage release, and is a beer to buy two of: one to stash or cellar, the other to drink on a very, very special occasion.

LOWER HUTT, NEW ZEALAND

### 787 Fill up on beer with a side of homebrewing supplies

Baylands Brewery has offered brewing supplies and tastes, cans and bottles, and fills of its beer to go at its cellar door since 2011. Much of its core range is available on tap, though some brews are exclusively in bottles (Van da Tsar Russian imperial stout, Glasgow Slasher barleywine), keg-only, or on handpull.

NEW ZEALAND

# Seek out these top five New Zealand hops

### 788 Motueka

A versatile hop with aroma (citrus) and flavor characteristics (orchard fruit, basil, rosemary) more suited to culinary creations, Motueka is used in hoppy or dark lagers and pilsners, or maibock, European ales, and wheat beers.

### 789 Nelson Sauvin

Named after the Sauvignon Blanc grape, this hop imparts that and gooseberry, fleshy tropical fruit aromas to IPAs, saisons, and some wheat ales since its availability in 2000. Pacific Jade is also used as its substitute.

### 790 Pacific Jade

Favored in pale ales, IPAs, and hoppy Belgians for its citrus, melon, and pungent black pepper elements, it's now easier to get this internationally. It can be used as a substitute for Nelson Sauvin.

### 791 Rakau

Developed in the 1970s, available in 1983 as AlphAroma, and renamed in 2007, Rakau is used in IPAs, hop-forward lagers, Belgian ales, American wheats, or American pale ales. It imparts ripe peach, stone fruits, grapefruit juice aromas, tropical flower, and balsam hints if dry-hopped.

### 792 Wakatu

Released in 1988 as New Zealand Hallertau and renamed Wakatu (Māori for "Nelson") in 2011, this hop imbues tropical fruit and fresh lime notes, and an earthy, sweet floral aroma in lagers, Belgian ales, and pale ales.

## 793 Get heady with Panhead Custom Ales

Starting up in 2013, Panhead Custom Ales was acquired by Lion in 2016, and seems set on international distribution, which has already seen it being brewed and readily available on tap in Australia. The Canheads range saw large cans with stunning art and subtle, unusual flavors—one of note being Lola Deville, a rosehip and hibiscus saison, and Johnny Octane, a red IPA. The best easily-acquired introduction to this brewery is through its Quickchange XPA or Supercharger APA. Naturally its core beers feature in its sixteen-tap tasting room.

### 794 Get schooled at Craft Beer College

Offering walking tours of breweries and bars around Wellington, Craft Beer College also runs beer tastings, and can customize services for workplaces and social gatherings. There are sessions for novices and for those wanting to delve deeper into beermaking. Join one of the set tours, which includes a visit to five beery spots, with lunch and a pint.

### 795 Enjoy fine dining in New Zealand's capital

Since 1996, Logan Brown restaurant has been serving contemporary New Zealand cuisine from locally sourced, sustainable produce in the country's capital city. Expect fine dining that comes with a lengthy drinks list that includes a decent range of beers ordered from lighter to darker styles and features breweries such as Epic, 8 Wired, Garage Project, and Emerson's.

### 796 Learn the best food and beer pairings

The family-friendly Fork & Brewer brewpub looks to showcase beer and food equally, and the forty taps pour its and other notable national breweries' wares (Tuatara, Hallertau, Moa, Mussel Inn, Liberty, 8 Wired, and Behemoth) alongside some international brews. Ask staff for suggested beer pairings on your food order (some brews are also used in cooking).

WELLINGTON, NEW ZEALAND

# Taste ten of the best Garage Project beers

### 797 Cockswain's Courage

An imperial porter brewed in freshly emptied oak bourbon barrels for eighteen months, expect notes of caramelized dates, vanilla-infused chocolate, and dark, strong spirits. Best cellared if you snag a bottle.

### 798 Cherry Bomb

A cherry chocolate imperial porter with excellently balanced flavors of red stone fruit, sourness, and unsweetened black coffee or cacao, on tap it pours a dark brown with a slight reddish tinge.

### 799 Demus Favorem Amori (formerly Death From Above)

Renamed in Latin ("we choose to stand for love"), this chile, lime, and mango US-style IPA uses Vietnamese mint and warming chile to provide something savory yet elusive, while hops and tropical fruit dominate.

### 800 Es Buah

This Javanese fruit cocktail sour is directly inspired by an Indonesian iced fruit dessert made of shaved ice and diced tropical fruits. Try identifying jackfruit, papaya, lychee, honeydew, and cantaloupe flavors.

### 801 Party & Bullshit

This East Coast American-style IPA is unapologetically hazy and cloudy, offering tropical fruit notes in line with the Simcoe and Mosaic hop profile, with little to no bitterness.

### 802 Pernicious Weed

Hops were once condemned as a "wicked and pernicious weed" (thought to be related to cannabis). Drinking this is anything but—due to the sweet, bitter, fruity hops used (organic Rakau and whole-cone Nelson Sauvin).

### 803 Sauvin Nouveau

Dividing beer purists, but delighting white wine drinkers? A clean, crisp, slightly acidic pilsner with no bitterness, Sauvin Nouveau contains Nelson Sauvin hop characteristics (Sauvignon Blanc grapes, peachy, or apricot aromatics).

### 804 Louisiana Voodoo Queen

Give this Brazilian coffee and chicory root-infused dubbel the chance it deserves—fragrant black coffee and warming spices make this one to sip and contemplate as a nightcap.

807

## 807 Explore New Zealand's boundary-pushing brewery

A massive enterprise for "three mates in a derelict petrol station" who started off as a nanobrewery in 2011, after brewing twenty-four different beers in twenty-four weeks—some of which are still part of the lineup today. Garage Project Brewery has produced nearly 400 unique beers and gone from its initial Aro Valley location in Wellington to brew at two additional places: Wild Workshop, also in Wellington (not open to the public; wild fermentation beers are brewed here), and B-Studio in Hawke's Bay. Drop into the Aro Valley Cellar Door for free tastings from eight taps, sales of cans and bottles to go, and fills (BYO vessels encouraged). You can then head across the road to visit its Taproom, which has eighteen taps that are changed weekly, two cask lines, and food. Its Kingsland Cellar Door in Auckland has twelve to sample from, and tasting flights with food, but you'll need a takeaway fill for anything bigger (on-the-spot crowler fills, and BYO vessels). Continually making its trademark zany, bizarre brews, several international breweries held in repute in their respective countries have collaborated with the Kiwi team. The list includes Beavertown, Kyodo Shoji Coedo, Modern Times, Moon Dog, Nøgne Ø, Sierra Nevada, Stomping Ground, and Stone—proving that there's some black hole in your knowledge if you don't make an effort to see what the fuss is all about.

## 805 Day of the Dead

Available on the Mexican *Día de los Muertos* and inspired by the Aztec beverage *xocolatl*, this black lager has boozy chocolate, chipotle chile heat, and a touch of smoky black coffee.

## 806 White Mischief

Despite its low ABV (2.8–9%), this white peach-based gose has a fleshy peach aroma and is moreish. The brewery's suggestion of it as a palate cleanser works well with (South Asian) Indian food.

**WELLINGTON, NEW ZEALAND**

## 808 Couple beer with Japanese-inspired snacks

Hashigo Zake is a specialist bar that aims to offer the best and most extensive range of imported beers. There are ten taps, and the website alerts punters as to what drops are scheduled to go on next. The bottled beer list shows the price if you imbibe at the venue, or choose to buy to go, and it has an online Cult Beer Store to match its cult beer bar vibe. Food is available: there are pies, Japanese-inspired bar snacks, house-made dumplings, and sourdough buns. There are weekly new-release nights, live music, and cult movie screenings.

**WELLINGTON, NEW ZEALAND**

## 809 Collect stamps along a boozy beer crawl

Like a beer-only scavenger hunt, it's recommended you download and print out the Craft Beer Capital Trail brochure, which lists all the venues from which you need to collect twenty-three venue rubber stamp imprints. The brochure has a detailed map, and there are prizes for collecting stamps in the three categories: CBC Classic (at least eight bars on the trail), Brew Pub Pilgrimage (all eight central brewpubs), and Suburban Sanctuary (all five suburban locals). After completing your map, submit it online with the required contact details to claim your prize. It sounds like a great way to get to know the city, and walk off the beery calories you're likely to drink while exploring Wellington.

**808** *Above:* Hashigo Zake offers an extensive range of imported beers

## 810 Sample irreverent brews from the Yeastie Boys

A play on the iconic American-Jewish rap act's name, Yeastie Boys'
website claims that it makes "irreverent ales made for all beer-loving
folk . . . at the opposite ends of the Earth in New Zealand and the UK,"
though it now also brews in Australia. Founded in 2009, it has a core
range of about ten regulars, including Pot Kettle Black porter, Rex
Attitude smoked beer, Gunnamatta Earl Grey IPA (the resulting brew
requested for GABS 2012), White Noise wheat beer, and xeRRex (a
doubled version of Rex). As you'll have noticed with xeRRex, the
brewery is fond of "beefing up" existing core beers to create limited
brews or for industry events and festivals—such as with the PKB
Remix series; Gunnamatta's fifth anniversary beer; and Royal
Tanninbomb the champion GABS 2012 double Earl Grey IPA.

## 811 Sip brews from an ever-changing beer list

At Ortega Fish Shack & Bar,
the drinks list features an
extensive beer selection, listed
by flavor or taste, and includes
a Juice Head Beer of the Day,
and Sour Beer of the Day if
you fancy something special.

## 812 Discover bliss at the Beervana festival

Craft beer is considered mainstream in Wellington, and indeed
perhaps throughout most of the country, as breweries find
evermore ways to incorporate native ingredients and influences
to come up with the next *enfant terrible* brew. Beervana festival is
the country's most popular beer festival. It began life in 2002 as
Brew NZ, organized by the Brewers Guild of New Zealand, and
was held at Wellington Town Hall with about 200 people in
attendance. That's since jumped to about 14,000, and tickets are
often available months in advance. Expect two days of great food,
hundreds of beers from around sixty breweries, wild collaborations, live dance, music, and interactive
entertainment, and an inundation of just what is available nationally, in Australia, and a handful of invited
international breweries. There are four sessions over two days in August, including a showcase for the
official international guest brewery, a homebrew competition where you can try your hand at beating
the industry pros, and special pop-up or dedicated bars such as the Pink Boots Bar (a female-only beer
collective). If the festival isn't enough excitement, the Road to Beervana is an option worth investigating
if you've got time to really do the hardcore tourist thing.

## UPPER MOUTERE, NEW ZEALAND

### 813 Drink in history at New Zealand's oldest pub

Moutere Inn's claim to fame is that it is the nation's oldest pub, in a building existing since 1850. In 2008, it became a thirteen-tap freehouse, some of which are handpumps. It also has three German-style beers contract brewed, and pub meals use as much locally sourced produce as possible, and change according to what's in season. There are some noteworthy weekly specials like steak-wine night, and Hops and Glory discounts and activities, with whiskey-cigar evening sessions or the odd live gig, and special banquet-type dinners that book out, and previously, there's been on-site accommodation. Other nearby attractions include the Sarau Festival, held at the beginning of the year, to celebrate the area's harvest, with music and a farmer's market.

## GOLDEN BAY, NEW ZEALAND

### 814 Discover beer made from pristine water

Set in a stunning part of the country, The Mussel Inn offers its beer in PET or standard glass bottles to go. The water for its beer is unique in that it comes from a hill with a bush-filtered stream behind the venue, that's low in dissolved minerals.

---

**TOP 10**

## WELLINGTON, NEW ZEALAND

# Take a trip to Wellington's top ten bars and breweries

### 815 Fortune Favours Beer

This brewpub is located inside an old industrial building in the Leeds Street district, and offers crowler fills, weekly experimental brews, beer flights, and great local cured meats and cheeses.

### 816 Bebemos

Translating as "we drink" from Spanish (*bi-beer-mos*), enjoy an array of choice from eleven taps, sixty-plus beers, a Latin American-inspired menu, and the Cabana—an all-weather beer garden.

### 817 Black Dog Brewery

Located in the city's central business district, this pet-friendly venue wields canine-puntastic core beers, growler and crowler fills, and collaborations with folks like Tuatara, Rhyme and Reason, and UK-based microbrewery Lord Almighty.

### 818 Golding's Free Dive

Not far from Fortune Favours, this Te Aro dive bar showcases both national beer and wine, and serves Neapolitan pizza from neighbor Pizza Pomodoro.

### 820 Little Beer Quarter

Beer geeks will find themselves in beer heaven in this Te Aro establishment. It boasts fourteen rotating taps, two handpulls, and more than a hundred refrigerated beers.

820

### 823 ParrotDog

The Flora range offers unexpected flavors in conventional brews, while RareBird pays one-off homages to Aotearoa's "quirky birds"—Puffinus Huttoni was a boysenberry sour brewed for GABS and Hawkeye is a canned session IPA.

### 819 The Third Eye

Eclectic Tuatara brews and collaborations feature at this "Temple of Taste," available as fills to go or six- and twelve-packs. Suitable for novices and geeks, you can book to attend its venue tour here and also at the brewery's tasting room in Paraparaumu.

### 821 The Hop Garden

Located in Mount Victoria, 2018 saw this beer bar stock sixty-two national breweries. Regular offerings include those from ParrotDog, North End, Boneface, Brave Brewing, Sawmill, and Eagle.

### 822 The Malthouse

The home of Tuatara Brewery since 2007, The Malthouse takes beer very seriously. You will find more than 150 national and international beers, plus six different temperature-controlled fridges to offer aged beers.

### 824 The Rogue & Vagabond

This child- and pet-friendly dive bar has several taps as well as a nitro and handpulls. It offers pub food staples, holds regular comedy and music gigs, and has a beer garden.

## 825 Sample beer made by a former winemaker

Moa Brewing was founded by the country's only qualified cicerone, Josh Scott, who was initially a winemaker by trade. Frustrated with the lack of choice at the time in 2003, he met now head brewer David Nicholls at the Marlborough Wine and Food Festival, and together they started Moa (pronounced "more")—named after a now-extinct giant flightless bird that used to inhabit the region. Drop into the Cellar Door and spend some time in the beer garden where a food truck will keep you fed. You can also book a tour—make trying the sour beers a priority!

## 826 Visit New Zealand during fresh-hop harvest season

Availability of fresh-hopped beers varies annually according to the yield, and when the harvest officially starts and finishes. In New Zealand, this occurs from around mid-February to late March. El Niño and La Niña (collectively known as El Niño-Southern Oscillation or ENSO) can have significant effects on the nation's rainfall, wind, and temperature, though this doesn't deter the enthusiasm when developing or breeding new hop varieties. The year 2006 saw the inaugural official harvest, and in 2018, seventeen New Zealand-specific varieties harvested (with four trial hops), with nearly 2.5% organically cultivated. New Zealand Hops head Doug Donelan cites Renaissance as an example of the nation's breweries making the best use of the end product.

## 827 Discover New Zealand's hop-growing heritage

At Founders Heritage Park Hop & Beer Museum you can visit McCashin's Hop Garden and taste the wares available, while having a meal or a coffee, before or after checking out the museum. It celebrates 160 years of hop growing and brewing history, starting with Nelson having a brewing tradition from 1843, with the city itself only being established two years before, claiming to be the country's beer capital (though Wellington might disagree). Be sure to check out the museum's replica hop kiln, learn about the arguments for and against alcohol prohibition in the Brewer's Office, and generally get a handle on the overall brewing process.

## 828 Enjoy English-inspired beer in New Zealand wine country

Cork & Keg is an English-style pub with accommodation (rates are higher during festive seasons) that includes one wheelchair-accessible room and courtesy pick-up and take-home transportation. The pub offers regular food and drink specials, and it's best to book early if interested in events like the Wine and Food Festival held in February, and the Grape Ride Festival held in March, given its proximity to the Marlborough wine region.

## 829 Visit both breweries and wineries on this tour

Though a largely wine-focused service (operating in one of the country's largest wine regions), Hop 'n Grapes brewery visits are an option if you book for a full-day tour—Moa Brewing and Renaissance are close by. After the tour concludes, you can choose to be left at either aforementioned breweries, or in nearby restaurants.

**MARLBOROUGH, NEW ZEALAND**

## 830 Drink beer in the land of Sauvignon Blanc

Most beer aficionados will know that Renaissance and Moa are in the area, though there are a few smaller ones, too. There are Sinka Beer Brewing Limited and Golden Mile Brewing, the latter of which serves sessionable beers. In October, there's the free-for-all-ages A Festival of Beer, and in December there's the ticketed (eighteen-plus) Summer Beer Festival—both run annually in Blenheim. There's also the gastropub Speights Ale House (not to be confused with the Speight's brewery in Dunedin), and the Hop On Hop Off Wine Tours company that can take you to the aforementioned Cork & Keg Pub.

### 831 Knock back a pint brewed with local ingredients

Renaissance Brewing emphasizes using local ingredients (hops and malt) in American, British, and European beer styles. It began when two Southern Californian brewers bought a lease on the Grove Mill in Blenheim in 2005. 8 Wired head brewer Søren Eriksen did a stint with the brewery from 2008 to 2012, and it has continued to grow and accumulate awards. It doesn't have its own taproom and recommends nearby Cork & Keg and Dodson Street Beer Garden for its beer and a good feed. Its Stonecutter scotch ale is one of its best-known brews, and if you're looking for a treat, the Abundance Baltic cherry porter even has suggested holiday food matches (turkey curry, mince pies, fruit cake). It also has a low-gluten beer range labeled Hepworth.

CHRISTCHURCH, NEW ZEALAND

### 832 Wander the shelves of the Beer Library

The Beer Library is a store that has a massive selection where you can go and get fills on preferred vessels you bring in (as long as it's clean and has a lid). Alternatively, you can order online and get your brews delivered free for orders over a certain amount.

CHRISTCHURCH, NEW ZEALAND

### 833 Celebrate beers from the South Island

While mainly a swish function space, historic Ilam Homestead is the location of the biannual South Island Beer Festival held in February—a celebration voted Best Canterbury Beer Event by the Society of Beer Advocates. Time a visit to coincide with festival dates. The venue also occasionally holds informal beer tastings.

CHRISTCHURCH, NEW ZEALAND

### 834 Grab a brew or two at the Great Kiwi Beer Festival

With more than 300 breweries represented, often with first-time participants, and thirty-five-plus street food vendors, get tickets sooner rather than later, and organize transportation for this annual, late-January festival. There's a Cooking Theatre with on-site demonstrations, the Pomeroys Craft Beer Academy with fun but entertaining chats with respected beer-industry figures, and live music crammed into a single day.

CHRISTCHURCH, NEW ZEALAND
## 835 Drink cask ales in a serene setting

Despite its clinical name, The Laboratory brewery is worth the pilgrimage, with seven beers on tap—four from The Twisted Hop—and a handful of guest beers and ciders. It specializes in brewing English-style "real ale," which means the brews are cask conditioned, undergoing final fermentation in barrels and handpumped at a warmer temperature than usually associated with beer.

CHRISTCHURCH, NEW ZEALAND
## 836 Taste real ales made with Kiwi hops

Since 2012, the English-style real ale brewery and gastropub The Twisted Hop uses locally sourced malts and New Zealand hops. It hosts lots of regular events (games and quiz nights, a math club, live music, and various beverage festivals), and runs informal beer tastings, with formally structured ones held throughout the year.

CHRISTCHURCH, NEW ZEALAND
## 837 Stay up to date on New Zealand's national beer scene

Self-described as Christchurch's least hipster, hipster bar, The Institution has five taps and a myriad of bottles on offer. You can get a fairly good idea of what the national craft beer scene is like by scheduling a drinking session here. The beers change frequently, so visiting is the only reliable way to find out what's on offer.

### 838 Explore local beer and food in a nineteenth-century hotel

Established in 1863, the Cardrona Hotel is one of the country's oldest hotels—and one of only two left over from the gold-rush era. Set in an area where some of the best artisanal food producers reside, the pub doesn't shy from incorporating this into its menu. Though the food, wine, and accommodation is the focus at this historic hotel, expect brews such as Panhead, Emerson's, and Speight's Cardrona ale on tap.

### 839 Quaff organic Belgian-inspired ales

Craftwork Brewery is pretty obsessed with Belgian beer. Since 2014, it has brewed small batches of idiosyncratic, multi-award-winning Belgian-inspired ales, and organized a small-group tour to Belgium in 2018, so folks could experience the brewery's muse firsthand. Locally, it supports the Society of Beer Advocates (SOBA), and uses national, organic brewing malts and adjuncts wherever possible.

### 840 Discover New Zealand fresh-hopped beers

In 2006, New Zealand brewers decided to start using fresh hops rather than dried hops or pellets in the chase for danker, hoppier brews. Two such debut examples are 8 Wired's Fresh Hopwired, and Mac's Brewjolais (the latter no longer in production). The most sought-after hops tend to be Motueka and Nelson Sauvin. Wellington's Craft Beer Capital Hopstock festival (usually held in April) had twenty-two venues and beers, including a trail to follow and collect stamps as you sip your way through. Craft Beer College also holds tours in Auckland, Christchurch, Marlborough, Nelson, Waikato, and Wellington on similar hunts, as the beers gradually pop up nationally.

# Asia Pacific

Over the past decade or so, the indie beer cultures of countries like Japan, South Korea, Thailand, and Taiwan have skyrocketed from backwater to mainstream. Now, nearly every major urban area in these regions features a distinct and increasingly mature beer market loosely reflective of (and heavily influenced by) ones found in North America. Think: hoppy Japanese ales, sour ales brewed with native Thai fruits, and Taiwanese imperial stouts. India, too, has experienced exponential growth in its market and now readily offers myriad options for local, regional, and craft brews, which are often offered in stylish, nightclub-like outlets.

Wherever you go, don't miss out on the opportunity to drink with locals. One of the finest experiences is hoisting pint after pint of ice-cold, refreshing bia ho'i amid the rickety plastic stools and tables on the streets of Vietnam.

MORIOKA, JAPAN
## 841 Say prost! at this German-style Japanese brewery

In one of the northernmost prefectures on Japan's main island is a small brewery focused on creating fresh, traditional beers for its local residents. Baeren (German for "bear") is the craft beer pride of Iwate prefecture, making its mark among the burgeoning Japanese craft beer scene with traditional German-style beers. Opened in 2003 with a brewmaster certified in Germany, it still uses a vintage copper German brewhouse. Its flagship, Baeren Classic lager—with a clean, crisp profile and immense drinkability—isn't the type of beer to blow your socks off, but rather a regional specialty that's made fresh locally and sold mostly within its hometown.

ICHINOSEKI, JAPAN
## 842 Sip a sansho-infused spring ale

Spring seasonals are ubiquitous whenever beer is made. That includes bocks in Germany, saisons in Belgium, and myriad light, refreshing springtime ales in the US. So it's no surprise that Japan would have specialty beers to welcome the blossoming end of winter. One of the best is Sekinoichi's peppercorn-infused Iwate Kura Japanese Ale Sansho—packed with notes of sage, pineapple, and a distinct floral quality unlike nearly anything else. Similar to, but less aggressive than, the Sichuan peppercorn, sansho peppercorn—pale green berries of a spindly Asian shrub—offers a slight tingling sensation. The beer is backed by big notes of papaya, lemon, and citrus. Sansho Ale is one of the most unique and refreshing beers in the world.

# Try five of the best Hitachino Nest beers

Japan's most well-known craft beer export is this little owl-themed brewery in the coastal Ibaraki prefecture north of Tokyo.

### 843 Nipponia

Nipponia is a Belgian-style strong ale unique for using two distinctly Japanese ingredients: Kaneko Golden (an ancient Japanese barley) and Sorachi Ace hops imparting flavors of lemon.

### 844 Yuzu Lager

Yuzu gets its citrusy kick from the addition of the orange-like yuzu fruit. Hitachino also makes a yuzu-infused saison.

### 845 Red Rice Barrel Edition

The brewery's regular Red Rice Ale (made with a historic amber-hued rice variety) is aged with wild yeasts in barrels made from sakura (cherry blossom) timber.

### 846 New Year Commemorative Ale

This special-release 8% ABV beer brewed each winter for New Year has Belgian-style yeast that lends notes of vanilla, coriander, and other spices.

### 847 Espresso Stout

This high-gravity, jet-black stout is infused with dark roasted espresso beans for a rich flavor and pleasantly robust mouthfeel.

### KAWAGOE, SAITAMA, JAPAN

## 848 Taste Japan's original sweet potato beer

Dedicated to making pure expressions of classic beer styles, COEDO is one of Japan's most quality-conscious breweries. Partially named after the former term for Tokyo ("Edo"), and located in the capital city's far northwestern suburbs, COEDO focuses on a core lineup of American- and European-inspired ales and lagers. Start with Kyara, an India pale lager bathed with highly aromatic hops, before moving on to Shikkoku, a pristine German-style schwarzbier named after the jet-black lacquerware of Japan. Perhaps its most well-known beer, though, is the Japanese sweet potato-based ale called Beniaka, a 7% ABV imperial amber ale. You can visit the taproom here—it is called Xiangmai, which means 'aromatic barley.' Its cuisine is handcrafted by a talented Japanese chef.

### MULTIPLE LOCATIONS IN TOKYO, JAPAN

## 849 Drink with the devil at DevilCraft

Inspired by the craft beer boom in the US, owners John Chambers, Mike Grant, and Jason Koehler began developing the idea for DevilCraft way back in 2008. By the summer of 2013, they had opened their first brewpub—the flagship DC Hamamatsucho—with twenty-one drafts of guest taps from other breweries. By 2015, the brewery license came through and the company was able to begin making its own beers, mostly riffs on American-style hoppy ales. Today, to serve its three locations, which now include Kanda and Gotanda in addition to the original outpost, DevilCraft brews its beers at an off-site facility in Oimachi. Each of the brewpubs serves hearty deep-dish Chicago-style pizzas to complement the American-style beers.

### TOKYO, JAPAN

## 850 Celebrate global breweries along with Japan's best suds

Mikkeller Beer Celebration Tokyo is a Danish import festival in early fall. It features dozens of breweries from the US, mainland Europe, and the UK, as well as locals from across Japan. Modeled off the original Copenhagen fest, it offers multiple day and ticket levels, including early access. Catch brews from cult producers like Richmond's The Veil, China's Great Leap, and Belgium's Bokkereyder in addition to Japan's own Anglo Japanese Brewing and Minoh Beer.

# Discover Tokyo's nine best beer bars

### 851 Mikkeller Bar Tokyo

Located on a corner spot in the uber-trendy Shibuya section of Tokyo, Mikkeller bar is a Tokyo gem pouring the best of the best Japanese, American, and European craft beers.

### 852 Bakushu Club Popeye

This brightly lit, wood-adorned tavern is Tokyo's OG craft beer destination. With seventy beers on tap, you're sure to find something delicious to tickle your palate.

### 853 Tanakaya Liquor Store

If you're seeking out rare and sought-after craft beer to go, check out this liquor store in the Toshima district for a mind-bending selection from dozens of Japanese and international breweries.

### 854 Pigalle

This tiny Belgian-themed bar in Tokyo's southwest suburbs serves rare and obscure beers in a sliver of a space. Check out the rotating drafts from Fantôme and Evil Twin, or grab one of seventy bottles and cans to go.

### 855 DevilCraft Hamamatsucho

DevilCraft has several locations throughout Tokyo, but this one is the best, featuring house-brewed IPAs alongside Chicago-style deep-dish pizza.

### 856 Beer Bar Ushitora Ichigo

This flagship bar for the Ushitora Brewery is located on the backstreets of Shimokitazawa. Of the thirty-five taps, roughly ten are from the brewery itself, while the others come from various Japanese and American breweries.

### 857 WIZ Craft Beer and Food

Housed on the first floor of a major shopping center in the central Chiyoda district, Wiz serves inventive pizzas to pair with Japanese, European, and American craft beers.

### 858 Titans Craft Beer Taproom & Bottle Shop

This no-frills Toshima spot offers around a dozen drafts, including many rare beers from the US, and a small menu of *gyoza* and vegetables.

### 859 Ant 'n Bee

This cellar-level tavern offers twenty taps (be sure to check out the "flux capacitor" draft system) along with bottles and a fun selection of Japanese whiskies.

TOKYO, JAPAN

# Sing your heart out at these beer-fueled karaoke haunts

Tokyo is a city of karaoke. Though the karaoke machine was actually invented in Kobe some 300 miles away, Tokyo is the capital of the sing-along pastime. And with karaoke nearly always comes beer. Here are five of the best spots to do it.

### 860  Big Echo

With locations throughout Tokyo and the rest of Japan, Big Echo is a fun, reliable chain of karaoke bars. Once you get to your private booth or room, simply pick up the phone and order pints or pitchers of your favorite beer.

860

### 861  Amour

For something a little more stylish and chic—Lady Gaga is said to have been a patron—check out this boutique karaoke room. Make sure you book in advance, as there are only four rooms.

### 862  Studio Himawari

The unique twist on this fun spot is the owners Takuya and Mimi Tachibana actually play guitar and saxophone along with you as you sing.

### 863  Karaoke Kan

Famously featured in the movie *Lost in Translation*, this spot in Shibuya is one of the top karaoke destinations in Tokyo for simply that reason.

### 864  Shidax

One of the other top players in Tokyo's karaoke scene is Shidax, a chain with more than a dozen locations around the city. A large selection of beers (though no real craft options) is typically available.

# Listen to tunes at these five record bars

Don't miss the uniquely Japanese record bars—typically tiny, intimate bars where the bartender spins a specific style of music on vinyl.

### 865 Small World

Pouring three drafts from the likes of Hansharo, Shiga Kogen, and Nihonkai Club breweries, this tiny space also offers a small crate of vinyl records for purchase.

### 866 Funky Chicken

Shibuya's Funky Chicken plays 1970s funk on both vinyl and a giant projector screen with a rather uninspired selection of watery beer. The overall experience is out of this world, though.

### 867 Big Love Records

Offering a wide selection of indie and experimental music on vinyl and cassette, Big Love pours three drafts of craft beers and a small selection of bottles.

### 868 City Country City

Also known as CCC, this spot is a combination coffee shop, vintage record store, bar, and pasta restaurant all rolled into one. The beer selection isn't always stimulating, but it's a fun experience nonetheless.

### 869 JBS Jazz Bar

The shelves behind the bar at this Shibuya spot are chock-full of jazz, blues, and soul vinyl. Pair the soothing sounds with a cold drink, but fair warning: loud conversation is not allowed!

ZUSHI, KANAGAWA, JAPAN

### 870 Head south of Tokyo to discover these great beers

The Kanagawa prefecture south of Tokyo is home to Yorocco Beer, which was opened in 2012 by brewer/owner Kichise Akio. Akio ran a bar on the nearby island of Enoshima for eight years before leaving to pursue his passion for beer at Baird in Tokyo. Today, his brewery shares a space with a local bakery (a friend of Akio's) and serves its delicious pale ales, wheat ales, and IPAs to visitors. The beers are decidedly American-influenced with big hop aromas and robust flavors, but display some Belgian influence, as well. The colorful labels—in bright green, blue, and yellow—are hip and easy to spot at beer stores throughout the country.

KARUIZAWA, NAGANO, JAPAN

## 871 Try an IPA brewed with bonito flakes

Japan's largest craft brewery is located about 105 miles northwest of Tokyo in Nagano prefecture. Founded in 1996, YOHO Brewing was part of the first wave of Japanese craft beer that swept the nation before fizzling out near the end of the turn of the millennium. YOHO survived on the popularity of its flagship Yona Yona Ale, essentially a Japanese version of Sierra Nevada's Pale Ale with a pronounced grapefruit aroma and striking bitterness. (Kirin, the Japanese beer giant, purchased a stake in the brewery in 2014 and now brews the majority of Yona Yona.) Other beers, most of which are American-style, include Aooni IPA, Tokyo Black porter, and Sorry Umami IPA brewed with bonito (dried fish) flakes. You can visit the brewery's various taprooms and pubs throughout the country.

### 872 Taste the *terroir* of Japan's rice and barley fields, in liquid form

Positioned in a spa town near Japan's west coast Ishikawa prefecture, the tiny Wakuwaku Tezukuri Farm Kawakita specializes in using locally grown and malted barley in its beers. In fact, all the malt used is grown among the barley and rice fields surrounding the brewery. While there, you'll find a small pub, restaurant, and covered "gardenhouse" where you can sample four different beers brewed on-site, including a simple pale ale, a Koshihikari ale made with local rice, a full-bodied dark ale akin to a porter, and a weizen made with Ishikawa-grown wheat. Adjacent to the brewery is a small general store selling local produce, meats, and other foodstuffs. Be sure to check into one of the local hot spring spas while you're in town.

**871**  *Left:* YOHO Brewing produces an array of mostly American-style craft ales and lagers

MIYAZAKI, JAPAN

### 873 Explore a mythical brewery

Located on the southern Japanese island of Kyushu, Miyazaki, Hideji Beer is the self-professed "mythical brewery" that is surrounded by several icons of traditional Japanese mythology, including Mount Mukabaki and Kyushu island itself. Hideji is located in Nobeoka City, which is said to be the place where the gods descend onto the Earth. Today, it is a modern city that incorporates much of this traditional myth into its local culture, including craft beer. Founded in 1996, Hideji brews some of the best beer in Japan, including the famed Kuri Kuro dark chestnut imperial stout, with rich, robust notes of dark chocolate and roasted coffee. Hokura Kin Nama, a German-style pilsner, is brewed with barley grown in the town of Takaharu in southern Miyazaki.

MULTIPLE LOCATIONS, JAPAN

### 874 Get to know one of Japan's first craft breweries

Often pointed to as an old hand in the Japanese beer industry, Baird Brewing began with the husband-and-wife team of Bryan and Sayuri Baird in 2000. After a pilgrimage to the west coast in the late 1990s, the couple, with support from friends and family, became the smallest licensed brewer in Japan. As one of the earliest foreign craft brewers in the country, Baird has expanded from its humble beginnings and has been growing ever since. It has an extensive lineup of year-round and seasonal brews that are produced in the rural Izu-shi brewery. If you're not able to make the trek, don't fret, as you can now find its affiliated taprooms around the country, which are known for utilizing local pub food, particularly *yakitori* and *izakaya* in tandem with its selections. This a great way to experience Baird's range in a traditional Japanese culinary context.

PYONGYANG, NORTH KOREA

### 875 Find a plethora of beer choices in Pyongyang

If you should ever find yourself in Pyongyang, the capital of North Korea, and in need of a spot to wet your whistle, this outpost may very well be one of your few choices. As one might expect, North Korea is rather austere compared to its southern neighbor. Nothing highlights this more than the abundance of choices found at the Koryo Hotel's microbrewery. You may try a "yellow" or "black" beer. Compared to the cosmopolitan South, which is experiencing a flourishing beer scene, it might seem spartan. However, the idea of "black" beer or stout was not an uncommon description in South Korea until fairly recently either. Either way, if you have the chance, you've reached one of the last frontiers in the craft brewing world.

**874** *Above:* You can order a "yellow" or "black" beer from Koryo Hotel's microbrewery

SOUTH KOREA

## 876 Indulge in some local *chimaek*

If there is one thing that you'll pick up from the drinking culture in Korea it is that it often, if not always, involves food. This often means having a couple of "rounds" involving drinking and eating. This increasingly means fried chicken and beer = *chimaek*. Basically, *chimaek* is a combination slang term for chicken (*chi*) and beer, which in Korean is *maekju*, hence *chimaek*. At one point there were thousands of fried chicken and draft beer restaurants operating on the peninsula. Popularized by a local TV drama, this style exploded, particularly on the banks of the Han River that meanders through central Seoul and is lined by loosely regulated public parks. Whether it's college kids on a date or workers blowing off steam, this is a worthy first round for your Korean beer adventure.

SEOUL, SOUTH KOREA
## 877 Drink superbly fresh ales on the outskirts of Seoul

MysterLee Brewing began in 2017 on the eastern edge of the sprawling Seoul metropolis as a collaboration between Lee Seung-yong and Lee In-ho, hence the MysterLee namesake. It produces a wide variety of special releases and has four year-round offerings. It aims to offer you the four "misters": Mr. Yellow, Mr. Purple, Mr. Green, and Mr. Black, which are aimed at satisfying a wide array of tastes. These two craftsmen emphasize "Drink fresh" as the company motto and it therefore does not distribute its beer outside the facility and pub. This guarantees freshness and quality, which is at the heart of the business and the center of the brewery's obsession. This does limit your ability to try these brews, however, but don't worry—they are easily accessible via the Seoul metro at Gongdeok station, which you can easily attach to a trip to Hongdae.

SEOUL, SOUTH KOREA

## 878 Explore the bars and bottle shops of Hongdae

Hongdae is an area around Hongik University (exit 9 of the metro station with the same name) that has become an epicenter for nightlife in Seoul. An amalgam of the space between multiple universities in the area, it naturally filled in with activities targeting students. There are numerous places to drink: outside, inside, on rooftops, or in bars, clubs, and pubs. More recently, it has embraced the craft beer boom in the country. Outside exit 3 there is an infill park on an old railway line that has become a popular place to sit with a beer—you'll find numerous bottle shops here. The further addition of the AREX express train to Incheon International Airport means this has become a popular spot to stay in the city and is easy to visit if you're on a lengthy layover.

SEOUL, SOUTH KOREA

## 879 See the super selection of Woori Super

One of the more unique experiences you'll find in the sprawling South Korean capital is the Woori Super. As the "super" in the name suggests, this was once simply a small local supermarket run by Mrs. Kim Yeong-Suk. Over time, it began to cater to the growing expat community in the neighborhood of Gyeongnidan, which is adjacent to one of the long-standing US military bases in central Seoul. Eventually, this led to its complete transformation into a full-blown bottle shop with outdoor seating. There is everything from your typical European and American mega-producers down to your pricier craft beer imports and, of course, local craft beer choices. Needless to say, it has become one of the hottest spots in one of the trendiest neighborhoods in the country. It is something you will want to check off in fall, spring, or even summer. This is not just for the temperature, but the lively vibe that the street picks up out front and the *super* selection at Woori Super.

SEOUL AND JEJU, SOUTH KOREA

## 880 Check out the magnificent Magpie Brewing

Magpie Brewing, much like many of its craft beer contemporaries, began with a husband-and-wife team and their two friends in Seoul. This was the beginning of the craft beer boom in 2011, and Magpie quickly expanded to become one of the most recognizable names in Korean craft brewing. Located along Gyeongnidan-gil (or road) next to Woori Super and down the road from The Booth, this area quickly became one of the hottest spots in the country to grab a bite and a pint. Magpie took full advantage with pop-ups and its in-house pizza (which some have said started the pizza-beer trend *pimaek*). Furthermore, with changes in the local regulatory environment, the Magpie team was able to switch from small batches and licensing its beer to opening its own brewery on Jeju Island. So, whether you're in Seoul or enjoying the beach in Jeju, Magpie is there for you.

## 881 Track down one of the oldest breweries in Korea

Platinum brewery is one of the oldest licensed craft brewers, not only in Korea, but in mainland China. It initially began as a brewpub in the southern districts of Seoul back in 2002, but in order to expand, it needed to build a brewery outside of Korea. After a chance encounter with a former UC Davis brewmaster school colleague in China, founder Junghoon "John" Yoon began brewing in China for export back to the Korean market in 2015. After some regulatory changes, Platinum was able to begin brewing in 2017 and is now one of the largest craft brewers in Korea. Yoon studied brewing in the 1990s in the US and during this time began to develop the recipe for his beers, in particular his signature Pale Ale. Platinum's brews are distributed throughout much of Korea now, so you shouldn't have trouble finding it.

## 882 Amaze your taste buds with these beers

Amazing Brewing is an ever-expanding chain of pubs and taphouses in Seoul. However, it all began in Seongsu, which is a gentrified industrial area that was tailor-made for a brewery. This location offers a great outdoor courtyard with a refreshing menu in which to enjoy the local and global selection on tap. On average there are sixty beers on tap with half of them brewed in-house. This brewery is also near subway line number 2, which circles Seoul, making it one of the most accessible breweries in the metro area. There is a local discount provided on a select beer every day, so if you happen to know someone residing in the district, be sure to bring them along. Amazing Brewing boasts an amazing selection of beers and locations—including in Jamsil and Incheon.

## 883 Crack a cold one at Craftworks

The South Korean capital has been at the forefront of the emergence of Korean cuisine and culture, but was never really considered a sophisticated beer market. Beginning in 2010, the Canadian Craftworks Taphouse & Bistro operation was one of the first to challenge the regulatory regime around beer. The licensing system basically made craft brewing outside of brewhouses impossible. With successful pressure, the rules regarding brewing capacity and distribution were changed, which allowed for a new generation of brewers. Craftworks focused on a particular localized form of beers, utilizing local mountain names for inspiration. In a country where hiking is a national pastime, this was highly effective.

## 884 Pair beer with a slice of "Spice Girls" pizza

The Booth in Gyeongnidan began as a small pub on a street that runs perpendicular to the Yongsan US military base at the bottom of Namsan. This quickly became a neighborhood associated with the craft beer boom in South Korea. The Booth took a modest approach to this location, utilizing simple stacks of pallets as tables accompanied by plastic stools commonly associated with Korean barbecue joints and street-food shacks. Don't let this fool you, as the beer is tasty and the open atmosphere blends well with the vibrant quality of the area. You can find The Booth in a number of districts in Seoul, such as Gangnam—yes, the one from the song—and Common Ground. Pizza by the slice is also a nice touch— try a slice of "Spice Girls" pizza to go.

SEOUL, SOUTH KOREA
## 885 Celebrate South Korean beer at Beer Week Seoul

Beginning with the IPA gold rush of 2011, the Korean alcohol scene started to see significant changes—and with it came an increasing number of beer festivals. They are now a regular fixture during spring and summer around the city. Beer Week Seoul is orchestrated by Booth Brewing, which operates a brewpub in Common Ground. It makes good use of its international presence and partnerships, providing a great opportunity to interact with local and international craft producers. Common Ground is an open courtyard catered by food trucks and surrounded by blue shipping container shops. It is conveniently located just off subway line number 2, making for an easy trip home.

SEOUL, SOUTH KOREA
## 886 Start or end your evening at this hole in the wall

Hair of the Dog is a bit of a hole in the wall—however, you can expect a current and consistent collection of domestic and international craft beer here. You'll also find a consistent collection of domestic and international residents that are approachable and engaging. Sounds like a winning combination, right? Hair of the Dog sits on the bend in the main artery servicing Haebangchon, which is where many expats live in Seoul. You'll find notable craft beer classics such as Platinum on tap, as well as not-so-classic Korean lagers like Max. There are also some classics on the menu: chicken Parmesan and reuben sandwiches.

## 887 Bounce into the Booth's pubs

The origins of The Booth Brewing lie with an infamous *Economist* article written by Daniel Tudor (one of the founders) that stated the superiority of North Korean beer over the South's. This buzz led to the collaboration between Tudor and the other founders, Heeyoon Kim and Sunghoo Yang, in 2013. The Booth is a domestic producer, but has its beginnings with its international partner Mikkeller, with whom it produced its first beer. It has partnered primarily with the Danish craft producer among others, while simultaneously operating a brewery in California and enlisting local Korean pop icons in its collaborations. The eye-catching design is hard to miss on the bottles, taps, and promotional material, and you can also find its pubs around Seoul. So, if you're looking for beers by The Booth, or its friends, you can try the brewery or any number of its pubs.

## 888 Tour the Korea Craft Brewery

The Korea Craft Brewery, located south of Seoul, is where the award-winning Ark beer is brewed. This facility resembles the concepts employed by vineyards in North America, combining fresh architecture, open spaces, and entertainment with its beers and pizzas. It has also sought to include performing artists in the process and often hosts movie nights, concerts, and Christmas parties, among other events. You can take part in two types of tours: the Classic, which is forty minutes long, or the Master, which is an hour with the brewer (limited availability). If you're concerned about transportation, the brewery offers a monthly "You Drink! We Drive!" tour that bundles transportation to and from Seoul into your tour.

**890** *Left:* Busan's Gorilla Brewing crafts beers with fresh hops grown on its very own hop farm

NATIONWIDE, SOUTH KOREA
## 889 Catch a movie with a cold one

It has been said that Koreans are the Irish of Asia and their penchant for drinking is no more apparent than in its inclusion in almost every activity, whether cycling along the Han River or taking in a movie at one of the many theaters. With a thriving local movie industry and one of the largest international box offices, Korea boasts a number of worthy entertainment options. Local theaters are still very heavily attended, and are also very competitive. You'll find a number of added services and special effects designed to lure in customers. 3D and 4D theaters are common and you can find large IMAX and Guinness record screens throughout Seoul. While you're at it, you may want to have a couple of cold ones in the theater, which are readily available on tap. At one point, you could even get Jägerbombs to wash down your popcorn! These days, you can also find Magpies' collaboration with CGV theaters in grocery stores, pubs, and the theater, of course. If you're in Korea during the summer, this is a great way to take a break from the sweltering heat.

BUSAN, SOUTH KOREA
## 890 Sample South Korea's freshest hops at Gorilla Brewing

Since 2011, the beer market in South Korea has changed significantly and nowhere is this more apparent than on the hop farm of Gorilla Brewing. The fresh hops make a real difference in the flavor and freshness of this beer, particularly the IPA. This British-owned and operated venture began in 2015 and has become an increasingly common presence in beer festivals and on bar taps across the country. This is emblematic of the growing success and familiarity of craft beer in South Korea. As the market has begun to mature, there has been a greater appreciation for the effort being put in by brewers. With plans moving ahead to increase its hops farm by fivefold, look to Gorilla Brewing to continue to be at the forefront of the market.

## SOUTH KOREA

### 891 Grab a four-pack of neigai manwon

If you visited South Korea before 2011, you would have found your beer selection to be lacking. Local laws and habits hadn't really embraced beer beyond its role as a partner for *soju* and food. The market was dominated by local producers, and craft beer licensing was highly restrictive. However, legal changes in 2011 helped to open the market to craft producers and free-trade deals opened the market to international mega-producers. This led to a popular beer promotion: *neigai manwon*. Initially, this was found mostly in convenience stores, but this expat favorite has reached cult status and is often offered in major grocery and department stores. Basically, major distributors offer four 500 ml cans of imported beer for "*manwon*" or a single 10000w note (which equates to around $9). So you should be able to find something to wet your whistle at a reasonable price.

PARO, BHUTAN

## 892 Discover beers made with native Bhutanese ingredients

A beautiful landlocked country with a population of around 800,000, Bhutan is home to Namgay Artisanal Brewery. Located at Dumsibu, the brewery was created by Dorji Gyeltshen, who makes beer using the exotic flavors from Bhutanese ingredients. Gyeltshen has a degree in hotel management from Les Roches, Switzerland, and has experienced the European brewing culture, which inspired him to open his brewery. He believes that beer will help in improving the Gross National Happiness of the country, which is also the government's driving philosophy. The brews include the flagship Red Rice lager made from locally sourced red rice, Wheat Ale, Dark Ale, Milk Stout, IPA, Pilsner, and an apple cider.

PANCHKULA, INDIA

## 894 Hop to this Indian microbrewery

Chandigarh's tryst with beer began in 2010 when Hops n Grains was set up. After gaining an MBA in Australia, Amritanshu Gupta went back to India to run a candy store. After about seven years of doing this, he moved to the beer industry and introduced Hops n Grains, a brand that has won every award that the brewery has been nominated for since its inception. In fact, Gupta was quite instrumental in changing the perception of nightlife in Chandigarh. He and his wife have innovated the personality of the city, turning it from a retirement town to a bustling mini-metropolis brimming with youthful energy. At Hops n Grains you'll find freshly brewed golden ale, weiss, German bock, and a brewer's special flowing on taps.

GURUGRAM, INDIA

## 893 Relax with a fresh brew and live music

7 Barrel Brewpub is a newer kid on the block and caters to youth looking to unwind with live music, dance, and of course, beer. Murals done by Delhi Street Art add an eclectic vibe, and great hospitality wins it brownie points. The malty Amber Red, full-bodied Premium Lager, the dusky, heavy-tasting Schwarzbier, and the all-time favorite wheat beer are the fresh brews on offer. This venue is a hit among live bands—one of the biggest Indian bands, Indian Ocean, has performed here!

GURUGRAM, INDIA

## 895 Come to the crease at this cricket-themed bar

Howzatt closely beat Pune's Doolally's to become the first microbrewery in India. It opened its doors to the public in December 2008 with an offering of four fresh lagers: Premium, Wheat, Light, and Dark. Today, Howzatt is a 2,500 sq ft (232 sq m) cricket-themed bar, with plasma TVs all around, making this the best choice for those who wish to enjoy a game with a glass of beer. The brews are also appreciated for being healthier compared to other options, thanks to a double-brewing process applied to the entire brewing process.

GURUGRAM, INDIA

**896 Visit a German brewhouse in India**

*Brauhaus* in German means Beer House, and 45°F (7°C)
is the ideal temperature to enjoy a freshly brewed beer.
So 7° Brauhaus is essentially a brewhouse serving
great German beers at recommended temperatures.
A visit to this microbrewery—spread across 12,500 sq ft
(1,161 sq m)—is reminiscent of the breweries in Bavaria.
Oak and maple wood furniture and vintage, rustic decor
give 7° an old-school charm, which also makes it one of
the finest dining destinations in Gurugram. It has even
experimented with its beers to create beer ice creams,
something that was only seen in Germany, and needless
to say, the crowds love it!

BANGALORE, INDIA
## 897 Join The Biere Club revolution

The palates of the beer guzzlers in Bangalore
underwent a massive change when the first
microbrewery popped up in 2011. Used to drinking
bottled beer, the frothy, bittersweet golden brews
that were being brewed at The Biere Club started a
revolution. Inspired from the breweries they visited
on their travels across Europe, Meenakshi Raju and
her brother Arvind decided to open a brewpub in
Bangalore. An idea that took form in 2006 came to
fruition only in 2011, as the laws were drafted and
passed in the Indian state of Karnataka. It was a
brand-new concept and, as The Biere Club educated
beer drinkers about the different types of brews, people
soon fell in love with the lagers, ales, and stouts.

BANGALORE, INDIA
## 898 Grab a beer and burger at Barleyz

It is the rooftop allure that continues to bring locals and
tourists alike to this 1,000-seater beer garden located in
Sony World Junction, within the hip neighborhood of
Koramangala. The open-air ambiance has been an instant
hit, and a dance floor and Bollywood weekends have
made this microbrewery a popular party destination. The
beer menu boasts of six brews: American Blonde, Belgian
Wit, German Wheat, English Pale Ale, Irish Stout, and
the highly recommended Special. This brewhouse has
also earned a lot of praise for its burgers. So if you've got
beer and burgers on your mind, you know heading to
Barleyz is a good idea.

**897** *Left:* The Biere Club was the first microbrewery to
pop up in Bangalore in 2011

BANGALORE, INDIA

## 899 Have a taste of ABC beers

Starting in Michigan in 1995 as a passion project, Arbor Brewing was a craft beer company that made its way to Bangalore in 2012. Known as ABC, it gave India its first American-style brewpub. The Brasserie Blonde, a spiced ale with a distinct flavor of orange, along with the sweet, spicy, and fruity Phat Abbot Tripel and the classic IPA, soon became the favorites of all those who walked through the doors of this hip brewpub, while pretzel bites and onion rings made for excellent accompaniments with those man mugs. Even non-beer drinkers fell in love with its Smooth Criminal, the honey lavender ale. ABC takes pride in stocking a selection of around eight original craft beers at any given time. Today, it is a buzzing center for beer and nightlife enthusiasts.

BANGALORE, INDIA

## 900 Prepare to party at Toit

Launched in 2010, Toit kicked off when colleagues Arun George and Sibi Venkataraju decided to quit their jobs in Singapore to realize their dreams of owning a bar. What started off as a place for beer drinkers to drop by for a pint of Toit Weiss (made using imported German wheat malt), Dark Knight (a dark, full-bodied, roasty, malty ale), or an IPA slowly revolutionized the brewing culture in Bangalore and, ultimately, India. Toit features gigs, rock shows, DJ nights, and performance tours. Today, a line outside the iconic building on 100 Feet Road in Indiranagar is proof of its popularity. Toit has also reached Mumbai and Pune.

BANGALORE, INDIA

## 901 Enjoy an ale with jazz tunes

The folks in Bangalore are brewing a sweet, niche culture. Live music enthusiasts, the sports squad, the party-hoppers, or the simple beer guzzlers all have a brewery that suits their mood. One such establishment for jazz music aficionados is Windmills Craftworks. Melody, harmony, and rhythm get together in soft jazz tunes at this warm, comfortable, and cozy microbrewery. The Stout, Golden Ale, India Pale Ale, and Hefeweizen are popular.

BANGALORE, INDIA
## 902 Drink your worries away at Vapour

Fresh, edgy, and youthful, the ambiance is what draws the crowds to this microbrewery. Vapour doubles up as a nightclub, too, so don't be surprised if you find yourself surrounded by many others waiting to let their hair down, thanks to the insanely low prices of alcohol. The hefeweizen and stout are a hit, and the seasonal specials create quite a buzz (the reviews of the mango mint beer proved this!). Vapour is the first eco watering hole in India, using eco-friendly LED lighting systems; it has other venues in Hyderabad and Gurugram.

**899** *Above:* Arbor Brewing, which began in Ann Arbor, Michigan, is a surprise hit with its location in Bangalore

**BARDEZ, INDIA**

### 903 Discover great Goan brews

Goa Brewing has a simple mission: to produce non-conformist beers. This homegrown craft brewery in the land of sun, sand, beaches, and parties is the brainchild of Suraj Shenai, a man passionate about beer and hospitality, who quit his impressive corporate job to follow his dreams. Goa Brewing is set inside an old Portuguese house, complete with an old school courtyard and lined by rooms that now store malts, barrels, and bottles. Creativity is the driving force behind the brand, which explains why doughnut-flavored beer and a cherry-flavored stout might soon be on their way. The "non-conformist" IPA is called Eight Finger Eddie, a tribute to the famous hippie from the 1960s who put Goa on the tourist map.

**PUNE, INDIA**

### 904 Toast to the weekend at TJ's

With Pune witnessing a boom in the cosmopolitan culture, TJ's BrewWorks opened its doors in Maharashtra with five beers on tap: Devil's Dark, Zen Weiss, Premium, Mystery, and Blonde. The city's second microbrewery boasts chic wooden interiors, an al fresco seating area, great finger food, and, of course, some of the best brews in town. TJ's soon grew to be the choice of watering hole that is frequented on weekends by those who love to dance, drink, and make merry.

**903**  *Right:* Goa Brewing's mission is to craft "non-conformist beers"

PUNE, INDIA
## 905 Indulge at India's second microbrewery

Prateek Chaturvedi and Suketu Talekar left high-paying jobs in Singapore to study the brewing culture in the country, and in 2009 opened Doolally—India's second microbrewery (after Howzatt in Gurugram). After facing much resistance from the government in terms of licenses, quantity control, investments, and permissions, the duo soon navigated their way to the top of the best microbrewery list. Their lager got the attention of the locals in Pune, and those in Mumbai started frequenting Doolally on the weekends. Wheat Beer, Santa's Ale, English Brown Ale, Greenlandic Ale, and the Apple Cider slowly grew to be the comfort that we needed at the end of a long week.

PUNE, INDIA
## 906 Imbibe independence at IBC

Independence Brewing is more than just a brewery; it is a start-up community that gets together to discuss business over beer. Shailendra Bist and Avanish Vellanki are change makers who are trying to build a community among start-ups in Pune by holding events around business at their brewery. IBC, as it is fondly known, sees young founders and entrepreneurs as customers networking their way through the night with freshly brewed lagers to keep them company. The season specials are the talk of the town, even pulling in crowds from distant neighborhoods. Fun fact: IBC offers a start-up discount, which is much more generous than that offered to corporations.

**905** *Above:* Doolally was just the second craft brewery to open in India

## 907 Slake your thirst at Thirsty City

The crash in 2008 suddenly left Gregory Kroitzsh without a job, and from living a comfortable nine-to-five life in New York, Kroitzsh found himself on a plane to India. This gave him a chance to revisit his entrepreneurial dreams, and combined with his love for beer, he started working on a concept that later came to be known as the Barking Deer. His passion drove him to try new beer recipes, and the crowd fell in love with whatever was offered. The signature Barking Deer India Pale ale and the Flying Pig Belgian Wit soon became Mumbai's most popular craft beers. In fact, the Flying Pig was one of the beers used to make the glitter beer—a beer we had heard only of on Instagram. Today, the Barking Deer goes by the name of Thirsty City 127.

## 908 Party down at the White Owl

White Owl Brewery started in 2014 and has slowly made its way onto the list of popular brews of choice that beer drinkers and party goers opt for. Walk into a swanky nightclub in Mumbai, Pune, or Goa and you won't be surprised to see the White Owl–branded beer glasses filled with its freshly brewed golden elixir. Javed Murad, a Harvard Business School graduate, launched White Owl in Mumbai in 2013 as a restaurant, and then converted it into a fully fledged brewery the following year. Its portfolio of beers includes: Shadow, an English porter; Torpedo, a punchy American pale ale; Diablo, an Irish red ale; Halcyon, an incredibly popular German hefeweizen; Ace, a French apple cider; Paulina, a German Kölsch; and Spark, a Belgian wit.

## 909 Drink beer without packing on the pounds

Bira 91 became India's favorite beer in just two years—and for good reason. Smart branding, a quirky positioning, and, of course, a high-quality and great-tasting beer made Bira 91 a household name within a few months of inception in February 2015. Bira 91 launched with two variants: Bira 91 Strong and Bira 91 Light. The Strong was the first strong beer based on wheat, with 7% ABV. Later, Bira 91 launched the low-calorie beer, one of the first few low-calorie beers on the Indian market. In fact, this light beer is said to have fewer calories than milk or even a glass of orange juice!

## 910 Wash down the wares at Woodside Inn

Woodside Inn was set up by Neighbourhood Hospitality Pvt. Ltd in 2007 in the stylish neighborhood of Colaba. It was the first pub in Mumbai that served craft beer without being a brewpub. It was a luxurious space in a locality of southern Mumbai that was otherwise a financial hub filled with hustlers. It offered what other establishments in the neighborhood did not: a laid-back luxurious space and craft beers. Woodside Inn went on to open another pub in the suburb of Andheri, and has built a reputation for great food and craft beer in each of these two locations.

MUMBAI, INDIA
### 911 Gulp classic beers at Gateway

Gateway Brewing was founded in 2011 by three men passionate about the business of beer. Navin Mittal, Rahul Mehra, and Krishna Naik have a single purpose: to brew the evergreen, classic beer styles with local ingredients and make them easily available and affordable to the masses. It was because of the consistent efforts of this trio that a comprehensive microbrewery policy for the state of Maharashtra exists—something that seemed impossible when they started out. Inspired by Mumbai's iconic landmark, Gateway of India, Gateway Brewing has now become a household name within the community of beer drinkers in this vibrant metropolis.

SHANGHAI, CHINA
## 912 Booze up at this "boxing" brewery

Established in 2008, Boxing Cat Brewery—a boxing-themed brewery with beer named after various fighting terms (Right Hook Helles, TKO India Pale Ale)—offers two locations in Shanghai to sample its beers. In addition to its core lineup, the brewery has also created numerous collaborations with companies like Mikkeller and Great Leap Brewery.

**BEIJING, CHINA**

**913 Take it slow at Slow Boat Brewing**

Slow Boat Brewing is a stylish brewpub featuring industrial-chic concrete columns, blonde wood flourishes, and honeyed leather banquettes. The beers are largely American-style hoppy ales, like Monkey's Fist IPA (made with Citra hops) and Zombie Pirate Pale Ale, named after China's most infamous pirate, Zheng Shi.

### 914 Try beer from this former homebrewer-turned-pro

With thirty-seven taps and nearly a hundred bottles, NBeer Pub offers one of the largest selections of beer in Beijing. It began in 2013 when Beijing Homebrew Society founding member Yin Hai launched the brand after winning multiple homebrew competitions. He now makes dozens of varieties and serves them in this sleek space.

### 915 Swill a Panda brew

Founded by Pan Dinghao and Kurt Xia, Panda Brew is one of the top craft breweries in China's emerging but still-young scene. Its pub is a haven for craft beer enthusiasts, with two floors of great beer and lively conversation surrounding the liquid. Be sure to check out Panda Eyes Red Honey Ale and Killed a Copycat Outlaw Witbier.

### 916 Partake in revelry at Asia's Oktoberfest

Qingdao International Beer Festival—aka Asia's Oktoberfest—is an annual summer bash that features a month-long celebration of all things beer. Like its German counterpart, this celebration features long tables filled with revelers swilling beer, dancing to traditional music, and enjoying tons of Chinese and Western food. Note: the beer is largely from international conglomerates (Heineken, Corona, Beck's, etc.).

BEIJING, CHINA
### 917 Taste beer infused with traditional Chinese ingredients

Established in 2012, Jing-A Brewing focuses on making classic beers with a Chinese twist by incorporating local ingredients into its recipes. Think: red rice koji, Sichuan peppercorns, ginger, and smoked local chile peppers. Other beers are takes on modern-traditional styles, like a Citra and Mosaic IPA, and an aggressively hopped Black IPA.

**918**  *Above:* Great Leap Brewing is based in a 115-plus-year-old *hutong*

## 918 Wander the backstreets of Wudaokou to find this brewery

Beginning in Beijing in late 2010, husband-and-wife team Carl Setzer and Liu Fang sought to combine some of the finer elements of Western brewing with some of the finer aspects of Chinese tradition and history. This is easy to see in Great Leap Brewing's striking branding, but also in its location. Not only does this brewery boast an extensive array of beer on tap, but it is also located in the backstreets of Wudaokou, a trendy university district. This 115-plus-year-old *hutong* is a traditional form of residential architecture that is vanishing quickly in a modernizing China and adds to the spread of historically inspired beers. There is a limited food menu at this location, but if you're hungry, you are encouraged to order in your own outside food. Great Leap has two more locations in Beijing, and both of these have extensive food menus.

SHENZHEN, CHINA
## 919 Imbibe Bionic brews

Bionic Brew is a pizza-and-beer brewpub that features American-style pies from local NYPD Pizza, paired with beers brewed right in-house. The citrusy Bionic Ale and Crickside, a Kölsch, are brewed year-round, while the seasonal offerings include Metropolis IPA and Sofro Wheat, a German hefeweizen.

HONG KONG
## 920 Check out this Asian beer bash

Founded in 2012, the annual fall Beertopia festival is Hong Kong's largest beer celebration, attracting more than 13,000 attendees each year. Expect in excess of 500 beers from all around the world at this event held over one weekend, under a backdrop of Hong Kong's Central Harbourfront space. Food trucks sling American, European, and traditional Asian dishes, and live music and DJs round out the experience.

HONG KONG
## 921 Explore Hong Kong's legitimately exotic brewery

Beginning late in 2013 on the south side of Hong Kong island, Young Master Ales quickly outgrew its modest facilities and added another more expressive facility. This second brewery is far more fitting to the mantra of this brewery itself, which thrives on creativity. That being said, if you're looking for something locally inspired and legitimately exotic, this is the brewery for you. There is no shame in Young Master Ales' game when it comes to providing a unique beer-drinking experience that is tied to Hong Kong. It is one of the largest craft brewers in the city and is a brand that embraces its locality. A prime example would be its Cha Chaan Teng Gose, which draws on local salted limes for its inspiration. As the south side of the island is off the beaten track, check major supermarkets, as the beers are often sold there as well.

## 922 Drink with the "door gods"

Also born in 2013, Moonzen Brewery is a husband-and-wife team that has sought to fill a void in the beer market. As the name Moonzen (or "door gods") suggests, this brewery takes a very local approach to its craft beers and experiences. However, it has a much broader scope, aiming to utilize local ingredients from every Chinese province in its future beer projects. The Dragon King Fujian Radler was added to its list and used honey pomelos to add a local twist to this summer favorite. Like most of its Hong Kong brethren, the Kowloon brewery is located in an industrial block that is tricky to find. Ask local warehouse staff—drink gesturing helps.

## 923 Taste Hong Kong's best food and beer pairings

Not far from the Yardley Brothers' brewery, you'll find a relatively new transplant to Hong Kong in Tsuen Wan called the Kowloon Bay Brewery. The product of the founders' desire to expand the beer market in China, they logically set up shop in Hong Kong in 2015. They have since developed a healthy range of beers both seasonal and year-round to meet growing thirsts. The brewery is keen on promoting food and beer pairings and collaborations, which may be worth looking into if you have a chance to visit. Furthermore, it has far more accommodating hours compared to other Hong Kong brewers, making it a more accessible option.

## 924 Sip beer from Hong Kong's largest craft beer facility

Over the mountains in the New Territories is the largest craft brewer in Hong Kong: Gweilo. The name, as some of the labels suggest, can be translated as "ghost chap" in its earliest references and is now largely a term used to describe foreigners in Hong Kong. This is fitting, as the brand originally came to Ian Jebbitt in a dream, which, in tandem with recipes from his childhood, led to homebrewing with his wife, Emily, and his friend, Joe Gould. Beginning in 2015, Gweilo has expanded quickly. Although not open to the public, Gweilo is very widely distributed across Hong Kong and Macau. You can find its core range of IPAs and pale ales—as well as limited batches—in most places on the island, whether in harborfront bodegas or large supermarkets.

HONG KONG

### 925 Wander the boisterous, hilly streets of Lan Kwai Fong

If you're visiting Hong Kong, you have probably heard about Lan Kwai Fong—or LKF, as it's commonly referred to. There is a little bit for everyone in this spot, from shot bars to proper dance clubs, but the real story is on the street on Friday and Saturday nights. This is where you get a healthy mix of people and a fairly relaxed attitude toward drinking in the hilly jackknife streets that constitute the district. This island neighborhood is a great place on the weekend to grab a couple of cans from the local 7-Eleven and take in the crowd. Be advised that there isn't much in the way of public toilets, so you may want to grab a spot on one of the many street-side patios and take in the shenanigans with a cool pint.

HONG KONG

### 926 Help yourself to a Hong Kong Bastard Imperial IPA

North of Kowloon, you'll find the Yardley Brothers nestled on the fifth floor of an industrial block in Kwai Hing. Yardley is a bit out of the way, but worth the detour. You will get a unique experience from not only the award-winning, year-round selections, but also the seasonal and collaboration ranges. The Yardley Brothers are a touch irreverent about their lucky beginnings in Hong Kong, and you'll taste that in the brands, such as the award-winning Hong Kong Bastard Imperial IPA. The Yardley Brothers are also brewers who border on mad scientists, as they seek to push the boundaries of beer in a number of directions. One example is in the hopless chile basil sour, the Thai Chilli Getaway, which is a tasty and unique experience.

HONG KONG

### 927 Sip beer at this seaside shack

The Lamma Island beer shack is the first manifestation of Yardley Brothers' beer experiments and aspirations. Although Luke Yardley began brewing in his home, he soon had an outlet for sharing his creations. In 2013, he found a seaside shack through one of his wife's friends. Since then, Luke has been able to provide an important service and quintessential beer-drinking experience up the road from Hung Shing Yeh beach. Whether you're looking to hang out on the beach or go for a hike, this is a nice place for a casual beer—or many. So, what are you waiting for? Grab a Lamma Island IPA on Lamma Island.

**927** *Above:* Taste the wares of Yardley Brothers at the Lamma Island beer shack outpost

TAIPEI, TAIWAN
### 928 Snag an American-style brew in Taiwan

Founded by two US brewers with a passion for rock climbing and craft beer, Redpoint Brewing creates American-inspired beers like Rock Monkey Stout, Disco Macaw Juicy Pale Ale, and Long Dong American-style lager. A neon-lit taproom offers the beers on draft and hosts an American-style menu.

TAIPEI, TAIWAN
### 929 Discover Taipei's best nanobrewery

Founded by Americans Brett Tieman and Matt Frazar in 2014, 23 Brewing is part of Taiwan's second wave of craft brewers. The duo brews small batches of American-style beers for distribution throughout the city's bars and restaurants. You can also visit the 23 Public in the city's Da'an district.

NEW TAIPEI CITY, TAIWAN
### 930 Drink beer from a retro Airstream trailer

Founded in 2013 by five partners, including the American–born-and-raised Peter Huang, Taihu Brewing is one of Taiwan's premier breweries. Huang left a job in finance to move to Taipei to pursue the development of this quickly growing brewery. Taihu now features a handful of locations throughout Taipei, including a research and development lab with rare beer releases and a barrel-aging facility, an outdoor taproom, and even a mobile location based around a renovated vintage Airstream trailer retrofitted with more than a dozen draft lines. Be sure to try the Kumquat Kölsch dosed with locally grown fresh calamansi juice, the flagship American-style Taihu IPA, and the mind-blowingly tart Smoked Plum Lichtenhainer, brewed with smoked plums.

**TAIPEI, TAIWAN**

# Enjoy Taipei's top five craft beer bars

### 931 23 Public Craft Beer

An outpost of Taipei's 23 Brewing, this brightly lit corner spot offers a dozen beers on draft from the host brewery along with Western-style bar snacks and pizzas.

### 932 Way Home Beer House

This small store has dozens of shelves lined with the best of the best Taiwanese, European, and American craft brews. Post up at the bar and order from the eight draft selections.

### 933 BeerGeek Micropub

This English-style pub features a scrappy but interesting array of beers from around the world, served with British-style snacks like chips and beans and savory meat pies.

### 934 Chuoyinshi Landmark

This sleek "drinking room"—one of Taihu Brewing's many locations—features twenty draft beers in a sleek, modern setting.

### 935 The Local Taipei Craft Beer House

This cool craft beer pub offers domestic drafts and bottles of imported beers from the likes of Germany's Ayinger and San Diego's Belching Beaver.

**NEW TAIPEI CITY, TAIWAN**

## 936 Check out one of this brewery's ten-plus locations

Founded in 2014, Zhang Men Brewing is one of the fastest-growing breweries in Taiwan with more than ten taprooms and bars throughout Taiwan, Hong Kong, and China. Focusing on modern styles like imperial porter and Berliner-style weisse sour ales, the brewery is helping usher Taiwan into the craft beer future.

**NEW TAIPEI CITY, TAIWAN**

## 937 Taste a tea-infused Scotch ale

In 2015, three craft beer geek friends cofounded Taiwan Head Brewers in their hometown, producing innovative craft beers made with local and indigenous ingredients. The brewery has won numerous awards from competitions around the world with brews such as Rain Water Taiwan Tea Ale 4, a Scotch-style ale infused with locally grown golden daylily oolong tea.

## 938 Catch a soccer match with a local ale

Exposed brick walls and handsome wood flourishes greet you at the small Craft Beer Pub in Hanoi's Hoàn Kiêm district. It's a great spot for watching international soccer matches while sipping on a cold local ale from Pasteur Street Brewing or Platinum Premium Beers.

## 939 Drink a frothy Milkshake IPA in Hanoi

Though it's not much to look at inside, the beer at FURBREW Beer Bar—an outpost of the local FURBREW Craft Beer—is outstanding. Twenty drafts are offered and range from the light and refreshing Sour Grapes sour ale to the frothy Milkshake IPA.

**938** *Above:* Hanoi's Craft Beer Pub is a great spot to sample local brews

HO CHI MINH CITY, VIETNAM

## 940 Give a wink to Winking Seal

Winking Seal Beer is a cool, bright spot that was founded in 2017 by Americans Brian Kekich, a TV producer–turned–professional brewer, and Mark Nerney, who has a design background. They've created one of Vietnam's hippest new breweries with a fun, colorful tasting room and an interesting selection of house-brewed beers. Check out the uber-hoppy One Eye Imperial Pale Ale, clocking in at over 10% ABV.

HO CHI MINH CITY, VIETNAM

## 941 Become a fan of Phat Rooster Ales

With a solid core lineup of six different craft beers and eye-catchingly colorful packaging, you'll find ales and lagers from Phat Rooster Ales in specialty beer bars throughout the city and in other parts of Southeast Asia, including in Singapore. Be sure to check out the amber ale for an updated take on the classic style.

HO CHI MINH CITY, VIETNAM

## 942 Settle into a secret craft beer oasis

Ong Cao Craft Beer is a hip craft beer oasis in the middle of the bustling Bùi Viên Street. It offers a mix of East and West brews, including Vietnam's own Pasteur Street Brewing and Fuzzy Logic Brewing. Over the speakers you'll hear a mix of hip-hop, rap, and R&B.

HO CHI MINH CITY, VIETNAM

## 943 Pair slow-smoked meat with local pours

Slow-smoked American-style meat is the specialty at Quán Ut Ut's craft beer and barbecue joint. Try the BBQ sampler, a butcher block platter packed with pulled pork, smoked chicken, and ribs, along with one of dozens of local draft pours from breweries like the local BiaCraft Artisan Ales.

HO CHI MINH CITY, VIETNAM

## 944 Take a sip from the Heart of Darkness

Founded by New Yorker John Pemberton, Heart of Darkness Brewery is one of Vietnam's fastest-growing breweries. The flagship bar offers twenty different varieties on draft, including the collaboration with Hong Kong's Little Creatures Brewing: Creatures of Darkness IPA.

**HO CHI MINH CITY, VIETNAM**

## 945 Enjoy West Coast–style beers with a Vietnamese twist

One of the most impressive microbreweries by world standards, East West Brewing combines classic Western flavors with a Vietnamese twist. The flagship Far East IPA features a blend of American Centennial hops and New Zealand Nelson Sauvin for a beautiful tropical aroma of grapefruit and white wine grapes.

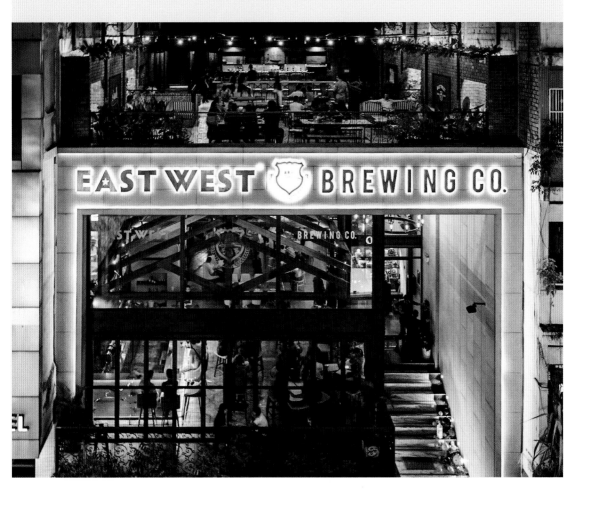

### HO CHI MINH CITY, VIETNAM
## 946 Sample a heady jasmine-infused IPA

Pasteur Street Brewing (PSBC) founder John Reid poached Alex Violette from Boulder, Colorado's Upslope Brewing to move to Vietnam and start this innovative brewery in 2014. With a mission to combine American craft beer know-how with traditional and local Vietnamese ingredients, Reid and Violette have grown Pasteur Street into one of Vietnam's most recognized and revered craft breweries. With six taprooms spread across Ho Chi Minh City and Hanoi, PSBC creates unique takes on classic styles. Must-try beers include Jasmine IPA, brewed with a blend of three American hop varietals and a dash of jasmine, and Passion Fruit Wheat Ale with the tangy sweetness of local passion fruit.

# Locate these places for *Bia hơi* in Vietnam

*Bia hơi* is a Vietnamese specialty street beverage consisting of uber-fresh beer delivered daily and consumed within hours. Mostly found in small bars and on street corners set with plastic stools and tables, the low-alcohol, supremely crushable beer is a cheap and fun way to get refreshment. Here are seven of the best places to enjoy it.

**947   Bia Ho'i Junction**
Corner of Ta Hien and Lu'o'ng Ngoc Quyen streets in the Old Quarter, Hanoi

**948   Bia Ho'i Ngoc Linh**
2 Đường Thành, Hoàn Kiêm, Hanoi

**949   Bia Ho'i Thiên Nga**
86 Trân Hưng Đao, Ho Chi Minh City

**950   Bia Ho'i 19C Ngoc Hà**
Ba Đình, Thành Phố, Hanoi

**951   Bia Ho'i 1a Âu Cơ'**
Near the InterContinental Hotel, Hanoi

**952   Bia Ho'i U Pháo Truc Bach**
1 Trân Vũ, Quán Thánh, Ba Đình, Hanoi

**953   Bia Ho'i Hài Xôm**
22 Tăng Bat Hô, Hai Bà Trung District, Hanoi

955   *Above:* Enter the tropical oasis of Botanico Wine & Beer Garden

### HO CHI MINH CITY, VIETNAM
## 954 Discover Vietnam's craft beer vanguard
Opened in 2015, BiaCraft Artisan Ales quickly gained a reputation as one of the city's best craft beer destinations. With sixty taps, it offers by far one of the largest draft selections in town. Drop in for a tap takeover from one of Vietnam's newest craft brewers or simply settle for a paddle of samplers to work your way through the overwhelming selection.

### PHNOM PENH, CAMBODIA
## 955 Follow the jungle path to this hideaway
To get to Botanico Wine & Beer Garden—a hideaway beer oasis—enter through the wooden gate below the sign and traverse the meandering rain forest–like path. You'll soon find a tropical beer garden of delight, pouring eight craft beers on draft and several more in bottles, with a focus on local and regional craft brews.

### KOH KONG, CAMBODIA
## 956 Procure a purple-hued brew
The magenta-hued Butterfly Pea Wheat ale from Stone Head is brewed with butterfly pea flowers, which lend it the brilliant purplish-blue coloring. In Thai cooking, butterfly pea flowers are used for dessert and in herbal teas, imparting a rich earthiness to nearly everything they touch, including this beer.

### SIEM REAP, CAMBODIA
### 957 Bend an elbow with expats

The Local Brew Pub and Guesthouse is a hostel-like café, bar, and pub that pours a variety of local and international brews to the roving crowd of expats and travelers wandering through its doors. Grab a seat at the bar and choose between eight taps, or pick a flight and nestle in at the couches in the front foyer.

### SIEM REAP, CAMBODIA
### 958 Take a walk down Pub Street

A walk down Siem Reap's Pub Street is unlike anything else in the world. An overwhelming number of bars, pubs, lounges, and restaurants greets you with an endless array of drink options. Though most do not offer high-end beers, there is plenty of sampling and street food to make the experience worthwhile.

### SIEM REAP, CAMBODIA
### 959 Check out this chic brewpub

With a high-end hotel pool-like vibe—low-slung wicker furniture, a koi pond, and an open-air floor plan—Siem Reap Brewpub might be one of the chicest brewpubs in the world. Try one of six house-brewed beers like the basic but cleansing Blonde Ale, or the rye malt-infused Saison Ale with a superb dry finish.

BANGKOK, THAILAND
## 960 Seek out spectacular views at this rooftop beer bar
Located on the twenty-ninth and thirtieth levels of the Radisson Blu hotel, the rooftop Brewski, a craft beer bar, pours more than a hundred different beers and is the highest and most scenic craft beer spot in the whole of Thailand. A daily "beer buffet" offers unlimited pours of local ales to pair with the breathtaking panoramic views of the city.

### BANGKOK, THAILAND
## 961 Catch a theatrical performance inside a beer hall

Tawandang German Brewery consists of a sprawling German-style beer hall—with communal tables stretching as far as the eye can see. It features theatrical performances nightly, including Egyptian-themed dancing, Thai pop hit covers, and comedic drag shows. The beer, brewed on-site, is basic but refreshing—you'll find a lager and dunkel dark, as well as a weizen wheat ale.

### LOEI, THAILAND
## 962 Go out of your way to find this small-town brewery

The small town of Loei is the unexpected home of Thailand's Outlaw Brewing, makers of some of the best craft beer in Thailand. The laid-back taproom offers a selection of the brewery's modern American-style craft beers, including Mosaic IPA, with notes of dank fruit and citrus, and The Beast DIPA, clocking in at 10% ABV. Pair these with a menu of Isaan Thai specialty dishes, including *yum nua* (mixed beef salad), spicy Thai chicken wings, and roasted pork. A small selection of imported canned beers is often available.

### CHIANG DAO, CHIANG MAI, THAILAND
## 963 Get tropical-outdoorsy at this beer bar

Microkosmos Craft Beer Bar is an outdoor bar whose surrounding tropical greenery and camp-like vibes—including a firepit and rough-hewn wooden tables and benches—make it feel like it's set smack in the middle of the jungle. The beer list is here to cool you down with drafts and bottle offerings like Deschutes's Chasin' Freshies IPA and Stone Vengeful's Spirit tropical IPA.

### CHIANG MAI, THAILAND
## 964 Pair international beers with fried bites

The small but stylish Craffity bar offers a diverse selection of bottles and drafts from American, Cambodian, and European brewers. Post up at a table inside or grab your beer and retire to the black-tiled front patio, where you'll find a smattering of tables and benches. A small selection of fried foods is also offered.

BANGKOK, THAILAND
### 965 Get a taste of Denmark in Bangkok

Feeling like there's a Mikkeller Bar in every corner of the world? You may be right. Mikkeller Bangkok was one of the brand's first expansions into Asia, and it features sleek, Scandinavian-style pale wood decor with high-top tables and outdoor seating. Thirty drafts are offered, most from US and European cult breweries.

BANGKOK, THAILAND
### 966 Match beer with Euro-Thai fusion cuisine

Thai-influenced European fusion dishes are the theme at the upscale Eat Me Restaurant in Bangkok's Silom district. Live music—think lounge acts—permeates the space, and a short but fun selection of beers, including the crisp Tuatara Pilsner from New Zealand, are on offer.

## PHUKET, THAILAND

### 967 Spend some time gazing at this copper-clad brewhouse

Home of the flagship Chalawan Pale Ale, Full Moon Brewworks is a sleek and stylish brewpub in Phuket. The copper-clad brewhouse is on full display in the dining area and bar, and an outdoor waterside area offers great views.

## BANGKOK, THAILAND

### 968 Crack a beer at this compact store

Known as BOB for short, Bottles of Beer bar is a small, compact, and impeccably clean little store that sells bottled beers to go and draft pours for on-site consumption. The offerings range from domestic craft beers to international beers from Evil Twin, Stone, and FrauGruber.

## BANGKOK, THAILAND

### 969 Earn reward points on a large craft beer selection

Offering one of the largest selections of craft beers in the country—with more than forty drafts at the original location and another twenty at a newer spot—Bangkok's CRAFT bar offers plenty for the beer geek and novice alike. A rewards program earns you points, which can be exchanged for more beer.

## SINGAPORE

### 970 Try your luck at Good Luck Beerhouse

Good Luck Beerhouse is an unassuming Singapore bar adorned with brewery memorabilia from Orval, Founders, and Stone, among others. It packs quite a punch with eight drafts from primarily local breweries, including Brewlander and Daryl's Urban Ales. The selection is small but diverse—you'll typically find a range of beers from light, refreshing pilsners to robust stouts and hoppy IPAs.

## SINGAPORE

### 971 Drink Japanese craft beer in Singapore

Located in the heart of Singapore's Orchard Road district, JiBiru Craft Beer Bar is a Japanese craft beer and *yakitori* pub owned by the local Eastern Craft Trading group. The beer selection features a surprisingly wide range of offerings, including everything from the basics like Sapporo Premium Lager to obscure international beers from London's Fourpure Brewing and Japan's Minoh Brewery. Regardless of style, all the beers pair well with the menu of grilled delicacies—chicken thighs with spring onions; tender, juicy pork belly; and chicken meatballs. A variety of prix fixe menus of various sizes and quantities will leave you feeling satiated and happy.

## 972 Sample from twenty-five drafts in a former pharmacy

Housed in a former pharmacy, the black-and-white–tiled Druggists space, with handsome marble-top tables and an overall sleek, minimalist vibe, offers around twenty-five beers on draft and a menu that ranges from burgers and hot wings to *banh mi* and tempura vegetables. If the weather's good, post up outside at one of the German-style *biergarten* tables in front.

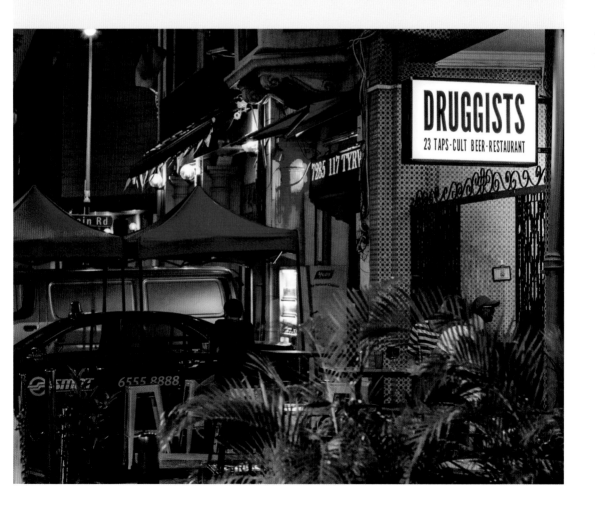

## 973 Sip beers from Singapore's first microbrewery

Brewerkz Riverside Point—Singapore's first and longest-running microbrewery—was founded in 1997 as a sports bar–themed spot for fresh beers. The core lineup includes everything from a Golden Ale to an Oatmeal Stout, and dozens of seasonals. A sprawling food menu offers satay, potato skins, fried chicken, and even American-style barbecue ribs.

## 974 Sample traditional Singaporean cuisine with house-brewed beers

Located along Singapore's foodie destination Joo Chiat Road/Katong district, The 1925 Brewing serves eight house-brewed beers alongside traditional dishes like *teochew* fish porridge and *sacha* rice with dried shrimp, garlic chives, and bird's-eye chile.

**974** *Above:* Pair 1925 brews with traditional Singaporean fare

## 975 Check out this indoor-outdoor smokehouse and beer hall

An expansive indoor-outdoor beer hall and smokehouse with seating for more than 400, Little Island Brewing serves up hearty portions of smoked meats and sausages on butcher-block platters and has a fun list of house-made beers. Pair a platter of smoked, roasted pork belly (*sio bak*) with a 19th Nervous Breakdown old ale that has notes of molasses, oak, and dried dark fruit.

## 976 Find world-renowned hipster ales at this tiny food stall

Beer geeks will find plenty to love about the Smith Street Taps, a small food hall nook (located inside the Chinatown Complex), which features a dozen rotating taps from around the world. You might find a juicy Simcoe and Mosaic-infused IPA from Cloudwater Brewing or something from Garage Project Brewing. Grab some street-style snacks from one of the adjacent stalls for a perfect lunch or dinner pairing.

## 977 Seek out Singapore's most Instagrammed beer

With two locations throughout Singapore, including Dempsey Road and Boat Quay, RedDot Brewhouse is an old-school microbrewery and pub featuring some traditional recipes and more modern offerings. It makes what is perhaps the most Instagrammed beer in the city: the Monster Green Lager, which gets its vibrant, verdant hue from an infusion of spirulina.

## 978 Enter through the red facade to find European delights

The strikingly bright-red facade of Mikkeller Bar Singapore on Purvis Street (located on the second floor of a heritage shop house) is difficult to miss. Enter and head up a flight of stairs, where you'll find the typical Mikkeller menu of lagers, ales, and experimental brews. Twenty-five drafts are offered, and the bar hosts regular bottle-share and brewer events each month.

## 979 Nosh street food with local and global brews

"Craft Beer for the People" proclaims the neon sign behind the bar at the lively, legendary Alamat Filipino Pub & Deli. Dig into a variety of street-influenced bites—*kare-kare* skewers, a platter of grilled sausages, and pickled vegetables—to pair with more than a dozen beers from domestic and international brewers.

SAGADA, PHILIPPINES

### 980 Drink beer brewed from native Filipino heirloom rice

A true one-of-a-kind experience awaits at the mountainous outdoor bar and brewery Sagada Cellar Door. Book in advance for the buffet of grilled meats and sausages—cooked over an open fire in the outdoor courtyard—to pair with the local brews. Andrew, the brewmaster and barkeep, makes his signature ale with a native heirloom rice called *balitinao*, along with several other varieties.

MANILA, PHILIPPINES

### 981 Sample wares from around the world

In 2008, Jim Araneta founded a beer distribution and importing company called Global Beer Exchange, dedicated to bringing in some of the best American, Japanese, and other beers. The Bottle Shop is his outlet for turning Filipino drinkers on to new and exciting beers that are a far cry from the fizzy yellow domestic lagers.

MANILA, PHILIPPINES

### 982 Hone your homebrewing skills

Joe's Brew is a homebrew supply store and brewery located in the heart of Manila. It crafts American-inspired beers aimed at the local Filipino market. Try Fish Rider Pale Ale or 34th Pursuit IPA on draft or in bottles to go. The small bar is a fun place to hang out and chat with other local beer enthusiasts.

MANILA, PHILIPPINES

### 983 Take a nip of Nipa Brew

The bright, bustling Nipa Brew offers nearly a dozen beers on draft, most of which are brewed on-site. Check out the citrusy Sun Stoked blonde ale, the Tropic Haze wheat ale, or one of several rotating beers from local breweries.

MANILA, PHILIPPINES

### 984 Celebrate the Philippines' beer scene

Manila's Brewfest MNL is the country's largest beer festival, held annually in late summer. It features forty local breweries, live music, and Filipino street food.

SAN PEDRO CITY, PHILIPPINES

### 985 Enjoy an Endless Summer Wheat Ale

Pedro Brewcrafters are homebrewers–turned-professionals, who honed their brewing skills during weekend garage sessions before deciding to open up a commercial brewery. Today, the trio—which includes Jill Borja and husband-and-wife duo Jaime Fanlo and Nadine Howell—offers their flagship Endless Summer Wheat Ale and other beers to bars and restaurants around town.

## SOUTHEAST ASIA
### 986 Crack a cold one in extreme humidity

There's nothing quite like cracking an ice-cold beer after a day spent in Southeast Asia's extreme humidity, whether sailing down the river or watching wildlife. On your next adventure, be sure to pack a cooler full of your favorite liquid provisions and enjoy the thirst-quenching power of one of the world's best beverages.

## ILIGAN CITY, PHILIPPINES
### 987 Indulge at this irreverent brewpub

A chubbed-up version of the famous Belgian *Manneken Pis* statue is the logo for the irreverent Filipino Fat Pauly's brewery and craft beer bar. Nearly ten draft beers are available—check out the coffee Sultan Stout—in a rollicking tasting room adorned with a mural featuring Jimi Hendrix, Janis Joplin, and Bob Marley.

## PALAWAN, PHILIPPINES
### 988 Meet the Philippines' first female craft brewer

The first and only craft brewery on the small Palawan archipelago province, Palaweño Brewery serves a niche community. The founder, Ayah Javier, lived in San Diego for years before she became the Philippines' first female craft brewer. The brewery was also the first in the country to offer tours of its facilities.

## ANYWHERE BEACHES ARE FOUND
### 989 Down some beer on the beach

One of beer's most intense joys is its refreshing and restorative power. Dig your toes into the warm sand and crack open a cold one. There's something magical about sipping an ice-cold brew on a windswept beach under the sun (local legislation permitting).

## 990 Tank up on Tahitian beer

The Tahitian brewery Hinano Beer crafts three styles of beer—a lager, an amber, and a golden ale—for distribution on the island and in export markets. Of the three, the amber Ambrée is by far the most interesting beer, with a strong roasted malt backdrop and a generous hop aroma.

## 991 Partake in the planet's "last happy hour"

About 2,600 miles west of Hawaii you'll find what locals refer to as "the last happy hour on the planet," a nod to the island's positioning near the international date line. The tiny Flying Fox Brewing crafts island specialties like Koko-Coco dark ale with roasted locally grown coconut, and Yolo Kipolo IPA, infused with Samoan kipolo limes.

## 992 Chill out with a beer on this stunning island

Founded in 2006, Matutu Brewing is a small brewery making English-inspired beers. The flagship is Kiva, an English-style pale ale brewed with Centennial and UK Goldings hops. Others include Mai, a German-style pilsner, and Maeva Celebration, an IPA made to celebrate Cook Islands' fifty years of independence. You can book a tour of the brewery's bungalow-like digs (including local transport) in advance.

KOMAVE, FIJI

## 993 Kill time with a Fijian lager

Located in the Beachhouse Resort along Fiji's Coral Coast, Kailoma Brewing's flagship beer is the light and refreshing Mokusiga Pacific lager. The words *moku* (meaning "kill") and *siga* ("the day") are a local colloquialism meaning "killing time," and reflect Kailoma's uber-relaxed approach to crafting local beer. Also try its new releases Cloudies Summer Ale and BBB (i.e. Bula Bitter Bomb).

FIJI

## 994 Taste a tropical brew in the tropics

Vonu Pure Lager is a surf-themed, "ultra-low-carb" pale lager that targets the athletic surfer dude and supermodel set that visits Fiji for rest, relaxation, and, yes, partying. Its claim is that the beer is made with "tropical water" from a local source, though the flavors are too delicate and ephemeral to really tell whether this makes a difference. The result: a crisp, clean beer for your Fiji partying pleasure.

## 995 Cool down with a Fiji Bitter

Produced by a subsidiary of the local Coca-Cola affiliate, Fiji Bitter is perhaps the most aggressively hopped of the country's locally made brews. It has a herbal hop profile and a floral note in the background that makes it downright flavorful. Not much character otherwise, but a good, cooling summer refresher.

### NOUMÉA, NEW CALEDONIA

## 996 Sip an ale in the sun

Stunning seaside views welcome you to the French-influenced Les 3 Brasseurs brewpub in New Caledonia's capital city. The beers themselves—blonde, amber, and a few others—aren't much to get excited about, but sipping them in the island sun is really something special. Pair with a *tarte flambée* or locally caught fish for a memorable meal.

### TAMUNING, GUAM

## 997 Guzzle the best beers on Guam

Ishii Brewing—Guam's first and only craft brewery—was founded by Toshiyuki Ishii, who trained as a professional brewer for years in the US and Japan before opening here in 2010. That influence shows in beers like the American-style pale ales and IPAs, and especially Green Tea IPA, a collaboration with California's Stone Brewing and Japan's Baird Beer.

### TAMUNING, GUAM

## 998 Bend an elbow at this craft beer bar

The laid-back, Irish-inspired Shamrocks Gastropub serves island-influenced dishes (coconut shrimp, tiki-flavored chicken wings) alongside Guam's largest selection of craft beers, mostly local and from the US. In addition to Guam-brewed Minagof beers from Ishii Brewing, try one of the other forty-plus options, including brews from Oregon's Rogue Ales and California's Lagunitas Brewing.

### VARIOUS LOCATIONS, GUAM

## 999 Pick up American craft beers to go

NEX Mini Marts—which stands for "Navy Exchange"—are a chain of US military–operated grocery, beverage, homeware, and clothing stores located throughout regions with active military bases. Guam's feature a solid selection of American craft beer, sold only to go, at reasonable prices. Note: you'll need to be with an active or discharged military member to shop here.

### PAPUA NEW GUINEA

## 1,000 Sit down with an SP Lager

South Pacific Breweries was founded in 1952 as Papua New Guinea's one and only beer producer. Its SP Lager (aka "Our Beer") is still the flagship and the country's most widely consumed beer with a mellow aroma and gentle but crisp finish.

# Index

# Acknowledgments

First and foremost, to Rica Dearman and Caroline Elliker for tirelessly reading, copy editing, and fact-checking nearly every word in this volume and seamlessly moving the entire project along while being infinitely patient with me. It's always a pleasure working with you both. Also at Quarto, to: Jacqui Sayers, Sorrel Wood, James Evans, Greg Stalley, Mark Searle, Chloe Porter, Eoghan O'Brien, Ginny Zeal, Katie Greenwood, and Jane Roe for all their hard work on the book.

I had plenty of help writing and researching the entries. Protima Tiwary wrote many of the entries in the India section, Gemma Mahadeo wrote all of the New Zealand and Australia chapter, and Robert Matthew James Watson wrote a lot of the Asia Pacific section. Thank you all for your strong contributions.

To Tomme Arthur for writing the foreword and continuing to be a leading voice and inspiration in the American and global beer cultures.

To my parents and Jason—thank you for your boundless support. And to Alex, Dave, D.G., Evan, and Harvey.

Finally, to Laura B., Cleo Love, and Izzycat—all the love, forever and ever.

# Image Credits

**t = top, b = bottom, l = left, r = right, m = middle**